THREE MEN WENT TO ROW

THREE MEN WENT TO ROW

*Fact and Fiction behind Jerome K Jerome's
classic book of the Thames*

John Llewellyn

Matador
9 Priory Business Park,
Wistow Road, Kibworth Beauchamp,
Leicestershire. LE8 0RX
Tel: 0116 279 2299
Email: books@troubador.co.uk
Web: www.troubador.co.uk/matador
Twitter: @matadorbooks

ISBN 978 1788037 433

British Library Cataloguing in Publication Data.
A catalogue record for this book is available from the British Library.

Printed and bound by CPI Group (UK) Ltd, Croydon, CR0 4YY
Typeset in 11pt Aldine401 BT by Troubador Publishing Ltd, Leicester, UK

Matador is an imprint of Troubador Publishing Ltd

To Jeannine, my wife and
constant boating companion.

Author's acknowledgements

The author would like to thank Dr Carolyn W de la L Oulton, Reader in Victorian Literature, Canterbury Christ Church University, author of the most recent biography of Jerome, *Below the Fairy City*, who read the manuscript, made suggestions, and gave much encouragement. Robin Newlands, retired Thames Conservancy inspector, who read the MS and shared his unrivalled knowledge of the river. Jeremy Nicholas, President of the Jerome K Jerome Society for allowing quotations from *Idle Thoughts on Jerome K Jerome* published by the Society.

Also thanks to Kiran Kataria of the Keane Kataria Literary Agency for helping to polish the MS.

Emeritus Professor Richard Ekin of the University of Ulster for use of his research on JKJ's residences in Bloomsbury and Fitzrovia. Peter Christie who has researched Jerome Clapp's years in North Devon. Göran Buckhorn for allowing use of his website article on *Three Women in One Boat*. The Rev Derek Winterburn, Vicar of St Mary's Hampton, for information on the tombs, and the parish centre staff for access to photograph them. John Leonard, former licensee of the Blue Posts in Berwick Street, Soho, for his story about the Huguenot saddlers. The late Michael Turk, grandson of Richard Turk who hired his boat to JKJ. Lynne Jackson of the *Architectural Review* for providing me with a copy of the journal dealing with Oatlands Grotto. Peter Delaney, secretary of the Wargrave Local History Society. Angela Houghton, of Reading Museum, Gordon Proctor, of CIMPSA, successor to the Institute of Leisure and Amenity Management, for allowing use of material from *The Grotto House* by Pam Pheasant. Janet Hurst, of the Goring and Streatley Local History Society; The Steam Boat Association archive; Dr Matthew Smith, curator of Egham Museum; SAS UK for information on Wittington House; Judy Dewey of Wallingford Museum; Richard Howard, trustee, Child Beale Park Trust; Mike Smith of the Institute of Structural Engineers; Ealing

Library for making Thomas Day's Sandford and Merton available to me; Richard G Williams, librarian and archivist at Mapledurham House. The British Library Newspaper section (then at Colindale) for access to the *Lock to Lock Times*; The British Library for access to *Dugdale's Topographical Dictionary*; *The Thames from its Source to the Sea*, by Sir Walter Armstrong, *Our River*, by George Dunlop Leslie and *Memoirs of the War of Independence in Hungary*, by General Klapka.

Dr Gabriel Ronay, the expert writer on Hungarian affairs, for help on Jerome K Jerome's name. The Thames Vintage Boat Club, in whose magazine *The Boater*, my first tentative articles on this subject appeared.

Permissions: Bloomsbury Publishing Plc for allowing quotations from *Dicken's Dictionary of the Thames*; F+W Media International for quotes from *The Thames Highway*. *The Times* for allowing extensive use of quotations from their archives. *Metro* for the article on the Caversham boathouse. Joseph Pearce for allowing me to quote from his book *The Unmasking of Oscar Wilde*, David Higham for quotes from *Thames Portrait* by E Arnot Robertson.

Oxford Local History Centre for providing a scan of the interview with George Wingrave, and *The Oxford Mail* for permission to reprint it. Newsquest Berkshire for permission to quote from the *Berkshire Chronicle* 1879-1887. The History Press for permission to refer to *Diary of a Rowing Tour*.

Dieter Jebens for allowing use of his photograph of the 1995 reconstruction of Edward John Gregory's painting of Boulter's Lock, Maidenhead and National Museums, Liverpool, for reproduction rights for the original painting; Orion books for permission to reproduce the photograph of the Edwardian boathouse at Caversham, and Citrus Studio Wokingham for the photograph of its successor.

Many thanks to those who took the time to respond to my many queries. Any errors of fact that remain will be of my making. I have made every effort to trace copyright holders, and I would apologise if I have omitted anyone.

CONTENTS

Contents

Collision with fishermen at Bourne End

The old Crown Hotel, Marlow

MARLOW

Temple

June 24
(hotel)

Bourne End

MAIDENHEAD

COOKHAM

Boulters

Hedsor backwater

BRAY

Defiant tin

Bray Church

Boveney

The first night

WINDSOR

Romney

RUNNYMEDE

Old Windsor

Bell Weir

Ankerwycke

Knights ride in

June 23
STAINES -UPON-THAMES

The Picnic, Ankerwycke,
since burnt down

Penton Hook

George arrives

River Wey

Thames Lock

CHERTSEY

Shepperton

Sketch Map of the Journey
With imagined dates June 23–July 3, 1888

Locks

Camping out

WEYBRIDGE

WALTON

Sunbury

Scold's bridle

KINGSTON

June 23

Molesey

HAMPTON COURT

Teddington

J and Harris depart from Turk's
Boatyard, Kingston

The Maze

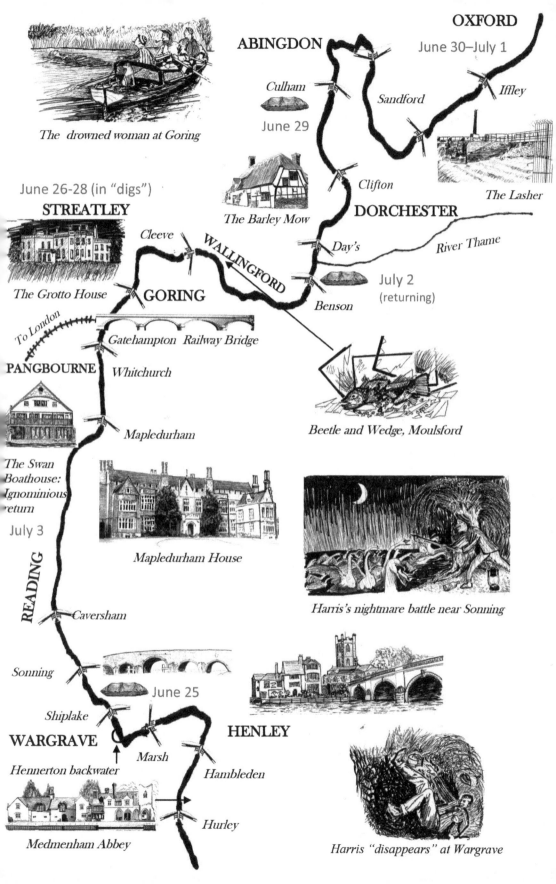

The drowned woman at Goring

OXFORD

June 30–July 1

Iffley

Sandford

ABINGDON

Culham

June 29

The Lasher

The Barley Mow

Clifton

DORCHESTER

June 26-28 (in "digs")

STREATLEY

Cleeve

WALLINGFORD

Day's

River Thame

The Grotto House

GOING

Benson

July 2
(returning)

To London

Gatehampton Railway Bridge

PANGBOURNE

Whitchurch

Beetle and Wedge, Moulsford

The Swan
Boathouse:
Ignominious
return

July 3

Mapledurham

Mapledurham House

READING

Caversham

Harris's nightmare battle near Sonning

Sonning

June 25

Shiplake

HENLEY

WARGRAVE

Marsh

Hennerton backwater

Hambleden

Hurley

Medmenham Abbey

Harris "disappears" at Wargrave

Preface

At the time Jerome K Jerome wrote *Three Men in a Boat* the Victorians were already complaining that the appearance of the Thames was being spoilt by housing developments and by unsightly iron and concrete weirs and bridges that were replacing the traditional wooden ones. It is a complaint that holds good today. I have been cruising up and down the Thames for over 25 years and have noticed the despoliation of its banks by ugly buildings and the cutting down of trees. The Thames Path runs 180 miles from the Thames Barrier to Kemble in Gloucestershire, passing through historic towns and beautiful countryside, but it has no single authority charged with conserving the landscape it passes through as is the case of a National Park. This task is left to local authority planning departments who too often seem to allow local interests to override the national one.

Jerome's work is a sharp reminder not to sully the 'golden fairy stream' that he loved so much.

The Three Men could set foot in places where we cannot go now — the grotto at Oaklands, destroyed by an act of vandalism in the late 1940s, Magna Carta Island, The grounds of Park Place, Henley, and the Gardens of Nuneham Park near Oxford for example. Landowners were more welcoming then, or at least ready to make money from admission charges during what had become a tourist boom. Now it is often the case that the super-rich and celebrities like to keep the public as far away as possible.

This book is intended as a commentary on the original work and aims to extend the enjoyment of those who have read it. It also serves as an unconventional guide for those making their own trips on the river.

The aim has been to make it as entertaining as it is informative, and I could think of no better way of beginning it than asking the Three Men to do it for me.

1

The Men and the River

*Thoughts on how to open a book – Snapshot of an undignified
moment – Harris the Russian teetotaller – Someone rats on
George – Advisability of taking a gun – The peril of dog stories
– When pulling the wrong string can be fatal – A feminist riposte*

*T*here were four of us – George, and William Samuel Harris, and myself and
Montmorency the dog. We were sitting in my room, smoking and talking
about the best way to open a book. Not about how to open a book physically, of
course, although someone like George finds this difficult. I should say at once that this
is not from excessive clumsiness on his part, but from chronic indolence.

Harris, who works in the printing line, said a publisher had once told him an
infallible way of attracting a reader's attention at the outset. You wrote the book and then
selected the most amusing, interesting or alarming paragraph you had written and twisted
everything round so as to make it your introduction. I said this sounded too much like the
sort of swindle where greengrocers buried their rotten fruit at the bottom of the box.

George was unkind enough to say that that was an appropriate example as some critics
had described my work as over-ripe. Then he settled back in his chair, puffed on his pipe and
mused: 'You know; the funniest book I ever read started with three chaps in a room just like
us chatting away about a holiday they planned to take on the River Thames. They joked,
insulted one another and told such hilarious stories about their friends and relations that half
the book was gone before they had even put an oar in the water.'

The book of course is *Three Men in a Boat,* published in 1889, and I hope
the shade of Jerome K Jerome, referred to hereafter as J, will forgive me for
ripping off his opening sentence. George, as imagined above, exaggerates. It
is more like a quarter of the book that is devoted to the preliminaries of the
great expedition, but the point is made that this is no travelogue. It doesn't
fall easily into any category in fact. It is a unique snapshot of the Victorians

caught at an undignified moment with their bottoms in the air, just as J and George were snapped by a photographer at Hampton Court after the nose of their boat snagged on a timber in the lock.

I was tempted by Harris's imagined advice, and if I had given in, I would have started the book thus:

They banged on the door with the back of a brush but there was still no reply. The strongest of the lodgers barged it with his shoulder and the rim of the lock gave way. A terrible sight was revealed: the young woman lay on her bed covered in blood. Her throat had been cut etc etc …

However, in a work of this kind there are certain prosaic preliminaries to be got through. The main characters need to be introduced and their exploits explained in the context of the Victorian Thames before we can begin our journey from Bloomsbury to Oxford. But I will take a cue from J himself and make no apology for wandering off the point for the sake of a good story, and will modestly attempt to settle arguments about where and why certain episodes occurred, indulging always in that pleasant Jeromean pursuit of teasing the reader.

Examine the text of this classic work closely and you will uncover many curiosities. In Bloomsbury I was mystified that so many pubs were called The Blue Posts, then I could not resist following the prurient interest of an inquest jury at the goings on in a brothel close to where J was to live. This was the scene of the 'Great Coram Street Murder' alluded to when J and Harris set out on their holiday. There is also the 'book within a book' — a musty old school textbook called *Sandford and Merton* written in 1789 by Thomas Day, an apostle of the Enlightenment. J hated it because of its priggish hero, yet he considered using the work as a template, and there are several references to it. Curiously the character he hated, Harry, morphed into the more appealing Harris.

On the river we encounter oddities like the steam-powered submarine and a disappearing island. Then there are ghosts, a suicide and fatal accidents.

The three 'real' men all have interesting stories to tell. Cash-strapped and upwardly mobile they lived in dingy lodgings but maintained a congenial lifestyle, regular eating in restaurants while tobacco never seemed to be in short supply. They prided themselves on attending every first night, and it was their interest in the theatre that brought them all together. J and George

Wingrave had shared lodgings for several years, and Harris, whose name was actually Carl Hentschel, met them through a playgoers' club.

At the time of their meeting to plan a holiday on the Thames J, who worked in a solicitor's office, was aged 28, George, a bank clerk, aged 26 and Carl was 24. In that gloomy room in a run-down house due for demolition[1], the joys of a summer holiday were eagerly contemplated. It was early spring in Tavistock Place, but no trees stood ready to mark the awakening of nature and the atmosphere was full of soot and smoke blown over from the great London termini of Euston, St Pancras, and Kings Cross to the north.

Despite being the youngest, Carl would have seemed the most successful of the three at this time. In 1887 he had set up his own business making printing blocks from drawings and photos for newspapers and magazines using a process he had invented. By 1894 he would be producing 60,000 blocks from three factories, the largest enterprise of its kind in the country. This was a business very useful to J as his friend could process the illustration for his books at cost.

George's career at the bank would lead to him becoming manager of a West End branch. But it was J, of course, who eclipsed them both as a distinguished author, now mostly remembered for his account of the hilarious Thames boating trip. He had already published two books and three plays and was to become very much part of the literary establishment of his day.

Much has been made of J's grim childhood in the East End, but while he was certainly not born with a silver spoon in his mouth, he was born to a mother who had a silver teapot in her hand.

The family name was Clapp, and in the normal course of events we should have known him as plain Jerome Clapp. He was from a modest Nonconformist family and his father was a lay preacher with a gift for words that his son inherited. The Rev Mr Clapp moved to Appledore in 1840 and two years later married J's mother, Marguerite Jones, the daughter of a Swansea draper. (J seems to have been rather ashamed that his mother's family was involved in "trade" and in his autobiography, *My Life and Times,* described her father as a solicitor, although draper is written on the marriage certificate. Of course there was no need to be ashamed of having a Welsh draper in the family. Think of John Lewis, Peter Jones and D H Evans.) On the death of his mother-in-law the Rev Clapp inherited a dairy farm with a substantial house. All might have been well and J brought up in this relative Eden instead of the grimy streets of Poplar, but his father's 'original sin' cast him out —or perhaps that should be 'unoriginal sin' — for this man of

God, in a moment of temptation, got a local girl pregnant. To compound his woes he had been persuaded by two conmen that there was silver under his fields and lost a large part of his fortune in a hopeless mining operation.

He sought a solution to his problems by moving to Walsall in Staffordshire in 1855, then the centre of a coal-mining boom. He dug a new pit, but things went badly wrong and it flooded, ruining him. Although he had remained active in the Congregational Church rumours began to circulate about scandalous behaviour in Devon and about this time he changed his name by making his first name his surname. When his youngest son was born in 1859 he named him after himself, Jerome Clapp Jerome.[2]

To escape poverty, Jerome senior was forced to leave his home in 1861 and seek work on his own in London. He ended up in the newly built suburb of Poplar close to the Lime House docks where he bought a chandlery business. As a professional man he had been reduced to working in 'trade' and it was one that eventually failed him. Sussex Street, on which he occupied a corner house, was a mixed neighbourhood with some households comfortably off and others poor.[3] The rest of the family found it socially demeaning when they moved in with him in 1862, and J writes of their days there as a continuous struggle against fate to achieve a lifestyle that they had enjoyed in former years. And no doubt the depressing signs of abject poverty were all around, not to mention cholera.

However, it is curious to find the inventor of the egalitarian 'new humour', accused by many at the time of being a vulgar proletarian, writing of his childhood in the following way:

> We lived in the biggest house in Sussex Street. It had a garden around three sides
> of it with mignonette and nasturtiums that my mother watered of an evening.
> It was furnished more beautifully, I thought, than any house I had ever seen
> with china and fine pictures and a semi-grand piano by Collard and Collard. In
> the dining room were portraits of my mother and father by Muirhead... when
> visitors came my mother would bring out the silver teapot...

His father wore a silk top hat and carried a walking stick with a gold head and J himself had a best suit for Sundays and 'visitings'; and always enough to eat even if it was sometimes only 'bread and slop'. Domestic servants came and went.[4]

His mother frequently reminded him he was a gentleman and no doubt dressed him as such, which must have been a provocation to the local boys who bullied him, making the mean streets of Poplar a place where hard lessons were learnt: his father thought it would help build his character, and no doubt it did.

It was not until J published his first book in 1885[5] that he replaced his middle name Clapp with Klapka. Perhaps this was because he wanted to distance himself from old scandals in the West Country, but why he should have chosen the name of a Hungarian rebel general fighting against Austrian rule long ago in 1848 is difficult to explain. It almost certainly had something to do with his belief that the Clapp family were of Viking descent and shared the indomitable characteristics of that race through an ancestor called Clapa. Klapka is a name of Germanic origin meaning "little Klap". By adopting it he was maintaining continuity with his roots.

The origin of this famous literary name is thus a complicated one, and there have been many erroneous accounts. Too lengthy to explain fully here, I have added an appendix at the back of the book.

After leaving school at 14, J worked as a railway clerk, an actor, a penny-a-liner newspaper reporter and schoolmaster. He occupied a series of insalubrious digs before moving to Tavistock Place, and it was from there in 1888 that he married Georgina Henrietta Marris (Ettie), a divorced woman, which was a socially daring thing to do.

★

J seized life's opportunities with both hands. As a sportsman he played cricket with J M Barrie, skied with Conan Doyle, played tennis with W S Gilbert and once skated in Dresden with a Crown Princess. He could drive a trap with spirited ponies and was a pioneer motorist. He stayed for extensive periods on the Continent, travelling as far as Russia where his fame had preceded him. He felt at home among socialists, aesthetes and bohemians, a man of the people although conservative in many ways, and a believer in 'breeding'. He was a patriot who toured America on the outbreak of the First World War lecturing on the justice of the British cause. Although far too old for the Army he joined a French ambulance brigade, the hardships of which broke his health and led to a premature death. He deserves to be remembered as a great humanitarian as well as an enduring literary figure.

J lived in Walsall for the first two years of his life and the town honoured its most famous literary son in 1927 by conferring on him the

Freedom of the Borough. It is now the heartland of the Jerome K Jerome Society, and Belsize House, where he was born, contains a small museum dedicated to his life and works.

★

His two boating companions became lifelong friends.

Carl Hentschel, who as Harris appears as a quintessential Englishman, was in fact Russian by birth, and could also claim to be Polish. His lengthy obituary in *The Times* when he died in 1930 at the age of 65 reveals that he was born in Lodz in 1864, then part of Russian Poland. He was brought to England by his father who was of Russian extraction. The family seems to have travelled to America before settling in England as Hentschel senior had American citizenship. Carl's father was an ingenious man who started a paper collar factory in Eastbourne but he does not seem to have had the business acumen to profit much by his innovations. Carl joined the family firm at a time when it was concerned with photographic printing plates.

J says Carl was brought low by the First World War when business rivals played on his name and accused him of being a German. This may be something of an exaggeration as Carl proved very resourceful in the face of such a challenge. In a move unprecedented in the business world of his day he changed his company's name to Knight's Manufacturing Co then started a new company called Carl Hentschel Ltd with £100 capital to act as 'trustee, agent or representative' for Knight's. In this way he retained his old company's goodwill.[6]

Carl took a very active part in public life, and contributed patriotically to the war effort as secretary to the London Volunteer Rifles and Royal Horticultural Society's War Relief Fund. J joked that he had ambitions to become Lord Mayor of London.

But at the time of his river trips with J, probably as a result of his family's own experiences, the real Harris was helping political refugees. While working at his block-making studio in Great Windmill Street, Soho, he was 'having to look after a lot of Communists, who had had to leave Paris'.[7]

There is a running joke through the *Three Men* that Harris liked a drink. J suggests that if Harris became a great and good man, signs might be put up outside the public houses he patronised, like the ubiquitous 'Queen Elizabeth slept here' – but no, there would be too many of them.

More likely: 'Only house in South London that Harris never had a drink in'.

In fact, Harris was a strict teetotaller, and on one of their boating trips made a great fuss after accidentally taking a sip of something alcoholic – well diluted with water.[8] This led to merciless teasing from J. Carl was relieved, no doubt, that his real name was not used.

George had his cover blown early on. It can only have been a mischievous person who contributed the following paragraph to the *Lock to Lock Times* weekly magazine[9] on 26 April 1890: 'I wonder what Mr George Wingrave of the London South Western Bank (Head Office) thinks of George in that raciest of river books *Three Men in a Boat?*'

Banks were very sniffy about what their employees got up to in those days, and being associated with a racy book describing the antics of the lowest sort of city clerks and using their slangy phrases cannot have endeared him to his superiors. George is portrayed as lazy – the sort of chap who jumped out of bed in the morning too late to shave before he went to the office. Harris is stung to make rude comments about George because he spent the morning of their departure at the bank, while the other two had to take the luggage and skiff all the way to Weybridge on their own.

He said his friend just sat behind a bit of glass all day trying to look as if he was doing something.

What's the good of a man behind a bit of glass? I have to work for my living. Why can't he work? What use is he there, and what's the good of their banks?

You can imagine eyebrows being raised by those superior people at the head office of the London South Western Bank if they had read those words. But perhaps they disdained to been seen with such 'vulgar trash'.

Certainly his career did not suffer. George eventually became manager of Barclay's Bank in the Strand, then one of London's most fashionable thoroughfares in the heart of theatre land. Many celebrities must have kept accounts at his branch and he would have known all their financial secrets – a social tightrope to be walked if he met one of them at J's literary gatherings.

George was introduced to J by a landlady who thought it would be a good idea if they shared a room in her boarding house. As the most prosaic of the Three, George felt a little out of place in the artistic milieu that gathered around his literary friend in later life, preferring the fine wine and cigars to the sophisticated chat. He never married, and he was the last survivor of the Three when he died in 1941.[10]

George is quoted rather stuffily by Alfred Moss, the first biographer of J, shortly after his friend's death.[11]

> We slept in the same bedroom for a number of years, we went on long walks together, and trip after trip along the Thames, and I got to know him through and through, and can safely say that a more high-principled man I have never known. He never got into bed at night without saying his prayers, and I never heard him say a base word or utter an unclean thought.

One likes to believe that the odd base word did escape when he was on the river.

George was more expansive when interviewed by a reporter from the *Oxford Mail* in 1933, when he was aged 71.

> Yes, we all three lived together, but not as you suggest in a triple-bachelor flat. The truth is we starved in one room. That room had to do for the three of us then. We were all making our way in the world, you see.
> As for the river trip which led to the book – well, it was a case of doing that or having no holiday. The important thing was it cost practically nothing. There was the beautiful river very near us and the boat, with room for us all to sleep on it, could be hired for a guinea a week [£1.05 in today's money].[12]

Of course it is the privilege of the elderly to exaggerate the hardships of their youth, and I think George is probably swinging the lead a little when he refers to 'starving' in the context of their life-style described above. I note later that on one of their river trips they took a leg of Welsh mutton bought from a famous supplier in The Strand. If J is to be believed, they spent a night in the most expensive hotel in Marlow as well as staying in lodgings in Streatley and at Oxford during their fictional trip on the Thames. But it should be remembered that their story is an amalgam of many excursions they made in the late 1880s and the timeline is based on J's honeymoon on the river. For at the time *Three Men* was written J was a married man living in rather superior accommodation – a flat at 104 Chelsea Gardens in what was then the most bohemian of suburbs.

★

Montmorency the fox terrier is fictitious, but an evocation of the kind of dog that Victorian young men cherished. He was always game for a scrap and usually emerged the victor.

Warnings were written at the time against taking dogs on river trips. They were forever fidgeting and upsetting the balance of the boat, or jumping on and off, wandering away, or going for a swim and shaking the water and mud off their coats on to the boat's occupants. But the celebrated artist George Dunlop Leslie RA, writing in 1881[13] thought these disadvantages were outweighed by security considerations. He told of a camping party that was attacked by tramps who took everything they could lay their hands on, and advised: 'A revolver and one or two good dogs should I think always be taken as precautions on these camping expeditions.'

This warning seems a little over the top. J was wise not to take a dog with him in real life, but it was good idea to include Montmorency in the book since dog stories were all the rage at the time.

As J wrote in *Novel Notes*:[14] 'It is a wicked thing to start dog stories among a party of average sinful men. Let one man tell a dog story, and every other man in the room feels he wants to tell a bigger one.'

The following is J's equivalent of a modern urban myth: the old, old story of a dog who had been in the habit of going every morning to a baker's shop with a penny in his mouth in exchange for which he always received a penny bun. One day the baker, thinking he would not know the difference, tried to palm the animal off with a ha'penny bun whereupon the dog trotted straight outside and fetched a policeman.

Montmorency is allowed his own voice at the beginning of the book and comments on the proposed holiday: 'If you ask me I call the whole thing bally foolishness.'

★

There is a fifth, unsung, hero of the adventure – the Thames double skiff. Designed for two rowers, it is a thing of great beauty, a symphony of harmonious curves created by its method of construction. Planks of overlapping mahogany are riveted together to create its basic form. It is a direct descendent of the Viking longships, and the top 'strake' or plank is called the saxbord, where the sea axe was hung recalling its ancestry as a ship of war. No modern ironmongery such as rowlocks spoil its line, the oars being held in place by wooden pegs – thole pins – which follow the outward curve of the gunwale. The stern has a delicate wine-glass shape, and in the back is a cushioned seat from which the rudder is worked by two ropes.

The original publisher should also be given his due. It was F W Robinson, editor of *Home Chimes,* who took J's first instalments of the book, then called *The Story of the Thames, its Scenery and History,* throwing out the 'slabs of history' planned for each chapter, but retaining all the humour. In this way he helped to create a masterpiece, J taking his cue and hitting on the perfect title half way through.

In his bachelor days J with George and Harris would take a train to Richmond on a Sunday morning and row up to Staines. Sometimes they would arrange to stay away for three or four days and camp out. A spell of bad weather would regularly break up their parties, according to Harris. On June 21st, 1888 J married Georgina, who had been divorced barely two weeks before, and they spent their honeymoon in a little boat on the Thames. If they were following tradition their honeymoon would have begun on that day, but the Three Men's trip, we are told, began on a Saturday – which would give us a starting date of June 23. This would have brought them to Henley the week before the Regatta, as described, because that year it was held from Wednesday July 4th to Saturday July 7th. On honeymoon J and Georgina would have spent their nights in cosy riverside inns, and the more leisurely pace allowed them to spend time at the Regatta. It was this holiday rather than the shorter excursions of the Three Men that provided the itinerary for J's immortal story. Put together from different trips, it is hardly surprising that the chronology goes a little astray now and again. At Cliveden it is early spring, at Henley, the last week in June, and at Sonning we are back in early June.

The success of his book written in the late summer and autumn of 1888 meant J could give up his plans for a career in the law, and holidaying on the Thames was given a boost.

*

His river exploits took place during what is now regarded as the Golden Age of the Thames. Commercial traffic had largely given way to pleasure craft and the river had become fashionable. But those living in a Golden Age rarely see it as such. For many late Victorians the rot had already set in. On the water, steamboats were threatening the peace and safety of rowers and punters. In July 1888 the *Lock to Lock Times* estimated that the number of steamboats on the river had reached 250, 'fifty per cent of which were objectionable'. Something should be done at once, it urged, to prevent enjoyment of the Thames becoming an impossibility.

The pioneer gentlemen steamboat enthusiasts were being taunted by riff-raff who prevented them from enjoying their innocent amusement, and drove them off the river. Their place was taken by a new breed of *nouveau riche* speed merchants.

No doubt the yobbishness directed towards steamboats was a rougher version of the cheeky bravado described by J – he and his friends lying relaxed in the bottom of the boat and pretending not to hear the hooting and shouts of an approaching leviathan urging them to get out of the way. But excursion steamers created a menace all of their own. They organised trips known as 'beanfeasts', which were notorious for drunkenness and loutish behaviour.

Some trippers in small boats had a bad reputation too. The *Lock to Lock Times* reported that there were 'certain men who go about dressed in the garb of gentlemen and who make "boating" an excuse for free living in every sense of the word'.

Those who had the welfare of the river at heart feared its banks were being despoiled by vulgar villas and public works. Picturesque wooden weirs and locks were being replaced by iron and concrete monstrosities. Worst of all, vulgar working-class people, the 'Arries and 'Arriets, were forsaking their traditional haunts such as 'Appy 'Ampton (Hampton Court) and, aided and abetted by the railways with their cheap fares, were desecrating the poetical upper reaches at Pangbourne, Goring and beyond.

There was some snobbery behind all this hand-wringing. The lower orders were beginning to venture into places where they had never gone before. A splendid example of their challenge to the social order is found in this anecdote of an encounter on Maidenhead Bridge.

An officer of the Household Brigade, a member of the Guards' Boating Club at Taplow, was crossing the bridge clad in his customary flannels with the Guards' ribbon in his hat. To him came a sickly looking youth of 5ft nothing with the anxious inquiry: "do you know that you are wearing the colours of the Lower Tooting Bicycle Club? Are you a member?" [15]

Hardly surprising, therefore, that J's book should attract criticism from those who saw it as confirmation of a decline in standards on the Thames. Not only did it sully the reputation of the river, it also poisoned the wellspring of the English language itself with such vulgar expressions as 'She was nuts on public houses, was England's Virgin Queen'. Punch famously dubbed the writer 'Arry K'Arry. But boating people were more sympathetic, and one reviewer wrote: 'To appreciate the book an acquaintance with the river is necessary, for this reason, if for no other, we heartily commend it to our readers.'[16] Time proved him wrong as the book had an appeal far beyond the boating fraternity. A vast new readership was coming into being that welcomed his casual style of writing. They took the 'new humour' J invented to their hearts and made his fortune. His book has never been out of print.

★

The world J reflected was very much a man's world. Women appear in the book as empty-headed and fashion obsessed or, more darkly, as victims seduced and betrayed. The hopeless situation of girls who became pregnant outside marriage leads us to a murder, a suicide and the horror of the Clappers, a weir at Caversham near Reading, where a diabolical 'baby farmer' disposed of the bodies of infants entrusted to her charge by desperate single mothers.

Women were victims in another sense too. They were expected to wear totally impractical clothing and gloves when they went boating. As we shall see, if there was an accident, they were the ones who usually drowned. It was often their task to sit in the back of the boat and steer it with ropes attached to the rudder while the men did the 'real work'. Of course Victorian men were obsessed with the idea that the lady might pull the wrong 'string'.

Anthony Trollope describes an accident caused in this way in his novel, *The Three Clerks,* of 1857. A rowing boat is trapped under Hampton Bridge and crushed by a passing barge.

'Your left hand, Katie, your left', shouted Norman; 'your left string.' Katie was confused, and gave first a pull with her right, and then a pull with her left, and then a strong pull with her right. The two men backed water as hard as they could, but the effect of Katie's steering was to drive the nose of the boat right into one of the wooden piers of the bridge.

The three fictional characters in the boat are rescued without harm, but I have found two court hearings in which confusion on the part of the woman steerer was suggested as a possible cause of fatalities.

Some feminists, or 'blue stockings' as they were called in those days, objected to J's blokeish new style and it wasn't long before they struck back. In 1891 Constance MacEwan wrote *Three Women in One Boat – a River Sketch.* Her three heroines were called Phoebe, Selina and Sabina, and as Phoebe put it:

> We were determined to show how we three women in a boat didn't make half such a mess of it as Mr Jerome's 'three men in a boat' — not by a long way.

They took with them a cat called Tintoretto, 'twice as well behaved as Montmorency'. The three women took their rowing very seriously, one had a boyfriend who was a champion at Henley, but the book was rather Victorian and stodgy and not funny at all. It has all but disappeared except for a few copies in university libraries.[17]

But I have a fantasy of those three young ladies meeting up with J and Co and an impromptu race resulting in which Selina, Sabina and Phoebe win, Phoebe shouting 'Go it girls!' and urging her crew on by singing feminist anthems. Montmorency would be barking in fury at an aloof Tintoretto and George, panicked by the unaccustomed hard work would lose his balance and fall backwards into the bottom of the boat.

A feminist riposte

2

The Great Coram Street Murder

*Seeking the point of the famous departure – Biggs's boy revealed – The life story
of a 'wretched harlot' – Comings and goings in a Victorian brothel – An inquest
punctuated with hilarity – A connection with Jack the Ripper.*

I THOUGHT it would be easy to locate the exact spot on a Bloomsbury
pavement where J and his friends set out on their Thames excursions. But
there are pitfalls for the unwary, two of them cunningly designed by J himself.

It is beyond doubt that Tavistock Place was Jerome's address at the time,
but finding the number of the house was more difficult. I first thought I had
located it at No 42. There seemed good evidence from the book; a delivery
boy shouts out on their departure: 'Hi! ground floor o' 42's a moving.'

This building certainly looks the part. Put up by speculative builders
early in the nineteenth century, it is a tall, narrow, sad-looking terraced
house of four stories and a basement that for most of its life must have
provided people with cheap accommodation. When I visited, it was a
small hotel boasting twelve rooms for tourists. The manager had never
heard of J. After I explained about this famous writer he asked: 'How old
was he?' I said that if he was still alive he would be 146. Undeterred, the
man persisted; 'Did he have a beard?' – No, a moustache. 'Because there
was a man last year who left some books behind ...'

★

It turned out that I was on a wild-goose chase. The Post Office had
renumbered all the houses in 1938 when the street was extended to include
the old Compton Street. In J's day the numbers stopped at 37, so he was
playing safe and not identifying a real place. Sir Arthur Conan Doyle played

a similar trick with 221b Baker Street as the home of Sherlock Holmes, but in his case someone struck lucky. That street was also extended, so the fictional address became a real one and a profitable place of pilgrimage. J omitted the name of the street, although he must have had Tavistock Place in mind. But despite the fact that the postal authorities have given 42 a spurious legitimacy, a better claim can be made for a spot across the road.

In his autobiography *My Life and Times,* published in 1926, J says that his old lodgings were demolished and the site occupied by the Passmore Edwards Settlement.[1]

Passmore Edwards was a newspaper proprietor and benefactor. J says he was a friend of his father when they were both young men, and the two had 'introduced golf to the South of England', playfully hitting a ball with a stick across the sands at Westward Ho when his father was farming land at nearby Instow. This seems unlikely as J's father was born c.1806 and Passmore Edwards in 1823, but they would have known each other as delegates to the Peace Conferences at Brussels and Paris in 1848 and 1849. They can't have been close friends, for when Jerome senior was cast into the outer darkness by scandal, no offer of a job came from the newspaper magnate.

The Passmore Edwards Settlement was an artistic commune where teachers and other professionals could live in return for instructing the local working class. The handsome Arts and Crafts building is now called the Mary Ward House and is a conference and exhibition centre. But as the actual point of departure it has a half-and-half sort of claim. The house J lodged in, then No 33, was half on the site of the back entrance to the Mary Ward Centre and half on the site occupied by a six-storey red-brick block of flats now numbered 11. You could not put up a blue plaque here – it would have to be cut in half.

Then I read an article by Professor Richard Ekins of the University of Ulster, who has made a study of the author's residences in Bloomsbury and Fitzrovia.[2] The English edition of *My Life and Times*, he discovered, omitted the following sentence: 'I shared the ground floor of number 19 Tavistock Place with a chum, George Wingrave by name.' This is confirmed by an entry in the 1885 Electoral Register for the Borough of Marylebone. So J lived for about a year there between 1884 and 1885 before moving across the road.

No 19, renumbered 32, still stands, and it bears a blue plaque recording J's residence there. But it is on the pavement where the flats (No 11) adjoin the Mary Ward House site that we should begin our journey. In later years Hentschel (Harris) told a friend, Douglas Sladen, that 'Jerome

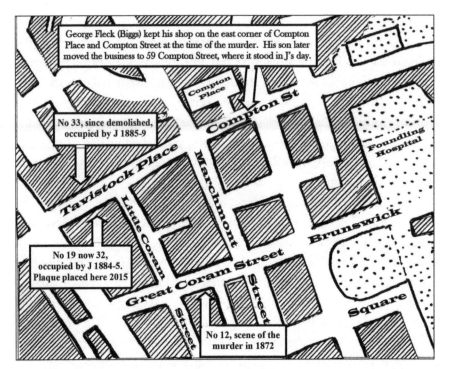

George Fleck (Biggs) kept his shop on the east corner of Compton Place and Compton Street at the time of the murder. His son later moved the business to 59 Compton Street, where it stood in J's day.

No 33, since demolished, occupied by J 1885-9

Foundling Hospital

No 19 now 32, occupied by J 1884-5. Plaque placed here 2015

No 12, scene of the murder in 1872

The scene of the Great Coram Street Murder and Jerome's lodgings 1884-89 based on an old map

and Wingrave used to live in Tavistock Place, now pulled down, and that was our starting point to Waterloo and thence to the river'. [3]

★

But let us return to J's account of the great departure and how the two were jeered on their way by a group of local urchins.

Biggs's boy was the first to come round. Biggs is our greengrocer, and his chief talent lies in securing the services of the most abandoned and unprincipled errand-boys that civilisation has yet produced… I was told that, at the time of the Great Coram Street murder, it was promptly concluded by our street that Biggs's boy (for that period) was at the bottom of it, and had he not been able in reply to the severe cross examination to which he was subjected by No 19 when he called there for orders the morning after the crime (assisted by No 21 who happened to be on the step at the time), to prove a complete alibi it would have gone hard with him.

16

The Great Coram Street murder was a sensation in its day. The scene of the crime was a little over a block away to the south of where J was to lodge twelve years later. It must have left a deep impression in local lore, and the person at No 19 could well have been J's future landlady. The Biggs's boy of the day was, I discovered, involved in the case not as a suspect but as a witness.[4]

From reading contemporary accounts of proceedings in *The Times* we can identify him as Joseph Connolly[5], who went into the witness box to contradict evidence given by his boss, the greengrocer George Fleck (J's Biggs), whose shop was a few hundred yards away from No 19 on the corner of Compton Street and Compton Mews.

The middle class and people in abject poverty lived cheek-by-jowl in those days. Compton Street was a respectable parade of shops, while Compton Mews was a rookery of tenements described in Charles Booth's poverty map of London as 'lowest class, vicious, semi-criminal.' Fleck's two shop boys lived there, so it is hardly surprising that they had a terrible reputation.

The old shop still exists beside a little arched alleyway leading from what is now Tavistock Place, but the mews is occupied by a smart art-deco style backpackers' hostel. Few of the young tourists who pass it by could guess the part this area played in one of London's most notorious murders. It retained its old number, 37, in the postal reorganisation. By J's day the business had moved a few doors to the west to slightly larger premises and was run by George Fleck junior.

Great Coram Street, like many of its Victorian residents, has fallen into reduced circumstances and is just Coram Street. Half of it was demolished to make way for an austere concrete housing development in the 1960s. No original buildings remain in what is left, so there is no trace of the house of ill repute where the murder occurred, but it stood on a site now occupied by the Post House Premier Bloomsbury Hotel.

★

The events in Fleck's shop on that fatal night are well recorded.[6] The greengrocery had stayed open late on Christmas Eve 1872 in order to catch the very last of the holiday shoppers. It was after midnight when a local woman the shop-keeper recognized as a 'well-behaved prostitute' entered the store with a male companion. She was wearing a black silk dress, black velvet jacket and a fashionable green hat with a red feather in it, the sort

17

of outfit that a 'gay woman', to use a contemporary phrase, would wear to draw attention to herself. Her companion was aged about 25, 5ft 9in tall, and looked like a working man on holiday. He had black hair, his face was unshaven and on his head was a soft felt 'Billycock' hat.

But perhaps the most remarkable thing about him was his face, which was covered in pock marks.

The young woman paid a penny for some apples and her companion bought oranges and almonds for eightpence. When she tried to persuade him to treat her to some grapes he replied very gruffly: 'No, no, no.' Those words caused the grocer to turn his attention away from the woman to the man because he thought they were uttered with a German accent. Also in the shop at the time were Biggs's two errand boys, and three pairs of eyes closely watched the couple leave the shop.

The streets were still alive with festive crowds, and the two paused to listen to carol singers. Songs of joy and hope filled the air as the woman, accompanied by the dark stranger, made her way back to her sordid little room on the second floor back of 12 Great Coram Street. It was the room in which she would spend her last night on earth.

★

The Great Coram Street Murder is a fascinating story with an importance far beyond the murder of a 'wretched harlot', to quote *The Times*. The case was bungled by the police, the inquest descended into farce, and a huge amount of public sympathy emerged for the man who had been wrongly accused. Even Prime Minster Gladstone contributed to a testimonial fund set up for him.

The victim was Harriet Buswell. She was born in the Cambridgeshire town of Wisbech, the daughter of a tailor, and had two brothers and three sisters.[7] After the death of her parents she came up to London at the age of 19 to work as a housemaid in Finchley. She was a good-looking and presentable girl, and it seems she became pregnant by the coachman to the household, who died shortly after. She moved to Islington to have the child and from that time took to an immoral life, frequently using the name of her daughter's father, Burton. It was as Mrs Clara Burton that she was known when she came to lodge in Great Coram Street. She had first found protection as mistress of a Major Brown, who lived in Southwark, and had two still-born children by him. Mrs Brown, or 'Brownie', was another of her aliases.

18

After that relationship ended she was befriended by a Mr Kirby, perhaps a 'do-gooder', who lived near Bloomsbury but who left for China at the end of 1870. He kept in touch with her and his letters were of a brotherly kind and full of good advice. He sent her money, £60 in all, sometimes in postal orders, sometimes in notes, and sometimes through a friend to give to her at so much a time. Days before she died, Harriet, who was illiterate, had asked a friend to write a letter to her sister, who lived near Hurst Green, Sussex, which was to be sent on to China.

Harriet was closest to that sister and had lived with her from time to time. She had been invited to spend Christmas in Sussex, which would have saved her life, but for some unknown reason she declined, even though her sister had offered to lend her the money for the journey.

She had gone beyond help. Superintendent Thomson, of E Division, Metropolitan Police, told the inquest that he had known Harriet to be a 'well-behaved prostitute for the past six years.'

So at the age of 28 the young woman was reduced to haunting the Alhambra Music Hall at Leicester Square, later a favourite place of entertainment for J and his pals. The theatre had nine bars and Harriet was well-known there, so the management does not seem to have been particular about morality, indeed, *The Times* referred to the place at this time as 'one of these open markets of vice.'

She led an unhappy life struggling to pay the rent in a succession of tawdry lodging houses, and was heard at least once to have threatened to take her own life. At first she paid 5s a week for her daughter Katie to be looked after by a respectable woman, but the guardian became attached to the girl: four years previously she had informally adopted her and subsequently received no money for her maintenance. Shortly before her murder, Harriet had asked to have her daughter, now aged eight, back to stay with her for the holiday. She wanted to buy her a present, but having no money she pawned a few pathetic belongings – five pairs of lady's drawers – for 5s.

We return to that fateful Christmas Eve. Harriet had left home at about 10pm to go to the Alhambra where she met a client who took her to the Cavour Hotel, the Alhambra's restaurant, and paid for them to dine on cold chicken and ham. (She begged for some slices of lemon: a strange craving. Was she pregnant?) Waiters later testified that they thought the man was German. The couple then proceeded to Great Coram Street taking the Brompton and Islington horse bus. Witnesses saw them get off at St Pancras Church from whence they walked down Judd Street, turned right into Compton Street and stopped at Fleck's shop before turning down Marchmont Street and into Great Coram Street.

The door of No 12 was opened by Harriet's landlady, Mrs Harriet Wright, as her lodger had no front door key. Wright was 'a bit merry' and invited her tenant into the kitchen for a glass of stout. Her companion, in the meantime, bounded up the stairs to her room as if he knew the way. Harriett had been given ten shillings by the man and gave nine shillings of it to Mrs Wright to pay off her arrears in rent. She put the remaining shilling back into a red morocco purse. Mrs Wright volunteered this information at the inquest but tried to deny it later. She had good reason to do so. It must have been apparent to the court and the public at large that by accepting money given for immoral purposes she was in effect living off the wages of prostitution, a criminal offence. If she had done 'the right thing', in the popular view, she would have ordered the man out of her house and there would have been no murder.

No-one knew exactly what happened that night. Mrs Wright and her husband said that they heard someone leave the house at 6 or 7am and gently close the front door. The Wrights were not surprised when Harriet failed to appear on Christmas morning but they grew alarmed after there had been no sign of her by lunch time. After banging on the door with the back of a brush, they forced it open and found Harriett lying on her bed in a pool of blood.

At first it was thought she might have committed suicide, but the surgeon called to the house soon disposed of that possibility. Her throat had been cut through to the bone in two places and he thought the wounds had been inflicted while she was still asleep, as her body was in an attitude of repose. The murder weapon, believed to have been a stout, single-edged knife, was never recovered.

Police began their inquiries. It seemed an open and shut case. Harriett had been murdered by her client, a German, and there were good descriptions of him. Scotland Yard in those days was zealous, if not intelligently led. By Christmas night, the description had been circulated and a watch set at all ports.

Two weeks before Christmas, a German emigrant boat, the 'Wangerland,' bound for Brazil, had put in at Ramsgate. It had run on to the Goodwin Sands and had to stop in England for repairs. For reasons never made clear, the assistant surgeon, Carl Whollebe, unexpectedly left his hotel in the town at 2am to return to his ship. This immediately aroused the suspicions of Buss, the local police superintendent, who thought the man answered the description of the Great Coram Street suspect and arrested him. An identity parade was arranged.

To the Rev Dr Gottfried Hessel, acting as chaplain on the 'Wangerland', such an accusation against his friend seemed preposterous. He decided to assist Whollebe by organising the identity parade, and persuaded a number of passengers of similar age to dress up in the appropriate clothing, placing himself among them.

George Fleck and his errand boys were taken down to Ramsgate with other witnesses to try to identify the murderer, but they all agreed it wasn't Whollebe. And then a bizarre thing happened. Some of the witnesses, including Fleck, were convinced that the unfortunate Dr Hessel was the man they had seen with Harriet Buswell. So Buss was not to be denied a suspect, and the unfortunate clergyman was arrested and taken up to London under threat of the noose. It was of no account that he had a cast-iron alibi, as he wasn't given the chance to produce it. Newsboys shouted in the streets 'Murder suspect found' — it was a German – no surprise – a clergyman – sensation!

To the Victorian public it was amazing that a man of the cloth should be accused of such a horrendous crime, especially after having the finger pointed at him in such a blatantly unfair way. German organizations in London also rallied to Hessel's support, and the Consulate of the German Empire made sure he had legal representation. Unfortunately for him, it transpired that he *had* travelled up to London on December 22 to spend Christmas in the capital with three people: his wife, Whollebe, and another passenger from the ship.

At least justice in Victorian times moved more quickly than it does now, and after the inquest began on December 28, full committal proceedings started on January 21 at Bow Street Police Court. The two hearings overlapped so that witnesses were required to give their evidence to both courts, sometimes on the same day. Things said in the coroner's court were elaborated on in the police court and vice-versa, so our account of proceedings combines reports from both places.

In the witness box George Fleck said that Harriet's companion had the appearance of a German: he knew this because he had many German customers. The man looked like a workman and he spoke with a German accent when he refused to buy the grapes.

The greengrocer looked at Dr Hessel in court and said: 'I feel all the responsibility of saying that he is the man, and I do say positively.' This was despite the fact that Hessel did not have a pocked-marked face and, as other witnesses remarked, did not look like a working man.

Fleck was followed into the witness box by his errand boy, Connolly, who testified that he too had been taken to Ramsgate for the identity parade. 'I said Dr Hessel resembled the man very much, but it was not he. I still say that. I am sure it is not the man who came into the shop.' Hessel was fairer, he said. Later in cross-examination he admitted that he had left Mr Fleck's service 'on my own accord'. 'I left because he was jawing me about being long on my errands, but that did not make me think different.'

The greengrocer was recalled – clearly the prosecution were seeking to prove that 'Biggs's boy' was motivated by malice in contradicting his former employer. Fleck said that he had had to discharge the boy for dishonesty (one senses hesitation here) or rather that the boy took some money for things and did not return. 'Did not return'? This seems to mean that he was merely late in coming back, as the boy lived only a few hundred yards away in Compton Mews.

There were, of course, two errand boys in the shop, but Connolly seems to have been the more dominant of the two since Fleck alleged that Connolly had told the other boy, John Murray, to say that Dr Hessel was not the man who had been in his shop. This Connolly denied.

When it was his turn to take the stand Murray had said: 'The prisoner is like the man, but has not such a rough look. The man who came into the shop was taller.' Testimony from a barmaid at the Alhambra supported this view about the man's height.

The evidence of identification was contradictory. But the whole case fell apart when the defence proved Hessel's alibi. He had been staying at Kroll's Hotel in Holborn, where an employee testified that he had been unwell and unable to go out over Christmas. His only pair of boots had been left outside the door of his room on the night of the murder.

So after eleven days in custody, to the sound of resounding cheers from the body of the court, the Rev Dr Hessel found himself discharged and a free man. By the time he resumed his voyage to Brazil he was £1,200 better off, a very substantial sum in those days, even allowing for his defence expenses. The money had been collected on his behalf by an outraged British public as a 'testimonial' to his character. The Queen herself had contributed £30.

It was as well that greengrocer Fleck had told the court during the case that he did not read the newspapers. He would have been spared the humiliation of seeing this *Times* leader:

It is due to most of the witnesses to acknowledge that they gave their evidence with care. An exception, however, must be made in the case of a greengrocer … He was the most positive of all as to Dr Hessel's identity, but as he was 'quite certain' the man was a German from the accent with which he said: 'no', it is not too much to suppose that he is apt to draw hasty conclusions.

The Times also thundered against the police: 'they have injured a worthy man, they have wasted precious time, and they have damaged their reputation for lack of a very little circumspection. Let us hope they will at least be more careful in future, and that they will recognize the fact that they have adopted a completely fallacious principle of investigation.' Never again would a case hinge on unsupported evidence of identification.

Fleck and the police were not the only ones to suffer the Thunderer's ire. The coroner also came in for a lashing. It does not make sense to us nowadays that one court charged with establishing the cause of death should be deliberating at the same time that another is engaged in the committal proceedings of the suspected murderer.

The inquest did not return a verdict of 'wilful murder by cutting throat' until February 4, five days after Dr Hessel had been acquitted. It had been unduly protracted mainly because the jury took a prurient interest in the comings and goings at 12 Great Coram Street, firmly supposed by followers of the case to be a brothel. We know this because one of the first witnesses to be called was Harriet's brother Henry. He was anxious to avoid scandal and got his employer to write a letter to the court asking to be excused. All the pleadings of a man as distinguished as the secretary to the Society of Antiquaries were of no avail, however; Henry had to appear. His employer had written: 'an account of what goes on in a brothel does not tend to edification and brings him into contact with a class of people he has not been used to. He is a very well-disposed lad and I want to keep him so.'

It was not all the fault of Mr Lankester, the coroner, that the inquest went on for so long. Juries held the whip hand in those days and had the right to call and question witnesses. The coroner seems to have encouraged them, however, and there is a sense that he was engaged in rivalry with the police to uncover vital evidence.

Of course we all share the inquest jury's prurience, and readers would probably feel cheated if we did not make a Jeromean-style digression here to lift the lid on this disorderly house. What are we to make of the landlady,

Mrs Harriet Wright, who literally frightened a Frenchman to death, if we are to believe *The Times*? In the course of the murder inquiry a Frenchman had come under suspicion. He was living with Mrs Wright's mother in Soho. When he heard that Mrs Wright was coming to stay with her mother he dropped dead from the shock. The usual witnesses, including Fleck and his boys, were taken around to view the body in a morgue, but all agreed he was not their man. It had been suspected that his 'shock' was due to the fear that Mrs Wright might have identified him as the killer.

★

Harriet Buswell had arrived at No 12 two weeks before Christmas asking if accommodation was available. Yes, she was told by Mrs Wright, but there was nothing suitable for a 'lady'. Fair warning perhaps, but the subsequent conversation made it quite clear that Harriet wasn't exactly a lady, for according to Mrs Wright:

> She said she had a friend who partially kept her and that formerly she lived with him. In fact she said she was visited by two friends, one of whom only came about money. One of these was an Italian. She told me her friend gave her £30 at a time when she needed money.

Later she tried to deny that Harriet had told her she was 'partially kept'.

'But you did say it!' Mr Lankaster retorted. 'It was written down. Did you mean you thought she was a kept woman?'

'I never went into that,' said Mrs Wright. Harriet was a respectable looking woman and she was only expecting her to stay for a week. The landlady was clearly skating on thin ice. She did not want to be accused of living off immoral earnings, and the Wrights had in fact engaged a solicitor, Mr Sydney, to protect their interests in court.

It had been a full house on Christmas Eve. The landlady and her husband slept in the kitchen, 'Mr and Mrs Nelson' slept in the ground floor back parlour, Mr and Mrs Martini slept on the drawing room floor, Mr Fernandez in the second floor front, Harriett and her companion in the second floor back. A Mr Hall slept in the front attic, and the back attic was occupied by the Wrights' two teenage sons.

When asked where a Mr Hooper was sleeping, Mrs Wright had to say that actually he was the man known as Mr Nelson. Much mirth was occasioned when Mr Sydney quickly interposed: 'And I have heard that Miss Nelson is to be married to Mr Hooper'. One of the jurors remarked facetiously, in the popular phraseology of the time, that this 'put a finish on the witness's evidence'.

This a good example of the lax and conversational way in which the hearing was conducted. *The Times* called inquests the most incompetent and purposeless of tribunals and the Great Coram Street one in particular a 'dreary and disgusting farce' that degenerated into scandal-mongering. The names of some of Harriet's clients were being aired in public. But, it sarcastically remarked, 'the tedium of the inquest, to be sure, is lightened to [the jury] by the playful humour of the coroner and the good things that are greeted by peals of laughter.'

Of course there was some humbug in all this *Times* ranting. The inquest had very usefully provided many avidly-read columns for its pages. And there was an element of snobbery too. Those witnesses who swore they had recognized the murderer had, 'as is so often the case with people of that class of life, done irreparable mischief by their stupidity and presumption'.

Some reports of the case said Harriet had once been a dancer at the Alhambra, and – according to Mrs Wright – she had told her daughter that she danced at the music hall in silk tights, but this may well have been fantasy. The Alhambra must have been under pressure to clean up its act after all the bad publicity, but it is no coincidence that the second victim in *The Three Men,* the woman who drowned herself in the Thames at Goring, could have worked at the Leicester Square establishment.

The plight of Harriet's daughter Katie is one of the saddest aspects of the case. She was in the house when her mother was murdered, although not listed among the occupants at the inquest.

When her unofficial foster-mother, Jane Smith, read of the murder, she went straight to Great Coram Street to pick up the girl. Mrs Wright said she was not there, but this proved a lie when Katie ran out to embrace the only woman she loved and trusted. Incredible as it may seem to us, she was not allowed to take Katie away from that house of horror. Mrs Wright insisted that the girl could not leave until all Harriet's debts were paid in full, so Mrs Smith had to leave the girl and go to Bow Street Court to seek custody. There she was told the matter could only be settled by Harriett's brother-in-law, presumably the one from Sussex, who eventually took the girl away.

The only beneficiary from this complete shambles was the murderer himself, who was never brought to justice. From a twenty-first century perspective the belief by the police that robbery was the motive looks naïve. The killer paid for Harriet to have a meal and gave her half a guinea. Why would he kill her for the sake of a few pathetic belongings – a purse with a shilling in it, a pair of jet earrings, a jet brooch and a pawn ticket? And why would he do so when she was asleep? She was twice stabbed in the throat, and each wound penetrated her windpipe through to the backbone. Either was enough to kill her but her murderer just wanted to be sure. He was obviously a very dangerous man who would probably kill again. We are now familiar with such cases: men with a hatred of prostitutes who kill in cold blood and take their belongings as trophies.

At the time J was writing *Three Men in a Boat,* the first of the Ripper murders was being committed in the East End. If Harriet's murderer was in fact a seaman, he could have committed other crimes wherever his ship took him, returning by chance to London seventeen years later when he was about 42 years of age, his manner of attack having grown more frenzied in the interval. It is not impossible that he was Jack the Ripper himself, but at the least he was certainly of his kind.

Harriet Buswell with her client stops outside the shop of George Fleck (Biggs) now numbered 34 Tavistock Place

3

Mystery of the Blue Posts

Bloomsbury to Hampton: Seeking J's favourite watering hole – Major success on the stage – Books touched by the master – We read of a terrible earthquake – A spectacular staircase – Waterman to the stars – Maps and Apps – Looking for a 'funny' tomb.

BOATERS sometimes find themselves going backwards, so I offer this as a lame apology for returning to the moment of departure of J and Harris from Tavistock Place to start the great adventure. I was so carried away by the Great Coram Street Murder that I forgot to mention that among the throng of youths who jeered them on their way was 'the empty can superintendent from The Blue Posts'.

This was a 'pot boy' whose job it was, in the days when pub customers had their own pewter pots, to return the cans to the appropriate peg after use. He also delivered jugs of ale to outside customers. I thought this must be an unusual pub name which would make it easy to trace as J's favourite hostelry where he hung out with George and Harris to discuss their boating trips.

An internet search revealed that the nearest Blue Posts to his lodgings can be found in Soho. I arrived there hoping there might at least be a Blue Plaque to confirm its importance in literature. There wasn't, but it was a nice cosy Victorian-style pub with a fireplace where you could imagine our hero leaning on the mantelpiece and holding forth with his hilarious anecdotes. So I asked the Australian barman if he had ever heard of *Three Men in a Boat*. He looked at me in a funny way and said: 'Dunno mate, never tried it'. This was, after all, Soho. Then he told me a strange thing. This was not the only Blue Posts, there were two other pubs of the same name within a quarter of a mile. I went to the one in Brewer Street where

I was told there were not three but *five* pubs all called the same and all within a mile of each other. The name was very prevalent in this part of London. When I got to the fourth of the Blue Posts, one of the customers told me there were in fact twelve. In the interests of research it was necessary to buy a drink in each of the pubs, so by now I was getting a bit confused. Wherever I asked about the origin of this obscure name I was told a different story. The hostelry in Kingly Street had a very artistic sign outside showing two blue posts with a sedan chair being carried between them, suggesting that the posts indicated a kind of walk-in taxi rank. This is the official Soho Society explanation for the name.

In Rupert Street I was told the posts marked the boundaries of a medieval royal hunting ground where merrie men in tights used to shout 'so-ho' in pursuit of the uneatable, thus giving the area its name and something of its reputation.

On the other side of Oxford Street someone in the bar said it was all to do with 'twopenny-blue' stamps and the second-class mail as there was a post office nearby.

A chap called John Leonard entered the pub at that moment and added to my confusion. He said he was a former licensee of the Blue Posts in Berwick Street, and had carried out some research into this oddity, producing the most complex explanation so far.

He said that at the end of the seventeenth century a community of Huguenots fleeing religious persecution in France established themselves in Soho. These asylum seekers of the day were very skilled leather-workers and had a high reputation, in particular, for making saddles. They lived and worked in very crowded and squalid conditions and were not allowed to buy and sell on the premises – a way of restricting their ability to compete with native craftsmen. They would arrange to meet their clients in pubs, and so that customers would know where to find them, blue posts were placed outside the door.

The pub-crawl through Soho was not a waste of an afternoon. I learnt a little history and certainly must have drunk in a pub frequented by J. The one furthest east, and probably closest to his lodgings, was in Berwick Street. It also had a theatrical air to it, being close to theatre-land, with a photo of Jessie Matthews prominently on display. Apparently she learnt to dance in a room upstairs. The pub's website claimed that stage celebrities were often to be found here. J was a theatrical type, so I would put my money on his being here *once*. However, there is safety in numbers. You can write what you like about pot boys or Australian barmen from The Blue Posts. No one can be sure which pub you are talking about.

When I returned home I looked up a book on London pub names. It said colours were used to identify houses before numbering was introduced in the 1760s.[1] This did not sound convincing, and for all my efforts I did not feel I had got to the bottom of this affair, which seems destined to be one of life's great unsolved mysteries.

★

Through all this confusion we have wandered from Bloomsbury to Soho. We need to retrace our steps to the British Museum, which once housed the reading room where J did all his historical and geographical research about the Thames. The Reading Room is still there where he read that medical dictionary and concluded he had every disease in creation, but all the books he consulted have moved to the other side of the Euston Road to shelves in the splendid new British Library.

Walking back to his lodgings in Tavistock Place he must have passed through Bloomsbury Place, the setting for his second most famous work, *The Passing of the Third Floor Back,* a short story that he developed into a very successful play in 1908. It is set in a boarding house which must have been similar to those he lived in. It is a very short street, so the address of No 13 given in the stage directions is fictitious.

The 'morality' play, as it was called, is not much performed now, being regarded as too sentimental for these more cynical times. It tells of a mysterious stranger who comes to take a room at the back of the third floor of a boarding house. He is a man with a strange stooping walk, as if he carried the world's troubles about on his back. J once saw such a man and he became obsessed by him. While the stranger stays with them the bickering and unpleasant lodgers are transformed into courteous and considerate models of society. To us, the character of the Stranger seems insipid, and it would require an actor with a powerful stage presence to bring him alive. J found such a one in Forbes Robertson, and his audience saw the character as a 'Christ-like' figure, which produced a frisson of controversy. The portrayal of Jesus was forbidden on the stage in those days of censorship by the Lord Chamberlain. How far could you go? Was he or wasn't he Christ himself?

★

There are three volumes we know J would have consulted before setting out to write his book and we shall be quoting from two of them on our journey.

First is *Dickens's Dictionary of the Thames* published in 1887.[2] The author is Charles Dickens Junior, son of the great novelist. It contains brief histories and descriptions of riverside towns and churches, and advice on bathing, boating and camping, plus all the minutiae required by the traveller concerning postal arrangements, police stations etc. There is a dour tone, understandable perhaps in the son of a literary genius forced to earn his bread with a book detailing early closing days and rail fares.

J told a friend that one of the first things he did after deciding to write the book was to read Dugdale.[3] This would be *The Topographical Dictionary of England and Wales* by Thomas Dugdale, published in 1848. On the strength of this I ordered a reprint of the book from the British Library Historical Collection. It proved to be a gazetteer listing all the towns and villages in the two Kingdoms in alphabetical order, and I was disappointed when I discovered it ended in the middle of the Bs. The book that J consulted was of four volumes and ended with Zennor. The last entry in my copy was Birches in Shropshire, and it provided a sensational cliff-hanger ending. In 1723 Birches was the scene of a 'violent convulsion of nature' ... 'a barn, after travelling 35 yards, was swallowed up ... The inhabitants fled, but were' – and there the facsimile of the original book ended[4.] I felt obliged to consult the internet to make sure nobody had been killed. However, being so detailed and taking up so many volumes, I concluded it would be the kind of book that contained all the information J's publisher decided to throw out.

Then there was *The Thames from its Source to the Sea* by Sir Walter Armstrong, printed in 1886[5]. The give-away here is that J quotes his claim that Culham Lock is the deepest and coldest on the Thames. It is certainly not the deepest, that distinction belongs to Sandford. Whether it is the coldest would be difficult to prove.

★

Dickens Junior tells us that the train journey to Kingston cost 1s 6d (7.5p) second class from Waterloo. Bribing the train driver to take the Exeter Mail to Kingston cost 2s 6d (12.5p) – J's joke. You got good value for money on the railways in those days.

It is at Kingston that we are told about the great oak staircase and, remarkably, it has survived a long saga of demolition and restoration. In the seventeenth century a great house stood on the market square. It was famous for its ornate staircase and panelled walls, and these survived when it became the Castle Inn. Towards the end of the nineteenth century the inn closed and the premises were taken over by a draper. J tells us that a friend of his bought a hat there on impulse and the grateful shopkeeper took him to see the staircase that would have done credit to a palace.

This led up to a drawing room that had been oak panelled, but the astonished friend was told that all the old woodwork had been covered with matchwood and wallpapered in a startling bright blue to brighten it up. J doesn't blame the shopkeeper for sharing the tastes of the time, he prefers it to phoney reconstructions of the 'old curiosity shop maniac'.

Despite redevelopment of the site as a department store, the staircase was preserved throughout the twentieth century. It was removed in 2001 and lovingly restored while the surrounding area was rebuilt. It now carries customers from a Next clothing store to a Costa coffee shop. I sat there once admiring the elaborate carving that includes a knight on horseback, a dragon, cherubs, bunches of grapes and the facade of a fabulous palace. Those in search of their lattes and cappuccinos never gave it a second glance.

Alas! nothing remains of the panelling described as adorning the walls all the way up the sides of the staircase, or of the carvings J describes in the room above. Kingston appears to have been careless with its panelling. An old photograph of Ye Olde Post House, which stood near the market square, shows painted on its front an advertisement for an oak gallery. This charming old building was demolished in 1954, an act of vandalism that puts the wallpapering shopkeeper in the shade.

It was at Kingston that J and Harris hired the skiff that was to take them up the Thames. Richard Turk, who had a boatyard on the river front, would have provided them with the boat and all the necessary camping equipment. It would have been in first rate condition, for Richard built his own craft and won many medals with them at international exhibitions. He even built a boat for Queen Victoria to use on a lake at Windsor.

Turk's is one of the oldest family businesses on the river, dating back to 1710. When I called on Michael, grandson of Richard, a few years back, he showed me around some boathouses which turned out to be an Aladdin's caves full of old movie props.

When Michael joined the family firm in 1956 his father, who was aged 80, had let the place run down, but he had initiated a glamorous line of business – working for films. And so a man from a family that had for generations been watermen on the Thames became waterman to the stars. As we wandered through sheds crammed with such things as model crocodiles, funnels and lobster pots, Michael pointed out a collapsible army boat used in *A Bridge Too Far* and a sailing dinghy that starred in *Swallows and Amazons*.

In addition to running the long-established family business of excursion boats and hiring skiffs, Michael travelled all over the world. He was boatmaster for the filming of *Murphy's War* on the Orinoco in Venezuela, and sailed a junk up the Yangtze for *Empire of the Sun*. He taught Jude Law to sail for his role in *The Talented Mr Ripley*.

In 1987 he commissioned a Turkish boatyard to build 'The Grand Turk' a 125ft replica of a three-masted 24-gun frigate that became familiar on television as 'HMS Indefatigable' in the *Hornblower* series.

With the coming of the digital age and advances in special effects, film makers had less need for elaborate props, so Turks held a great auction of their boats and other properties in 2010. The royal barge used by Henry VIII in *A Man for All Seasons* was bought by the Watermen's Company, and you might be lucky enough to see it being rowed in the annual Great River Race. Michael told me that J regularly hired boats from his grandfather, and the yard built the double skiff for the 1950s film of the book. Michael died in 2015 and his son Richard is now running the company. Let us hope it will continue for another 300 years.

It is only a short pull from Kingston to Hampton Court and its 'dear old wall' as J describes it, with its '50 shades and tints and hues in every ten yards'. J waxes so lyrical about that riverside wall that we feel it would outdo the combined resources of the Flower Show held here every year – 'don't bother with the plants, just look at this wall'.

Behind the wall is the famous maze where Harris boasted to a country cousin that he could find his way through in ten minutes. Harris said he had studied a map and the secret was always to take the first turning to the right. Harris could have found the map that was rather unsportingly printed in *The Book of the Thames* written by Mr and Mrs S C Hall and published in 1859.[6] You can take a Google street view of the maze, superimpose it over the old engraving and find that nothing has changed; it is still remarkably accurate. Harris's complaint, therefore, that the map must have been got up as a practical joke, sounds pretty lame. But no map, however accurate, is any use if you don't know your exact position on it.

The latter-day show-off would say: 'Nothing to this, I've got my iPhone with me and a GPS app that will show me exactly where I am to within a centimetre. Trust me, I'm a hedge fund manager – know all about hedges, ha-ha-ha'. Of course he would get lost with his foolish followers as surely as Harris. Maps and apps are useless in the hands of those too overconfident to use them properly. Harris's visit is still remembered here. A sound installation provides the atmospheric noises of rustling skirts, children's voices – and that of Harris losing his way.

It was while passing through Molesey Lock that Harris told J about his maze experience. This lock is in the centre of 'Appy 'Ampton, close to the railway station, which was only 45 minutes away from Waterloo. The cockneys thronged there and local people dressed in their Sunday finery to watch them. It was, says J, 'one of the gayest sights I know of near this dull old London town'. Perhaps a less agreeable aspect of the scene was the touts with their cries of 'tow you up to Sunbury, Shepperton, Weybridge!'[7]

But when the two passed through the lock they found themselves on their own. This was because it was a Saturday morning and the Weekend had not yet been invented. *Sunday* was the day for the river. Wage slaves like George had to work Saturday mornings and could only enjoy the afternoon. If they were shop workers they had to work the afternoon as well, but it was a legal requirement that they should have another afternoon off during the week to compensate. Early closing days are difficult to imagine in these days of seven to eleven shops and all-night supermarkets. But then they were a trap for the unwary traveller as towns chose different days to close their shops, usually on a Wednesday or Thursday. You needed someone like Dickens Junior to tell you, or you would be surprised to find the town centre silent as the grave.

Harris wanted to leave the boat at Hampton Church to go and see Mrs Thomas's tomb.

'Who is Mrs Thomas?' I asked.
'How should I know?' replied Harris. 'She's a lady that's got a funny tomb, and I want to see it.'

I am grateful to the Rev Derek Winterburn, Vicar of St Mary's, Hampton, for filling in this blank in Harris's knowledge. He sent me part of the parish history from which we learn that Susannah Thomas, who died in 1711, was the only daughter of Sir Dalby Thomas, a plantation owner in the West Indies at the time of the slave trade, so she was in fact, *Miss* Thomas. The marble sculpture shows her, book in hand, seated by the side of her reclining mother as if reading to her during an illness. The tomb, which commemorates both ladies, although Susannah is the first mentioned, is very sedate and classical – not funny at all, so Harris was in for a disappointment.

I think he had got it mixed up with the much cruder tomb of Sibel Penn, nurse to Edward VI, also in the church. Edward, born at Hampton Court, was the only legitimate son of Henry VIII, who died after a short reign at the age of 15. Dickens Junior describes it as a very curious monument with a recumbent female figure under a canopy 'bearing a singular resemblance to one of the ladies in the children's Noah's arks'. This tomb is rather remarkable because of the way it has been crammed into a confined space below the tower so that mirrors are needed to show Sibel's face and provide a view up her petticoats: 'funny' as Harris put it.

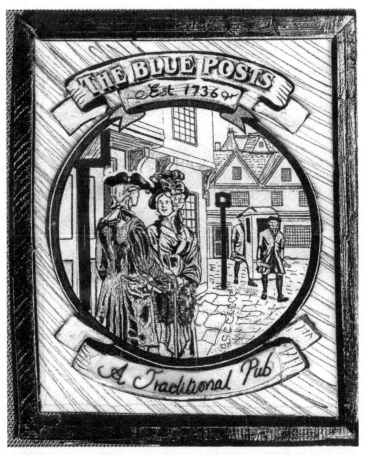

Drawing of the inn sign in Kingly Street, Soho, showing the blue posts (in solid black) as markers for sedan chair stops.

4

Oolite and So Forth

Hampton to Chertsey: Blackmail on the riverside – Unusual way of funding a golf club subscription – A fabulous grotto and a dogs' cemetery – How not to write about the river – The perils and advantages of towing.

HARRIS'S wish to stop at Hampton was an irritation to J, who was anxious to meet up with George for their appointed meeting at five o'clock. Nevertheless they had time to stop for lunch under the willows by Kempton Park. A pretty little spot J called it, but alas, it has gone forever, buried under high banks of clay when a water company dug out filter beds in 1892.

Kempton Park is now known as a racecourse which is some distance from the river, but the original park extended down to the Thames before it was despoiled to slake the thirst of the Metropolis. It is on the opposite bank from the towpath where there is public right of way, and this might have seemed a more obvious mooring. But it was not the place for a quiet picnic; you might be disturbed by the towlines of other boaters trudging along the path, or, even worse, a rough gang of men hauling a barge; 'scuffle hunters' they were called for their readiness to get into a fight for the chance of work.

The two boaters chose to stop on the other side, which was private land, although the owner of the park in those days seems to have taken a benevolent view on mooring, and J was pretty sure of his ground when a passing 'rough' tried to cheat him out of a shilling for the right to tie up the boat there.

He refused to pay, with Harris, 'a well-made man of about number one size looking hard and bony', backing him up. Not surprisingly the would-be blackmailer sloped off muttering that he would fetch his master – but of course he never reappeared. This kind of extortion was frequently practised on Victorian boaters and is not unknown these days. It was based on a real incident which J told of in a letter to the *Lock to Lock Times* in August 1888.

The other Sunday I camped for lunch on the favourite bit of ground under the willows at Kempton Park. As is getting so usual now, a man came round to know if everybody knew that this was private ground etc. I saw many people give him a shilling – he must have made some half-a-sovereign in about ten minutes … Who was he and what did he do with the money, and what would you call the people who are simple enough to part [with it]?

Lazy and timid is what J called them in his book.

Of course there are still people around on the river trying to extort money from the unwary. A resident of an Upper Thames village told me once of a farm manager who used to boast in the pub about 'those stupid boaters' who paid for his golf club subscription and running his Land Rover. He had been charging £3 a night mooring fees quite illegally and without the knowledge of the landowner. The moral is: Never pay up unless there is a notice clearly stating that mooring fees are payable and giving the amount.

As the two boaters proceeded towards Shepperton, reference is made to Oatlands House. This stands on the site of an old palace, which J notes was stolen by Henry VIII. The bluff old rogue did this in his usual devious way. He was negotiating its purchase when the owner, William Rede, died, leaving the estate to his heir who was just a child. The king made his henchman Thomas Cromwell guardian of the boy and it was no surprise when Henry quickly emerged as the new owner.

He needed it in a hurry to build a palace for Anne of Cleeves, to whom he was betrothed. This was the lady described as a Flemish mare, and Henry lost no time in ditching her when he discovered what she really looked like. Although put up hastily, Henry took the time to adorn its floors with decorative tiles taken from Chertsey Abbey, which he had recently suppressed. One of the barges carrying them down stream was wrecked and its precious cargo rediscovered in the 1950s, when the Thames Conservancy had to call in police to stop it being looted. (I was allowed to tell this story provided I did not give away the location.) The palace remained in the possession of the Crown and various Royals frequently popped down there. After being burned down and rebuilt several times, it had, by the late eighteenth century, passed into the hands of the Duke of Newcastle.

Grottos were the fashion at this time, and the Duke set about building one that would make all rivals engaged in this gothic fad turn as green as their ferneries.

Grouchy old Dickens Junior says it took 20 years to construct at a cost of £40,000, and remarks: 'How £40,000 could have been spent in constructing two or three rooms and a passage of oyster shells and cement is a mystery.' Other Victorian commentators perpetuated the myth of its extraordinarily long construction period by claiming that an Italian grotto-builder and his two sons laboured away for 20 years on the structure. In fact it was built in six years by Josiah Lane and his son who came from Wiltshire.

There was an elaborate cupola over the principal chamber composed of satin-spar stalactites. All the inner walls were inlaid with many fine specimens of minerals and shells placed with endless patience and skill. It is sad that after all this effort references to it are universally sneering.

Wasted labour and misapplied ingenuity seems to sum it up in contemporary accounts, while Horace Walpole sniggered and said the main chamber 'was square, regular, and, which never happened to a grotto before, lives up one pair of stairs, yet only looks on a basin of dirty water'.

J remarks that the grotto is supposed to be very wonderful and that you can see it for a fee, 'but I cannot see much in it myself'. This seems rather an ungracious comment about the painstaking assemblage of shells and minerals from a man who in later life would enjoy creating a floor for his summerhouse from chicken bones – and this I will touch on later. Many of us would gladly pay the fee if we could see the grotto today, but we cannot. It was the victim of a particularly flagrant piece of municipal vandalism in the late 1940s. Walton and Weybridge Urban District Council, as it then was, demolished it as a dangerous structure. *The Architectural Review* noted at the time: 'that a building of the very special kind of importance of the Oatlands grotto should have been destroyed without chance of a public appeal to save it is almost incredible and ought to be quite impossible'.[1]

It is strange how the hammer of the demolition man falling on a building suddenly transforms it into a priceless piece of our heritage. Under the heading 'Vandalism Triumphant', Marcus Whiffen wrote in the same issue:

'The simple fact is that it was a work of art. It was a work of art not merely because its ornaments, the tufa and the ammonites and spars and corals and cowries, were applied with a feeling for their distinctive decorative possibilities, but even more because the ingenious involutions of its plan and an extraordinary skilful use of light gave a sense of mystery and size to a structure which on paper is not of remarkable dimensions. And Oatlands grotto was also – what is perhaps even rarer than a work of art – a work of fantasy.'

Whiffen witnessed its sad destruction under pickaxe and pneumatic drill. Its core was of good solid brickwork and any unsoundness could not have been of a radical nature, he concluded. Was it the wasted labour of six man-years or a place of magical fantasy? We can no longer judge.

J has not finished with Oatlands, he goes on to describe another remarkable feature of this estate – a dogs' cemetery. This was established by the Duchess of York – the one who died in 1820 – the Yorks having bought the house from the Newcastles. Interred in a secluded dell were fifty of her pets, each marked with an appropriate tombstone. (Some Victorian guidebooks claim that there were seventy). J says she was very fond of dogs and kept an immense number of them. On the other hand, she may not have been very good at looking after them. A Regency Beau and property speculator called Edward Hughes Ball, known to his friends as The Golden Ball, bought the estate from the Duke of York when the latter fell on hard times, and it was broken up into building lots. The house, in Italianate style, was converted to a hotel.

The Oatlands Park Hotel, as it is now called, is magnificently situated with views high over the Thames to the flatlands of Middlesex, only slightly spoilt by the hangars of Heathrow Airport. It makes much of its historic grounds on its internet home page. You may find traces of the grotto, and some of the headstones from the dogs' cemetery have been set in a lawn surrounded by a tasteful white plastic chain-link fence to protect them from desecration by hind-leg salutes of their doggie descendants. There are no inscriptions to be read. They have either been worn away or the stones placed upside down. It does not seem to have been much of a loss. R R Bolland[2] visited the hotel in the 1960s and recorded such lapidary gems as

Dinah
A faithful companion
Died much respected
22 June 1881 aged 7 years
Mab
Aged 15 years
1889

He counted 69 of them, some dating from the 1930s.

Their new location is near the lounge bar patio, so you can now saunter out and view the stones with glass in hand. Harris would have approved of that.

Walton itself suffered more than any other town on the river from 1960s developers who destroyed much of its character. The rebuilding of the shopping centre swept away many fine buildings dating back to the eighteenth century. The crass concrete structures incorporating a multi-storey car park have since – happily – been demolished themselves and replaced with something more fitting. It is pleasing to record that the great destroyer itself, Weybridge and Walton council – having built a monstrous town hall in 1965 – was abolished in 1991 under local government reorganisation. This unsightly monument to overweening pride and bureaucratic destruction has since been knocked down and replaced by a supermarket.

Before leaving Walton I recommend male chauvinists of the old school to make a pilgrimage to St Mary's Church, where they can see one of the few scold's bridles left in the country. This is a metal frame which was fitted over the head of malicious gossips and has a two-inch iron prong to protrude over the tongue.

J jocularly remarks that these instruments of torture fell out of use because there was a shortage of iron and no other metal could be found that was strong enough. Walton's benefactor in 1632 was one Chester, said to have lost his estate because of a gossiping, lying woman.

The bridle was stolen from its glass case in 1965 by someone who obviously had urgent need of it. It was almost falling to pieces due to the vitriol in which it had been bathed during its active career. Fortunately, the verger at the time had made an exact copy, and this is on view in the original display case, on the front of which is the following charming couplet:

Chester presents Walton with a bridle,
To curb women's tongues, that talk so idle.

Before we leave Walton I should remark that of all Thames towns it has been the most unlucky with its bridges. The pleasing modern structure opened in 2013 is the sixth attempt to span the river here. The first was built in 1750 out of timber, and so ingeniously designed that any one piece could be removed and replaced without disturbing the rest. This 'mathematical bridge' was very picturesque and the subject of a painting by Canaletto. It had clay ramps at either end and, as the old nursery rhyme of London Bridge has it: 'Wood and clay will wash away', so in 1787 a stone bridge was needed to replace it.

This collapsed in a storm in 1859 and the Victorians replaced it with an iron structure which 'bent and bowed' after being hit by a Second

World War bomb. Two temporary bridges were then built before the present elegant reinforced concrete rainbow arch was erected at a cost of £32.3m and opened in 2013. Of course it is not traditional like the lovely old stone and brick bridges that we meet further up the Thames. But as we pass under it we can sigh with relief that so many delightful towns from here on have avoided Walton's fate.

Just above the bridge is 'Corway Stakes', where J says Julius Caesar and his army forded the river during his second invasion in 54 BC, despite pointed stakes having been hammered into the bottom by his British opponent, Cassivelaunus.

The place is usually spelt Cowey or Coway Stakes, so Corway looks like a misprint. In any case the story about this early equivalent to barbed wire has long been pooh-poohed by historians. They point out that those wooden stakes ran directly across the river rather than as a barrier lengthwise, and the course of the Thames has changed since Roman times anyway. They were probably the footings for an Anglos Saxon weir or primitive bridge. Even Charles Dickens Junior dryly dismisses the tale as recorded by Bede. 'It does not appear that the venerable one himself had ocular demonstration of the fact.'

The pointed stakes, whenever they were dredged up, were much prized as historic relics and created a market for sharp old pieces of rotten timber. Many found their way into museums and the private collections of antiquarian gentlemen. If you come across one, don't be fooled.

J says Halliford and Shepperton are both pretty spots, but there is nothing remarkable about either of them. Modern boaters would see this as much to their credit after Walton's experience. It is strange that a chap as lively as Harris should take such an interest in tombs and epitaphs. As Shepperton is reached, J becomes so anxious that his companion will want to see a memorial in the church that he knocks his hat off to distract him. Perhaps it is just as well that Harris forgets all about his beloved graves, for this is a particularly sad one, a maudlin moment would be out of place here.

The tomb was one of the weepiest on the Victorian grave enthusiasts' itinerary and carries a poem written by Thomas Love Peacock on the death of his three-year-old daughter in 1826. Poor Mrs Peacock never got over this bereavement and the disastrous consequences blighted Peacock's career. This is particularly sad from our point of view, as he was a pioneer of leisure boating on the Thames. He used memories of holidays on the river with Shelley in his novel *Crochet Castle*, which describes how a party of elegant people sets off from the eponymous stately pile – probably Park Place at Henley – for a journey up the Thames and Severn Canal, and through the Ellesmere Canal from which the romantic scenery of North Wales is reached.

> Four beautiful cabined pinnaces, one for the ladies, one for the gentlemen, one for the kitchen and servants, one for a dining room and band of musicians weighed anchor on a fine morning from below Crochet Castle and were towed merrily by strong trotting horses against the stream of the Thames.

They were 'going it a bit' as J and his pals would have said, and it would seem that we are in for some exquisite Downton Abbey version of the more famous jolly jaunt. But we would be disappointed.

> They passed from the district of chalk, successively into the districts of clay and sand-rock, of oolite and so forth. Sometimes they dined in their floating dining room.

This luxurious cruise could hardly be more different to that of the rough and ready voyage of the Three Men. But whereas the mundane became a masterpiece under J's light touch, what promised to be a glittering excursion is turned into dross by Peacock's literary style. 'Oolite and so forth' just about sums it up. He is more interested in recording the clever conversations of his companions than giving a straightforward account of their adventure, and so robs us of a rare chance to glimpse pleasure boating in those far off days of the romantic age.

Earlier, J had written that it was planned to pick George up at Shepperton at 5pm. In fact, they picked him up at Weybridge, where the River Wey navigation meets the river at Thames Lock. To do this, they had to make a diversion of a quarter of a mile up a weir stream. It is a short journey from Weybridge station to this lock compared to the two miles George would have had to trudge with his luggage from Shepperton Station to Shepperton Lock, so they were doing him a favour. His arrival was greeted with such a row that the lockkeeper feared someone had fallen into the water and went to get his grappling irons.[3]

This jubilation was quickly over.

George brought an unwelcome surprise package with him – a banjo. He didn't know how to play it, so he brought an instruction book along as well. Minstrel music from the Deep South of the USA was all the rage then and pale imitations of the real thing resulted in songs more suited to the Mississippi than an English river.

As a writer to the *Lock to Lock Times* put it[4]: 'You will agree with me, I think, that the banjo is the instrument of the Thames, and the Thames has been very badly treated by the writers of banjo music and song'. He quotes as an example:

As we was floatin' down de ribber in de ole steam boat
When a great big shark come and set us all afloat.

He suggested that songs should feature those great adornments of the river, the houseboats.

Of course, if you were a notoriously bad singer like George and didn't know how to play the accompaniment, it hardly mattered what you sang. But it was better perhaps to sing some rubbish than desecrate a cherished melody that had never done you any harm.

George, after a hard morning's work at the bank, the railway journey and walk to the river, welcomed the chance to flop down on the cushions at the back of the boat, while his companions rowed another quarter of a mile to take them back on course up river. This did not go down well, and J wrote: 'we made George work now we had got him'. Harris replied to George's protestations that he had a hard time by saying: 'Ah! And now you are going to have a hard time on the river for a change', and the new arrival is put to work towing the boat on from Shepperton to Penton Hook Lock, a distance of four miles.

Towing from the bank was the most popular means of making progress up the river at this time. Evidence had been given to the Select Committee on Thames Preservation in 1884 that 'the practice of tracking or towing is driving out rowing as far as going against the stream is concerned.'

While it is more efficient to have a point on terra firma from which to move a boat it is no longer an option today. Bushes and trees have been allowed to grow along the tow path and would obstruct any line.

This is a great shame as towing is an undeniably green way of shifting a boat and does not seem to require any special skill. Perhaps it should be re-introduced on appropriate stretches of the river and bankside vegetation removed. Indeed, the ghost of J hovers over me and says it should be made compulsory. He would dearly love to see the owners of large plastic 'gin palaces' get out and pull them.

The great inconvenience of this practice was the need to carry a long tow rope which inevitably tied itself into knots or got tangled with stuff in the bottom of the boat. This could cause much argument and ill-feeling, as J notes.

The basic rule was, and remains, that when a boat is coming upstream it gives way to a boat being towed down with the current because that boat has greater difficulty stopping. Of course, if you came up against a gang of 'scuffle hunters' you would not argue the point.

J tells with delight of the misfortune attending a party of men who had chosen the lazy option of paying a boy with a donkey to pull their skiff. They were going at a cracking rate when one of them pulled the wrong rudder string and they were hauled up onto the bank and thrown out of the boat.

Another hazard was that the tow rope might become detached from the boat while the tower plodded on regardless. This was a handy way of getting rid of that bane of Victorian courtship, the chaperone. Simply slip the rope and Mamma or Aunt Flo would drift harmlessly into the rushes, while the loving couple could stroll on with no one to interrupt their flirting.

Towing in those days was carefully regulated by the Thames Commissioners. They ordained that 'no vessel – unless in case of necessity, through strength of current – is to be towed from the bank otherwise than from a mast of sufficient height to protect the banks, gates, &c, from injury.'

This was no problem for the Three Men, who had a mast tall enough to carry a sail. But pulling a rope attached to a high point on a narrow-beamed skiff made it relatively unstable. Accidents happened, and as we shall see, they were sometimes fatal.

The late eighteenth-century grotto at Oatlands Park, Walton-on-Thames, demolished in the 1940s

5

Gallant Knights Ride In

Chertsey to Penton Hook: Steam powered submarines – A town with an image problem – The most ancient English yew – Arguments over the spot where Magna Carta was signed – Modern perils of boiling a kettle – The dangers of being on the River at night.

J WAS right to be rude about steamboats. There was some pretty dangerous stuff about on the Thames in his day. At Chiswick, John Thornycroft was building gunboats, while up at Chertsey – through which the Three now pass – was what Dickens Junior scathingly described as the Des Vignes torpedo boat manufactory.

If steamboats engendered fear and loathing in the breasts of Victorian boaters, then they would regard the pioneer engineer George Des Vignes as the chief demon. Today he is revered among steam enthusiasts as a technical genius. But in his day a reputation for recklessness led to him being charged with manslaughter at the Old Bailey, although he was acquitted.

It was his practice to take the fast umpire boats he had built to regattas up and down the river so that he could demonstrate their speeding potential and sell them off to sporting gents who wanted to make a splash.

Fast steam boats led him on to building the new-fangled torpedo boats which he supplied to the Turkish navy. The sight of one of these sinister craft, the cutting edge naval weapon of its day, moored up in peaceful Chertsey, must have jarred with those out for a quiet Sunday row. Furthermore, the enterprise and ingenuity of this boatyard resulted in it producing a secret weapon of more deadly potential. Deadly, that is, for people foolish enough to try to navigate it. For this was the – totally impractical – steam powered submarine.

It is worth taking time out from our journey to consider this wonder. It came about because the Turks had heard that the Greeks had got hold of submarines, and they did not want to get left behind in the Balkans arms race. Naturally they turned to their torpedo boat supplier.

The disadvantages of driving a submarine by steam are obvious to any schoolboy or girl. But this did not discourage Des Vignes or his clients. The way it operated was as follows.

First you had to raise steam. As the almost submerged steel hull of the sub acted as a pretty efficient heat sink, this might take you up to 24 hours. You then had to rake out the fire, remove the funnel, close the smoke escape valve and seal the fire door. You were then left with sufficient pressure in the boiler for the steam engine to work *theoretically* for four hours if you were able to survive the dreadful heat and fumes.

The designers were not mad enough to make a craft that could actually sink, so it did not have the ballast tanks seen in modern subs. The vessel had just enough buoyancy to keep it on the surface and it dived by means of horizontal propellers mounted on the deck. When the engine ran out of steam, the propellers stopped and the craft automatically returned to the surface.

The first submarine of this type was designed by the Rev George Garrett, curate of Moss Side, Manchester. He gave it the name 'Resurgam' meaning 'I rise again', emphasising its fail-safe principle in a word with religious overtones appropriate for a man of the cloth.

The idea was taken up by the Swedish industrialist Thorsten Nordenfelt, and it was his design for 100ft-long boats with a beam of 12ft that was adopted by Des Vignes. Chertsey, however, was not an ideal place to build such large craft. They had to be constructed in three sections so that they could be carried down-river on barges for shipment through the Mediterranean, then bolted together again.

Des Vignes had the reputation of being a bit of a chancer, and I am tempted to wonder if he ever secretly tested his submarines on the river. I like to imagine that on some earlier jaunt Harris might have shouted out as he passed through Chertsey: 'I say you chaps, isn't that one of those new-fangled thingummy-jigs – what-you-ma'-call-its – SUBMARINES!' George and J would have looked at each other knowingly and checked the whisky bottle.

In the event, the submarine enterprise was doomed to failure. Only one of the boats was ever reassembled and the Turks were unable to find sailors foolhardy enough to test it. They rusted away on the Bosporus, remaining as a scary item on the Turkish Navy list until 1910.

Although a mechanical genius, Des Vignes' talents did not extend into the world of commerce. In 1887 he went bankrupt, so that when the

Three Men passed by they would have seen a For Sale sign rather than the sinister weapons of war.[1]

This was perhaps fortunate. If the Three had chosen to play a game of chicken, pretending not to notice a high-speed steam boat driven by Des Vignes, I have no doubt about who would have been the losers.

J and friends covered just over twelve miles and six locks in their first day. They found the last pull hard going, and would have settled for a spot between a coal barge and a gas works; they were so weary and anxious to moor up for the night.

This would have been Staines, noted in their day for the manufacture of linoleum floor covering, and this would have produced an unpleasant whiff for those seeking a place to lay their weary heads.

It is generous of J not to name the town – just to mention the coal and gas. Staines has always suffered from an image problem, which is inevitable when the name is a synonym for grot. As the late Kenneth Horne once joked: 'How do you get rid of Stain(e)s? – blow up the bridge and burn the cinema'. Or: 'How do you get rid of stains in beds? Answer: Don't worry. It's not in Beds but Surrey.' In May 2012 the town officially changed its name to the more genteel Staines-upon-Thames, supposedly because it had become too closely identified with Ali G, Sacha Baron Cohen's spoof rapper, who had his fictional home here.

Then in 2013 when the Thames Path was voted the second best urban walk in the world by the *Lonely Planet* travel guide, *The Times* wrote that Staines was the one industrial blot on the landscape. A resident quickly sent a letter to point out that it was in fact a green and leafy place now, with no industrial estates near the river.[2] The only reference to its slightly whiffy past is a statue representing lino workers in the high street.

The Three Men had originally planned to push on to Magna Carta Island, but instead stopped for the night at Picnic Point, Ankerwycke, a popular spot with Victorian pleasure seekers. It was only 400 yards away from their intended destination anyway. Dickens Junior refers to a small cottage or folly here known as The Picnic. This was burnt down in the 1940s causing the death of its reclusive occupant. The river here takes a sharp bend to create a little peninsula, and there was a pleasant nook under a very great elm tree, where the boat could be moored to the spreading roots.

The bank at Ankerwycke remains wooded to this day, and Ankerwycke Park, which includes ruins of the ancient priory, is now in the care of the

National Trust, so public access is allowed. J refers to this spot as one of the places where Henry VIII courted Anne Boleyn.

The great glory of Ankerwycke is not mentioned by J, however. This is the ancient yew, thought to be around 2,500 years old, and among the oldest in Britain. It has lived so long by generating new trunks around its original roots, and now has a girth of 26ft (eight metres). It is much venerated by present-day mystics and pagans, and little votive offerings are left attached to its boughs. It is even believed by some that Magna Carta was sealed beneath it.[3]

A lot happens here in the book. It is the Three's first night spent on the river, and there is all the fun of erecting the camping cover over the iron hoops that fitted into sockets in the sides of the boat. These were hinged in the middle for easy stowage and were of different sizes, so they had to be attached in the right order. Needless-to-say the Three, after a great struggle, fitted them the wrong way round and had difficulty pulling them out in order to start all over again. George and Harris managed to get themselves rolled up in the cover and Harris was almost suffocated.

It is possible for those who wish to embark on a Thames adventure in the most authentic Victorian way to hire a skiff of this kind with all the necessary accoutrements. Nowadays it is made simpler by not having to pull a heavy tarpaulin over the boat at night. Synthetic weatherproof fabrics will keep both boaters and boat dry at a fraction of the weight and space required by the nineteenth century equivalents.

But sleeping in an open boat still requires the chore of emptying practically everything out of it in order to create enough space to lie flat. Your stores will need to be protected from any overnight rain, and everything will need to be packed neatly back into place the following morning.

Do not follow J's practice of boiling a kettle in the front of the boat, especially if you intend to turn your back on it and ignore it – he says you should do this because if it sees you are impatient for it to boil it will not sing. Very popular today are the little flat stoves which work with butane gas cartridges. I have known one to erupt in a mass of flames, and the Environment Agency issued a warning concerning them a few years back. Always use them on the bank and keep a beady eye on them. Not everything has improved.

It is not surprising that J has an uncomfortable night and awakes after a nightmare to get out of the boat and contemplate the stars. He launches into a long poetic passage and tells the story of a goodly knight who becomes parted from his companions and lost in a dark forest. Near to death, a stately maiden takes him by the hand and shows him a wondrous vision whereby he is saved.

And the name of the dark forest was Sorrow; but of the vision that the good knight saw therein we may not speak or tell.

A few pages later knights appear once again. 'Gay-cloaked companies of knights and squires have ridden in, all travel stained and dusty.' It is 1215 and they have come for the sealing of Magna Carta, a short distance from the boaters' overnight stop. J describes this in the chapter heading as a historical retrospect, specially inserted for the use of schools.

It is certainly the excuse for another passage of purple prose, and it is in striking contrast to the chatty style we have become used to.

No Victorian could have been said to have 'done' the Thames without visiting Magna Carta Island at Runnymede, which was well prepared for the tourist industry. George Harcourt, who lived in the old Ankerwycke House, rebuilt his fisherman's lodge on the island in splendid style. He decorated it with a series of coats of arms of the various barons present at the sealing, and installed an octagonal stone. It solemnly reads:

BE IT REMEMBERED, THAT ON THIS ISLAND, 25 JUNE 1215, JOHN KING OF ENGLAND SIGNED MAGNA CHARTA; AND IN THE YEAR 1834, THIS BUILDING WAS ERECTED, IN COMMEMORATION OF THAT GREAT AND IMPORTANT EVENT, BY GEORGE SIMON HARCOURT, ESQ LORD OF THIS MANOR, AND THEN HIGH SHERIFF OF THIS COUNTY.

So this is clearly not the stone on which the charter itself was sealed – King John could not write his name as J seemed to think. It is just a nineteenth century commemoration of the event, which may, or may not have taken place on this island, according to which historian you choose to believe.

J refuses to commit himself on the point, although he seems to accept the authenticity of the stone. He is 'inclined to give weight to the popular island theory'. If he had been one of the barons at the time he would have preferred to meet the king on the island where there was less chance of dirty tricks.

I needed an authoritative view on where the Charter was actually sealed (they didn't sign documents in those days), so I spoke to Dr Matthew Smith, curator of nearby Egham Museum, who was organising an exhibition to mark the 800th anniversary in 2015. He told me that the current thinking was in favour of Runnymede meadow. King John would not have risked being trapped on an island at a time of armed insurrection.

This is perhaps fortunate as we cannot visit Magna Carta Island today because it has become private property and its fishing lodge has grown to a seven-bedroom house with a swimming pool surrounded by 3.72 acres of grounds. The whole lot was put up for sale in 2014 with a price tag of £3.95 million. It was described at the time as the place where King John, with the protection of a circle of walnut trees and gentle curve of the river – which would keep enemy longbows out of range – met with his rebellious barons. Surprisingly there was no outcry about saving this precious plot for the nation and a few months later it was bought by a Chinese family.

Reverence for the Great Charter has created new memorials to visit. At the instigation of the American Bar Association, a granite pillar was set up within a small domed pavilion in 1957. It carries the words: 'To commemorate Magna Carta, symbol of Freedom Under Law,'[4] and is said to be on the very spot where the charter was sealed. Those prepared to climb a path up through the woods on Cooper's Hill will come to another modern monument. This is the memorial stone to John F Kennedy unveiled by the Queen in the presence of Jackie Kennedy in 1965. But the scene is dominated by the Air Forces Memorial completed in 1953 on a hill overlooking the historic meadow. It commemorates the 20,456 allied air men and women who have no known graves.

★

The Three Men were wise to moor up for the night before it got dark. Being on the river in a small unlit boat is always perilous, and I am prompted to tell a cautionary tale from my own experience. The year was 1994 and celebrations were being held at Richmond half-tide lock to mark its centenary after a £4m refurbishment by the Port of London Authority. It was originally built to keep the water in the river between Richmond and Teddington at a respectable level during low tides. After the removal of the old London Bridge, which acted like a dam, the Thames here could be reduced to a smelly trickle between muddy banks when the tide went out.

I had a slipper stern launch in those days, a fancy affair of varnished mahogany and polished chromium whose stern swept down to water level in a sexy curve. We had been asked to help 'dress' the lock chamber with other vintage wooden boats so that it would look good when Prince Andrew passed by to perform the ceremony.

I was joined by my wife, son and his girlfriend, and we were all dressed in best boating costume. As is often the case on these occasions, it rained all day.

My wife had to change into her 'fifties dress in a public lavatory before we could row out to the boat, which we had brought down river and left on a mooring.

We stayed most of the day in the boat while rain drummed on the hood. We did see the tops of some umbrellas, one of which might have been held over His Royal Highness. After it was all over, the plan was to take the boat back to Penton Hook Marina near Staines. I was meeting a friend at Teddington Lock to help me with this, allowing the family to dry out.

It was a miserable journey. We passed disconsolate rowers and punters soaked to the skin in their smart white shirts and ties. At every lock a sign was going up 'Caution stream increasing', the rain was having its effect.

The engine was running badly and the increasing current meant that we were making slower and slower progress. All the lockkeepers had gone off duty and we had to operate locks ourselves, which delayed us even more. We consoled ourselves by drinking from a bottle of red wine.

At Chertsey Bridge we thought we saw a curious thing – a boat moored up right inside one of the arches. As we approached, we found this was not the case but an optical illusion compounded by the dark. It was in fact tied up to the bank. I was so distracted by this phenomenon that we went through the wrong arch, the one leading to the weir stream instead of the lock.

I only realised this when I saw a patch of ferocious white water running ahead of us at right angles to the boat. I put the engine in reverse but it spluttered and stopped. The boat drifted onwards into the maelstrom and we were carried sideways against the hull of a steel barge. There was a mighty crack and a plastic wine glass was flung across the boat from one side to the other. I thought the boat had been split, but she drifted on into a patch of reeds without any sign of leaks.

I got the engine started again and we crossed the weir stream by pushing with our hands against the barge. We went the right way round through the lock, but our troubles were not over.

Penton Hook Marina is at the top of a horseshoe-shaped meander – the lock is across the narrow neck – so it was necessary for us to travel up this weir stream, which was running very fast, and at one point we were not making any progress at all. I grabbed a paddle to assist the engine, letting go of the steering wheel for a few seconds. The current swung us round and swept us back the way we had come, broadside on.

It was some distance before the stream relented and I could regain control of the boat. This time we were ready with two paddles to assist the engine, but even this was not enough at one point. Fortunately there were some moored boats which we were able to claw our way past.

It was past midnight before we arrived at Penton Hook Marina, to the relief of our wives. There were no mobile telephones in those days.

This story underlines the danger of navigating at night even in familiar waters. Some Victorian commentators such as Leslie, the artist whom we met earlier, thought it should be banned completely. He heard of a young man at Pangbourne who had been drowned in the lock in the late evening. His boat had been caught on the side of the lock and as the water rose he was flung out. Although a good swimmer, he was dragged down and sucked through the sluice hole, 'thus paying the penalty of his folly for being on the river in the dark.'

It was a bad enough risk for young men, but now, Leslie noted, women and children were frequently out at night. The contemporary 'bold and adventurous' girl made it hard for a young man to be prudent, he said, as she egged him on. 'I can see nothing for it but to order the locks to be closed at dark.'

This seems drastic to us, but Leslie would have been familiar with the tragedy of which we tell in the next chapter.

The Picnic, a small cottage at Ankerwycke

6

Disaster at Dockett Point

Chertsy: Fatal meeting between steamboat and skiff – Men with swords set a speed trap – Distinguished engineer on trial at the Old Bailey – Terrible loss of life on paddle steamer recalled.

I T ALL began as a pleasant outing on a Saturday evening in July 1880. Herbert Newcome, who kept a skiff on the Thames at Hampton, was rowing up to Staines, accompanied by his wife Amy, and another couple, William and Sarah Ballard, who had their two daughters with them, Nellie, nine months, and Edith, aged three. Newcome was an advertising agent, one of the newer occupations in the burgeoning Victorian middle class. He was aged 35 and had been active on the river since he was ten years old. Ballard was a jeweller and had been living for a while in Manchester, so had less boating experience.

The party's intention was to enjoy a light late evening meal – a meat tea as it was called then. It was a toss-up whether they would row home afterwards or take a horse-drawn carriage. Fatefully, they decided to row. Although it was a moonlit night, heavy clouds occasionally cloaked the water in darkness.

Further down the river a regatta had been held at Kingston and George Des Vignes, the celebrated boat builder and engineer, had taken his fast launch 'Wolverine' there to carry the umpires and hopefully pick up an order from someone impressed by her speed. He was on his way back to Chertsey, and such was his reputation that two Thames Conservancy Rangers on horseback, swords at their sides, were on the lookout to catch him for speeding. The Conservancy enforced its regulations by the sword in those days.

At Dockett Point, between Chertsey and Shepperton, Newcome and his party were in collision with the steamer. They were tumbled out of the boat and the two women and children were drowned. Des Vignes and his stoker, Harry Dagwell, were charged with feloniously killing and slaying all four.

The case was opened before Staines magistrates, where Newcome told of the terrible events of that evening. [1]

On July 24 his party had set out in a 25ft boat fitted with outriggers. These were iron frames on which the oars could be pivoted because the boat was too narrow to have rowlocks or thole pins, unlike the Three Men's skiff, and therefore less stable. He left Hampton for Staines, rowing part of the way together with Ballard and towing the rest. His wife, who was an experienced oarswoman, steered there and back, he said. The two women were sitting in the back on cushioned seats, the smallest child on Mrs Ballard's lap and the three-year-old between them.

They arrived at Staines at 7.15pm and went to The Angel where they had their meal and left in the boat at 8.45. They came through Penton Lock at 9.15 where they met a large steamer travelling in the same direction and asked it to give them a tow. The steamer refused because it was heavily laden and it was very late – another twist of fate.

The accident happened about two-thirds of the way between Shepperton Lock and Chertsey Lock, about 200 yards from Dockett Point. Mrs Newcome had called attention to a light from an approaching steamer.

Her husband looked over his right shoulder to confirm this – like all oarsmen, he had his back to the direction of travel. He thought the very small white light was close down on the water's edge and looked as if it was on a small boat. His wife suggested they should steer closer to the right-hand shore, and they did so.

By moving over to the right and keeping closer to the Surrey shore, the skiff was following the rule of the river – the opposite to that of the road where you keep left. The approaching steam boat, on the other hand, was on the wrong side. It was their practice when going up stream to take whichever side of the river on which the current was the slacker. Water runs faster along the outside of a curve because it has further to go, so Des Vignes was taking the inside of the curve around Dockett Point to save on coal.

About two minutes before the collision, the party in the skiff heard a whistle. Newcome did not hear the launch coming along but happened to know it was a '"noiseless" boat built on torpedo lines.' It made no more noise than a sewing machine.

Two seconds later, he looked around and saw the steamer heading into them at an angle of about 40 to 45 degrees. He got up when the steamer was close to try to stave her off – thinking she was only a small vessel – but she struck his skiff on the port bow. He was thrown into the water and did not come up for what seemed a long time. He could see nothing then but the hull of the launch about 100 yards away. He shouted out but got no answer. He swam to the shore where he was helped from the water by George Edwards, one of the rangers.

Five minutes later he saw the boat float down, but could not say whether she was capsized, as she lay so low in the water. In fact the boat remained upright and floated away with only three inches of water in her.

Ballard, who was a non-swimmer, was also thrown out of the boat but managed to grasp an oar until rescued by a life-buoy thrown from the launch.

Asked at what speed the launch was travelling, Newcome replied, 12mph, whereupon the chairman of the magistrates remarked: 'That is a great pace, as great as done by the Oxford and Cambridge boats at Putney.' Newcome said a piece of the boat's side 2ft 8in long was cut out as cleanly as if by a knife and the other side was damaged, two planks being knocked out.

After the collision, the steamboat took the two survivors back to Shepperton Lock and Des Vignes encouraged them to dry out by leaning on the boiler. Newcome complained that the only light on the steam boat had been too weak, to which Des Vignes replied: 'Don't make it too hard for me'. Ballard thought it very unmanly that the steamboat skipper should make a remark like that – he seemed to be thinking only about himself. Although Des Vignes had done everything possible to save those in the water, it was his general lack of sympathy that caused Newcome to instigate criminal proceedings.

At Shepperton the lockkeeper commented: 'Ah Mr DesVignes, I told you what would happen'. Des Vignes made no reply.

Questioned about the speed of the boat, Ranger Edwards said that after the launch left Chertsey Lock, he walked his horse around Dockett Point at three to four miles an hour keeping pace with it for about 100 yards before it steamed away at twice its previous rate. He heard the Des Vignes launch exchange whistles with the 'Formosa', travelling in the opposite direction. Two or three minutes later he heard a crash and a scream.

He hastened to the spot, took off his sword and scabbard and used it to pull Newcome out of the water. He asked how many more were in the river and Newcome replied: 'My dear wife is drowned, and I wish I was also'. The officer went for drag lines, and the Shepperton lockkeeper – with several young men who were camping near by – came up to render assistance.

Henry Joyce, lockkeeper at Sunbury, told the court that the launch had no light on passing through the lock, a serious matter as Conservancy rules decreed that a steamer travelling at night without lights should not be allowed to travel any further. Des Vignes asked Joyce to lend him one. It had a large glass lens – known as a bullseye – and a double-wick. This was better than those carried by some steam vessels, Joyce said.

James Newble, keeper of Shepperton Lock, remembered saying to Des Vignes when the launch was in the lock: 'Be careful Sir, I believe there is a "plant" on tonight'. By that he meant that a horse patrol was out to see if Mr Des Vignes was going to travel fast or not. 'I did not say to Mr DesVignes, as Mr Newcome was standing by; "Oh Mr Des Vignes! I told you what would happen"'. But he did comment that 'There would soon be another "Princess Alice" disaster if things were allowed to go on this way.'

To his embarrassment, Newble had to account to the magistrates for the absence of up-to-date entries in his log book around the time of the accident. Not surprisingly, he was dismissed by the Thames Conservancy in 1882. Boats passing through locks had to pay a fee in those days, so it looks as if Newble was pocketing the cash. And he had betrayed the confidence of his employers by revealing the presence of the 'speed trap'.

Charles Burgoyne, skipper of the 'Formosa' said it was very dark, and the spot where the collision occurred was one of the worst on the river. He could not tell from the one light on which side of the river the launch was coming.

Very surprisingly, the Conservancy in those days only required one light above the tidal limit at Teddington, and not green starboard and red port lights which is now the universal rule. Burgoyne always carried green, white and red lights, and had written to Captain Burstal of the Conservancy advising that these be made compulsory.

William Burgoyne, his brother, estimated the speed of the Des Vignes boat at 10mph. He did not think the boat could have been travelling as fast as 12mph at the time of the collision as that would have caused the skiff to be cut in half. He also said that if the rowing boat had been hit by the straight-stemmed launch at an angle of 45 degrees travelling at the speed described by Newcome, the outriggers would have been torn away.

The barrister defending Des Vignes did not call any witnesses at the conclusion of the committal hearing, preferring instead to rely on contradictions in the prosecution's evidence. His client had been charged with gross negligence in the navigation of his launch, amounting in law to felony, a crime that carried a stiff prison sentence. Yet, he submitted, the evidence did not stand up.

It was alleged that no whistle had been sounded, but Newcome, the rangers and William Burgoyne had all said they had heard one. Then it was said that Des Vignes was not showing sufficient light, yet the Sunbury lockkeeper had told the court that he thought the light was sufficient. Charles Burgoyne had said the light could be seen at 100 yards, and Edwards the ranger confirmed that its rays could be seen across the river.

As to speed, Newcome's estimate was founded only on a guess. The Thames ranger had said the launch kept pace with his horse at 3½mph, then had speeded up to 7mph. If the skiff had been struck at an angle of 45 degrees at 12mph, experts said it would have ended up on the bank.

The defence submitted that the accident had occurred because the people in the skiff had panicked and altered their course at the last moment.

Surprisingly, in the light of the evidence, the magistrates still found against Des Vignes and he was committed for trial at the Central Criminal Court – the Old Bailey. But the case against the stoker was dismissed.

Going beyond the evidence, the chairman pursued a line of his own, remarking that an old admiral had told him that 75 per cent of marine accidents were due to keeping a bad lookout, and if there had been a proper lookout on the steamboat the accident would not have happened. Keeping a good lookout was not always easy on those early steamboats. Evidence had been given that the launch had a funnel 4ft high on a plinth which obstructed the view from the steering position behind it.

It was only after the committal was announced that Des Vignes addressed the court. He said: 'I have only to say that the accident only happened in consequence of the actions of the people in the row-boat. When we were within a short distance of them, they altered their course and pulled straight across our bow. We were not going at more than about five miles an hour and should have gone quite clear of them if they had kept on their course. The collision was entirely their own fault.'

When the trial opened at the Old Bailey the prosecution witness, Newble the Shepperton Lockkeeper, denied he had said to Des Vignes, 'I told you what would happen.' His words were: 'Oh Mr Des Vignes, how did this happen?' His remark about the danger of another 'Princess Alice' disaster had applied to another launch that had passed in the afternoon, he said.

This time defence witnesses were called, principally the stoker, Harry Dagwell. He said that the whistle was sounded while going round Dockett's Point, and after travelling about 100 yards he saw a rowing boat about 90 yards away on the Middlesex side. They were travelling at about 4mph. When the boat got to within 15ft of them it shot under their bow. After the collision he was ordered by Des Vignes, who was steering, to reverse the engine, and the launch came to an immediate stop. If the rowing boat had not changed course there would have been room for them to pass safely.

Des Vignes did not elect to give evidence, and therefore could not be cross-examined on his actions prior to the tragedy. Expert witnesses were called to give evidence that the skiff had been struck at an angle of 45 degrees, consistent with it having turned across the launch's bows and that the latter could not have been travelling at any great speed.

An expert witness from the London Rowing Club said he thought the rowing boat was not safe to carry ladies on the river at night.

Newcome had said that his wife, who was very experienced with boats, had been steering, but it was Mrs Ballard who had the steering lines tangled round her arms when her body was recovered from the water the following morning. The rudder was still attached, having floated free from the boat. The defence claimed that in her nervousness, inexperience and excitement she might have pulled the wrong string and brought the boat across the bow of the steam launch at the last moment.

Before considering their verdict, the jury were asked to look through a window of the court at the damaged skiff. After a few minutes consultation in the box they found the defendant not guilty, and the judge remarked: 'I think that that would have been a very hard verdict if you had found to the contrary.'

The Marine Engineer, commenting on the trial, was less sympathetic, and said:

Mr Des Vignes has little reason to complain that he was put on trial on such a serious charge, since it has resulted in clearing up the case against him.

The effect of this calamity and of the trials which have arisen out of it has been to make the owners of steam launches a good deal more careful. But this is only a temporary result… It is up to the Thames Conservancy to take the whole subject in hand at once and put an end to the reign of terror which really exists on the river.

The journal believed that a total ban on steam launches on the Upper Thames, advocated in many quarters, should only be resorted to if regulation proved impossible. There should be severe limitations on speed and clear rules for avoiding collision.

There was one positive result from the tragedy. Red and green navigation lights became compulsory on the non-tidal Thames thereafter. The rule of the road was enforced as it already had been on the tidal river – always pass each other on the right.

The 'Princess Alice' disaster referred to by the Shepperton Lockkeeper had occurred in 1878, when the paddle steamer of that name crowded with trippers was in collision with the 'Bywell Castle', a collier, as she came up the Barking Reach. About 650 lives were lost – nobody could be sure exactly how many – making it one of the worst peace-time civilian disaster in British history.

Almost everyone in the East End of London had family or friends who had taken a trip on the 'Alice'. Her captain, William Grinstead, was a local celebrity so it was not surprising that rumours soon started to circulate that the captain of the 'Bywell Castle' had been drunk on the bridge.

But the facts speak for themselves. The captain of the collier was on the bridge together with an experienced Thames pilot who had responsibility for the safe navigation of the ship. On the 'Alice', however, an inexperienced crew member was at the helm. But it was a year later that the Court of Appeal finally put the blame for the tragedy on the paddle steamer.

Many passengers were trapped within the wreck. Piles of bodies were found around the exits of the saloon when the boat was raised. Those who jumped into the water were drowned in the poisonous effluent of London's sewers, which had been opened to release their toxic waste into the ebb tide.

There are similarities between this disaster and the smaller tragedy up-river two years later. A steam boat was on the 'wrong' side of the river in order to take advantage of the slacker current while proceeding upstream in order to save on coal, as custom had allowed it. The smaller boat changed direction at the last moment and was struck at a right angle. It took a few years, however, before the navigation rules for the tidal river were established – that boats should always pass each other port side to port side, and that they should always keep to the right.

Take even a small boat down the estuary today and drift carelessly away from the right-hand shore, and the radio which you are obliged to carry will crackle into life and the voice of someone who has been tracking you on the all-seeing radar will reprimand you and order you to take the correct course.

The 'Princess Alice' disaster would have had a peculiar horror for J.[2] When he was a youth of 13 he had taken the last 'moonlight excursion' that the 'Alice' was to complete. He would have been able to visualise passengers, so like the ones he had known, gripped in that last sudden panic as the singing stopped and the terrible screaming began.

The fatal meeting between a steamboat and skiff at Dockett Point near Shepperton in July 1880.

7

Snubbing a Royal Borough

Runnymede to Cookham: The indignity of a postcode – The ditch where Falstaff was dunked – Dearth of mustard at Bray now remedied – Fast and steamy affairs under the railway bridge at Maidenhead – Delights of a completely new river – A bad-tempered duke and a dodgy businessman.

J WROTE that after leaving Runnymede nothing important happened until they reached Monkey Island near Bray. This is a tremendous snub to Royal Windsor, which they would have passed through on their way. The castle looming over the river here is one of the most famous views in the world, but the river's greatest populariser chose to look the other way.

Windsor, since it occupies such a privileged position in our national heritage, must expect to be put in its place occasionally. The Post Office offended the town when it introduced post codes back in the 'sixties. The address of the royals was vouchsafed to Slough for safe delivery, and wits began to refer to it as the Latin Quarter of the place associated with dismal industrial estates. This could perhaps be true in a literal sense because of all those Eton schoolboys pursuing their traditional studies. Slough itself was famously rubbished by Sir John Betjeman:

Come German bombs and fall on Slough,
It isn't fit for humans now.

Residents of the Royal Borough of Windsor and Maidenhead occasionally protest about the slight on their social status, but they should consider that if SL is good enough for the lady whose head appears on the stamp it should be good enough for them.

★

To leave out Windsor, however, as J did, is to a leave a great hole in the course of our journey up the river, so I will attempt to fill the gap. It is a curious place – a fairy-tale castle silhouetted against the sky, the comings and goings of royalty and the presence of all those Etonians in fancy dress otherwise known as school uniform: an overblown train station and hordes of overseas tourists. It is, in fact, a Disneyland for real, and the wonder is that the council never thought of suing old Walt because they had the idea first.

Yet, among its historic streets and humdrum suburbs there beats the same heart that may be found in any small English town, despite the overpowering presence of privilege. Shakespeare had the measure of the place in his *Merry Wives*. The town's womenfolk must have had a rather dubious reputation in his day. Their virtue was forever under assault from gorgeously arrayed lords and knights and various hangers-on at court. But the Bard portrays them as gossipy, sharp-witted and virtuous.

One likes to think that they were, and not just because, as tradition has it, the play about Sir John Falstaff in love was specially commissioned by the Virgin Queen herself. I felt I could not pass by the town without trying to find the spot where the boisterous old soak was dunked in the river in a buck basket.

That delightful couple, Samuel and Anna Hall, had the answer in their guide book published back in 1859.[1] The scene of Falstaff's adventure was Datchet Mead, a low–lying area between the river and Windsor Little Park. Here the 'muddy ditch close by the Thames side' existed until the time of Queen Anne, when it was converted into a covered drain known as Hoghole. When the Albert Bridge was built here in 1851, the embankment forming the approach destroyed the last vestige of this literary curiosity – but it marks the immortal spot.

★

An entertainment lost to us now, but an excitement in Victorian times, was the spotting of Royals taking the air along the river bank. Strict security has done away with all that, and mooring is banned along the riverside in The Home Park.

Boveney is worth mentioning for the sake of a good story. There is a small wooded island called Bush Ait where the Clewer Millstream branches off. A little way downstream of it stand the remains of an old inn that is almost invisible except in winter, when ivy covered walls can be glimpsed. It was called Poison Ducks, a corruption of the Norman French *Poisson Duct* meaning a weir to trap fish. Back in the mists of time it was a bawdy house patronised by bargemen, but it became of much concern to Eton College when boys who were supposed to be sculling on the river dallied there. It was a case of swing, swing together with someone else's body between the knees, to paraphrase the old *Eton Boating Song*. This unhealthy activity was only stopped when the college bought the house and installed a caretaker.[2] It was not the first time pupils had been tempted into sin on the river. In 1730, a boat moored on the Eton side of Windsor Bridge was banned from selling wine because the boys were spending their time in idleness there.

But there is no longer any risk of the Thames enticing young Etonians into vice. The school has built an enormous rowing lake, which keeps them away from all such temptation. Eton Dorney was the venue for the 2012 Olympic rowing events and is frequently used for international championships, so do not be surprised if you hear the roar of a great crowd as you pass the lonely little church of St Mary Magdalene.

Left uncared for after its parishioners drifted away to live in less damp places, the church was declared redundant. It is a rare example of an unspoilt twelfth century place of worship, so it is fortunate that it was adopted by the Friends of Friendless Churches, who restored it with the help of grants. It is close to the river because it served the needs of bargemen, who must have been much more religious than they were in J's day.

Nothing exciting happened to the Three Men until they drew up for lunch at a spot just below Monkey Island, near Bray. The meal was ruined because they had forgotten to pack mustard, and the cold beef just didn't taste right without it. They would have given anything for a jar. Their mood improved when George drew out a tin of pineapple from the bottom of the boat. But they had forgotten to bring a tin opener, and their attempts to open it provide one of the most hilarious passages in the book.

It is ironic that Bray should have been the scene of this culinary frustration. It is now one of the swishest places to dine out. At the time of writing there were only four restaurants in Britain with a three-star Michelin rating and two of them were here – Alain Roux's Waterside Inn and Heston Blumenthal's Fat Duck, the latter run on 'molecular gastronomy' principles. It is a shame that the Three were not able to enjoy Mr Blumenthal's menu. A mustard ice cream in a red cabbage gazpacho soup might have ended their craving for the condiment for a while.

Monkey Island derives its name from Monks Eye, eye or eyot meaning island in old English. It inspired the Third Duke of Marlborough, who built a fishing lodge here in 1723, to decorate the walls and ceiling with pictures of monkeys. They are dressed in eighteenth century costume and shown hunting, shooting and fishing. His eccentric buildings have been incorporated over the years into a very handsome white-walled hotel, accessible now across an iron bridge built in 1956.

We cannot leave Bray without mentioning the vicar in the old song who, like the weather vane on the church tower, turned with every change of the theological wind to keep a grip on his pulpit. True to type, he is difficult to pin down. No one can be sure if he lived through the Protestant Reformation of the sixteenth century or the Glorious Revolution of the seventeenth. There was more than one incumbent during both these periods. Whoever he was, (favourite candidates are Symon Aleyn and Francis Carswell) tradition has it that he was buried under the central aisle of the nave.

★

After their debacle with the pineapple tin, which was finally thrown intact into the river, J and his friends hurled their curses at it, jumped into the boat and rowed away from the spot passing quickly through Maidenhead.

J didn't like the town. He thought it a haunt of the 'river swell' and his overdressed female companions, not to mention the showy hotels patronised by dudes and ballet girls. It was in his day the next best thing to France if you wanted a summer holiday away from your spouse.

You could pack your wife and family off to the country and moan that you were having to spend those hot dusty days working in the City, but actually nip down to Maidenhead (such an innocent name!) for a little recreational sex with a woman of disrepute. Less well-heeled men had to make do with a camping skiff moored on the river bank, and a Japanese parasol could hide a multitude of sins in a punt.

Here is Brunel's marvellous brick-arched railway bridge. It is the custom of those passing underneath it to give a shout and hear the multiple echoes reverberate around them. I like to think that the Three Men would have given a cheery hullo, with Montmorency adding a bark, to test the properties of the 'sounding arch'.

The bridge is the subject of J M W Turner's immortal painting 'Rain, Speed and Steam.' There were some pretty fast and steamy affairs going on beneath it too. A row of Victorian villas along the riverbank soon acquired the name Gaiety Row. Show girls from the Gaiety Theatre rented them in order to cater for the tastes of gentlemen from the Guards Club just over the bridge.

The grandest place to stay was Skindles Hotel, which is close to the road bridge. As Leslie RA noted in 1881, it was rather overdone by pleasure parties from London, whose gaiety, show and fashionable slang clashed unpleasantly with the gentle dignity of the river. Moralists will be sad to learn that the roof of this palace of vice only fell in as late as 2013 after a snowstorm and many years of neglect. The building is not without merit and there is a campaign to preserve it as part of a redevelopment.

Of course, many boaters on the river here were ordinary decent people out enjoying their innocent pleasure. I count my grandfather among them. He was born in 1869, ten years later than J, but still able to experience the last of those 'golden' river days, and I was able to learn about them at his knee. I was very young then, but one incident fixed itself in my mind. A group of 'roughs' had thrown open the sluices to their fullest extent while my grandfather was in the lock at Maidenhead, causing his boat to be thrown about in the turbulent waters. This was a dangerous prank, since if he had fallen in, the undertow could have done for him – and for me!

The escape from Maidenhead was through Boulter's Lock, and this rivalled Hampton in providing a colourful boating spectacle. It was of course much more up market. The grandest occasion was the Sunday after the Ascot races, when Lord Astor would bring his house party from Cliveden through in his private steam launch. Lesser celebrities, who knew that this was the place to be seen, crowded through with him, and the bank would be thronged with local people in their Sunday best hoping to catch a glimpse of the famous, and a whiff of scandal.

The scene was captured in sketches by Edward Gregory in 1885, but it took the artist until 1897 to perfect the oil painting to his satisfaction. His work was bought by William Lever, the soap manufacturer, later Lord Leverhulme, who used it in advertising to promote his Sunlight soap. This iconic image of the Thames has been widely reproduced ever since.[3]

In 1995 I took part in a boating pageant to mark the 110th anniversary of the painting. The organisers had arranged for vintage boats and people in period dress to re-create the scene in the lock, and many photographs were taken. (See plates section)

It was after lunch on a Sunday when the Three Men went through. It must have been a very busy time, though not as busy as on Ascot Sunday afternoon in 1888 when 800 boats and 72 steam launches passed through the lock. No wonder J had another great objection to Maidenhead as a 'witches' kitchen from which go forth those demons of the river – steam launches'.

There must have been many entanglements of boats in the lock, resulting in argument and acrimony spoiling an otherwise tranquil afternoon. Even a very adept boatman like Leslie RA could not prevent the nose of his punt from hitting the rudder of the then Duke of Cambridge, who had taken the helm himself. In what was clearly an understatement, the artist said 'it did not seem to please him'. Given the Second Duke's reputation for having a fiery temper[4], no doubt the distinguished Royal Academician suffered an embarrassing tirade.

There cannot have been many dukes out on the Thames in J's day, and one is reminded of his remark that 'the *London Journal*[5] duke always has "his little place" at Maidenhead'. This magazine pumped out cheap romantic fiction for the likes of housemaids, and its fantasies would have been all the more believable as it was known that there really was a duke hereabouts who kept a mistress and was a notorious womaniser.

We now have a brand new Duke of Cambridge of a very different disposition, and if he should wish to take to the river there is a magnificent golden royal barge at his disposal navigated by expert watermen and surrounded by security. There will be no unseemly incidents in locks for him.

The other side of Boulter's Lock finds us in some delightful scenery. As J notes, Cliveden Woods in their unbroken loveliness create the sweetest stretch of all the river.

It is a shame that in the latter half of the twentieth century scandal drifted up-stream to this tranquil spot like a miasma from the Maidenhead of the naughty nineties. In 1963 a small boathouse here became the trysting place of a young prostitute, Christine Keeler, and the Secretary of State for War, John Profumo. It was said that she was the mistress of a Russian spy, and Profumo had to resign after lying about the affair to the House of Commons.

Although Cliveden house and estate are now owned by the National Trust, the stately pile is leased out as a hotel. The ill wind of disgrace will always fill somebody's sails, and guests can now enjoy a Profumo Affair Break, which will give them the opportunity 'to experience the sumptuous luxury of Cliveden while finding out more about the events leading up to the greatest political and sexual scandal of the last century'. In J's day people made their own fun in hotels rather than spending their time finding out about other people's.

This is a glorious reach of the Thames, and it is even better now that we have two rivers instead of one. The Jubilee River, opened in 2002, the year of the Queen's Silver Jubilee, was dug to provide a flood relief channel. It leaves the river just above Boulter's Lock and rejoins it downstream of Eton. Although not navigable along its length, it is a very pleasant place for a walk, especially in winter, when the low sun illuminates the stems and branches of the reeds and trees carefully landscaped over more than a hundred acres.

★

Teatime saw the Three mooring up in a backwater just below Cookham Lock. Earlier in the book J had railed against riverside landowners who closed off backwaters to boaters with posts driven into the bed and chains across from bank to bank. Then they nailed up notice boards on every tree. He said he wanted to tear each one down and hammer it over the head of the man who put it up until he had killed him.

Hedsor Water, up which they could only venture a short distance, was the most notorious of these forbidden places. As the Thames historian Fred Thacker noted in 1920:

> This long half-mile of beautiful Thames scenery, not be it understood, a backwater leading nowhere but the ancient navigable highway, became entirely closed to the public; the unique example, I think, of the complete alienation of a length of the main Thames to private use and enjoyment.[6]

The villain in this case was the fifth Lord Boston, who complained after Cookham Lock was built in 1829 that it deprived him of the revenue from barges. The new lock short-circuited a hazardous bend in the river that flowed through his land. When the Thames Conservancy built a weir across the old waterway eight years later to keep the water high enough for the lock, Lord Boston retaliated by building a weir at the other end to trap eels, thus effectively preventing any access by boaters from either end.

In 1894 at the Committee Stage of the new Thames Conservancy Bill, lawyers for the sixth Lord Boston argued that public right of navigation must have been lost because for many years Hedsor Water had been effectively closed by two impassable weirs. Although it was an underlying principle that people should freely navigate the whole of the natural course of the river, the drafting of the Bill was ambiguous and the right to navigate here became a source of contention.

For the next 130 years, generations of Thames boaters believed they had no right to enter the backwater; the fish weir had gone, but in its place was a forbidding 'Private' sign board. By the end of this time the surrounding estate had been acquired by another man who was no stranger to litigation, Rowland 'Tiny' Rowland, whose activities involving the Rhodesian mining company Lonrho, were described by Prime Minister Edward Heath in 1973 as 'the unpleasant and unacceptable face of capitalism.'

In 2002, his widow, Josie Rowland, annoyed that her privacy was being infringed by pleasure boaters, sued the Environment Agency, the successors to the Conservancy, for a declaration that public right of navigation over Hedsor Water had been extinguished. But the Chancery Division ruled against her.

The exception made in 1894 was found to be unsound. The notice of the type so reviled by J has now disappeared and small boats may venture up the backwater, provided they are wary of the shoals and a low wooden footbridge, and do not land.[7]

★

It was evening by the time The Three had passed through Cookham Lock, and there was a following breeze so they could put up a sail and leave the work to nature. As the course of the river twists so much, a breeze that will bear you along quite happily in one place will threaten to blow you over in another. A skiff is a very light craft and has no keel or centre board to balance a lateral force against the sail. But, given a lucky wind, as J was, it will take very little to shift it. Indeed, a large sturdy umbrella will do the job and 'umbrella racing' is one of the more light-hearted events at regattas up and down the river.

Serious competitive skiff sailing takes place in Holland, and occasionally clubs come over to England to show how it should be done.

The Three Men were now entering famous Thames sailing waters. The river is broad and open here, and at Bourne End one of the oldest sailing clubs on the river was founded. J described sailing as coming as near to flying as man has got to yet. There was no more thrilling sensation, apart perhaps from taking off over the handlebars of a bicycle. It would be more than twenty years before men really flew about here. A little restaurant called The Bounty stands just above Cookham Railway Bridge on the site of what was once a large establishment known as The Moorings Hotel. Photos in a back room show light aircraft parked on the flat meadow behind it. They belonged to a German flying club who came here as part of an excursion to England in 1912, a short while before such visits were to be deprecated. After the war it became the fashion to buzz down for the weekend in the 'old kite': Bertie Woosters on butterfly wings. Regulation of private flying was pretty lax in those days.

Flying or not, J certainly had his head in the clouds and headed the skiff straight into three old gentlemen fishing in a punt. They were knocked off their chairs and fell in a heap at the bottom of the boat. Their swearing was comprehensive – worthy of a duke, you might say.

It is a shame that Harris had lost his interest in unusual tombs at this point. Cookham Church has a monument on the wall of the north aisle to Sir Isaac Pocock, who died of a heart attack in 1810 while taking a trip in a punt. The drama is graphically depicted on a stone tablet. An angel takes Sir Isaac's head upon her bosom while the man with the punt pole looks fixedly ahead as if this was an everyday occurrence.

Harris thought the three old fishermen should have been grateful for some excitement in their lives. But it is lucky none of them had hearts as weak as poor old Sir Isaac.

Collision with a punt near Cookham

8

Some Friends Remembered at Marlow

Bourne End to Hurley: Celebrities in the Wild Wood – Battle of the flowers between Marlow and Henley – American chooses a spot for his own grave – The long arm of coincidence – A pie made with dead puppies – Rivalry between a man of soap and a man of tea –The Lady Macbeth of the sports centre.

AFTER the collision with the punt George insists that J is unsuited, as an artistic, dreamy person, to be in charge of steering a boat and takes over himself. At least this would have left the author free to contemplate one of his favourite reaches of the river. He loved Quarry Wood with its narrow, climbing paths and winding little glades. Kenneth Grahame, who lived for a while at Cookham, also delighted in this spot and it became the Wild Wood in *Wind in the Willows*.

Many desirable residences have been built among the trees since those days, and if, in the middle of a snowstorm, Mole and Ratty were to stumble on a door in the 'Wild Wood' now, the chances are that it would be opened by one of the many TV celebrities living around Cookham. The wood was already becoming fashionable with actors in the 1930s, and the other most famous fictional characters living here after Badger must be the dreadful Bliss family in Noel Coward's *Hay Fever*.

The comedy is set in a country house with lawns reaching down to the Thames from which 'on a clear day you can see Marlow.' This is indeed true, and on exceptionally clear days you might even spot Shakespeare in far-off Warwickshire. In the play, house guests are driven away by the terrible rudeness inflicted on them by the family, who are left alone to continue their perpetual bickering. Lucky Ratty and Mole did not blunder in on *them*!

★

Coward was familiar with this spot. Beatrice Lillie, one of his leading ladies, had a place at Henley. The two of them would cruise about in a beautiful electric canoe called 'Beazie'. The boat is still around and you may be lucky enough to see her gliding silently along powered by her original motor, but the red velvet cushions touched by so many famous theatrical bottoms have had to be replaced.

In J's time the idyllic scene around here was under threat from developers who planned a big housing estate on the bank opposite Quarry Wood. Fortunately nothing came of it, but a boatyard built below the wood in anticipation of the trade it would bring still exists. Happily so, for the old quarry quay still resounds to the sound of hammers and chisels involved in the renovation of rare and beautiful boats.

Below the wood, curiously styled country retreats have been built. One has a facade completely covered in patterns of rough-hewn branches. Another is known as the 'cardboard castle' because its battlemented roof line makes it look like a toy fort.

The Three Men spent the Sunday night at the Crown Inn in Marlow, which is up the High Street and away from the river. It was as well that they had not chosen the more fashionable Compleat Angler Hotel next to the lock, which was popular with gentlemen who hired punts with professional fishermen – they might have been recognised.

★

J introduces us to Marlow in a rather teasing way, adopting the tone of a tedious old pedant to trot out a potted history cribbed from Dickens Junior's dictionary.

> Our fancy travels back to the days when Marlow Manor owned Saxon Algar for its lord, ere conquering William seized it to give to Queen Matilda, ere it passed to the Earls of Warwick or to worldly-wise Lord Paget, the councillor of four successive sovereigns…

Only joking, of course, and we are soon back again on the Thames. 'Marlow is one of the pleasantest river centres I know of', he writes. When the actor Rodney Bewes brought his one-man show based on the

Three Men to the Kenton Theatre in Henley a couple of years ago, he was brave enough to repeat those words and earned a chorus of catcalls.

For there is a strong rivalry between Henley and Marlow, and it is clear which town J preferred. He granted his ultimate accolade to Marlow by going to live there. The rivalry came to national attention in the 'battle of the flowers' in 2005. Henley, a regular winner of the regional Britain in Bloom competition, lost the title to Marlow. Enraged by the defeat, the town's councillors sacked the flower basket contractors and ordered the removal of the town's 146 hanging baskets.[1] At the height of this rancour, a Henley woman told *The Times*: 'It's like a sibling rivalry: we're always squabbling. Both towns are very similar but *we've* got the bigger Waitrose.'

★

J's classic description of passing through a lock comes to mind at Marlow:

> I like sitting in the boat and slowly rising out of the cool depths up into new reaches and fresh views; or sinking down, as it were, out of the world, and then waiting, while the gloomy gates creak, and the narrow strip of daylight between them widens till the fair smiling river lies full before you, and you push your little boat out from its brief prison on to the welcoming waters once more.

The lock here has a rise of seven feet – one of the deepest on the river – and perhaps on a busy day before entering it you have been kept waiting in the narrow, dreary lock cut. What joy when you emerge through the gates and into the sunlight again with the great weir sparkling to your left and the spire of Marlow church soaring magnificently on your right. Even the churchyard looks as inviting as a churchyard can possibly be.

J in his autobiography[2] writes of his friend, the theatre producer Charles Frohman, who on sunny afternoons could often be found 'sitting on his own grave there – or rather on the spot he hoped one day would be his grave: a pleasant six foot into four of English soil, under the great willow that overhangs the river. He was still in negotiation for it the last time I saw him there.'

Frohman shared his love of Marlow Church with one of his leading ladies, Pauline Chase, who came over from America to play Peter in *Peter Pan*. She had a country retreat at Farnham Common, five miles away from the town, and would pick up the impresario from his train at Slough to drive him to Marlow. She wrote that she was to be confirmed in the church, and he replied:

I am glad about Marlow. That little church is the only one in the world I care for.

Bizarrely, he arranged for the body of Pauline's mother to be removed from its resting place in Washington and re-interred in Marlow churchyard.

But the impresario's wish to buried at Marlow was never realised, for he was drowned when the 'Lusitania' was torpedoed off Ireland in 1915. His body was recovered and taken back to America for burial.

Frohman is best known for his association with J's friend, J M Barrie. As a producer, he first brought *Peter Pan* to the stage. You may have seen him played by Dustin Hoffman sporting a beard in *Finding Neverland,* the film that starred Johnny Depp as Barrie. In fact, Frohman was a beardless, baby-faced roly-poly looking man. Born in humble circumstances in Sandusky, Ohio in 1856, he rose to become a dominant figure in the English-speaking theatre, and at the height of his career controlled five theatres in London, six in New York and more than 200 throughout the rest of the United States. J as a playwright trusted him implicitly and never bothered him to sign anything. They would fix terms over a cigar and shake hands.

★

It was another friend of J's who introduced Frohman to Marlow. This was Haddon Chambers, an Australian-born dramatist, whose work is forgotten now. As he struggled to establish himself in London he contributed articles to J's magazine *The Idler,* and later collaborated with him on a play. The Jerome daughters taught him how to play croquet, and in return he told them stories about bushrangers and Dame Nellie Melba when she was a little girl.

Chambers had a summer retreat in a cottage at Bisham on the opposite side of the river to Marlow. After Frohman's death, on a visit to the United States in 1915 he gave an interview to the *New York Times* in which he described the impresario's relationship with the Thames-side town.[3]

It was 15 years ago, I should say, that Mr Frohman first came to see me at Marlow. I was spending my summers there and he had been staying at Maidenhead. He loved the river, and as Marlow is on the Thames and much the same sort of town, only smaller, simpler and more reposeful, I thought he might like it better. So he came to visit me and from his first glimpse of the place he fell in love with it, and as his knowledge of it ripened, he came to look upon it as his spiritual home. After that first visit he never failed to include a stay at Marlow in every trip to England.

He always stayed at the Compleat Angler, and it was Frohman's delight to wander up and down the High Street purchasing 'unconsidered trifles' as an excuse for chatting with the shopkeepers. His simplicity of manner, humour and sympathy won him many friends there. Among his favourites were Muriel Kilby, the daughter of an innkeeper, and Clark, the butcher.

Chambers told the reporter: 'Clark kills his own meat and Mr Frohman was always vastly interested in the butcher and his immaculately kept shop with its sawdust covered floor, and its neat rows of carcasses prepared by the hands of this pocket edition of John Bull strong enough to lift an ox.' His old premises are now occupied by the fashion chain Monsoon.

The New York Times article headlined the fact that a drinking fountain was to be erected in Marlow to commemorate the American producer. And there it now stands on a little green between the High Street and the church. No willow overhangs the churchyard bank, and the naked young lady who sits atop the memorial presides over a waterless fountain. But she has not been forgotten: her toes, which crumbled away over the years, have recently been replaced.[4] The family names of generations of tradespeople have long disappeared from the shop fronts, to be replaced by the ubiquitous Café Rouge, Boots, Slug and Lettuce & Co. But the spirit of Frohman would no doubt be happier here close to the High Street he loved than in his final resting place across the Atlantic, and J must have passed this memorial to his friend many times.

Alas for Haddon Chambers; unlike Jerome, all his words as a dramatist seem to have passed through the great sieve of time leaving only one tiny nugget of a quotation behind. Search on the internet and you will find only: 'the long arm of coincidence' from his play *Captain Swift*.

It is that same High Street and its obliging shopkeepers that was made famous more than twenty years before Frohman's death by the account of the 'imposing spectacle' as J, with his two companions accompanied by shop boys, hangers-on and dogs proceeded in ceremony back to their skiff having completed their 'marketing' for three days' supplies.

> We had insisted at all the shops we had been to that the things were sent there and then.

When they reached the landing stage with such a large load, the delivery boy asked sarcastically: 'Was yours a steam-launch or a houseboat?'

It is here that Montmorency made 'an awful ass of himself' when he was outfaced by a large black tom-cat.

There was a popular story going the rounds about Marlow, which J must have known. Tradition has it that a local innkeeper left a pie outside his door beside the river. A passing bargeman saw it and, bargemen being bargemen, had no scruples about eating every last crumb, he even boasted about it and said how good it tasted in the innkeeper's hearing the next time he passed.

In due course another pie appeared outside the inn to be eaten by the same bargeman. It did not taste so good this time, especially after he was told that it had contained a litter of dead pups. And that is why in Victorian days unruly urchins would shout down from the bridge at passing barges: 'Puppy Pie!'

Just above Marlow is Bisham Abbey, rich, says J, in melodramatic qualities. It has certainly had an exciting past. The Knights Templar built it, only to be evicted when the order was brutally suppressed. Then it became the place where Princess Elizabeth, later Queen Elizabeth I, was held under house arrest during one of England's most perilous times. But the real crowd-puller as far as Victorian visitors were concerned was Lady Hoby, mistress of the house in the sixteenth century. J puts her story concisely: 'The ghost of Lady Hoby, who beat her little boy to death, still walks there at night, trying to wash its ghostly hands clean in a ghostly basin.'

The legend has been much embellished in guide books. It is said that the lady became exasperated by her son's untidiness in his school work and espoused harsh educational principles. In expiation of her terrible deed, her ghost was said to walk continually washing its hands preceded by a silver bowl – going one better than Lady Macbeth. Some guide books naively assert that when renovations were carried out to the house, a blotted copybook was found behind the plasterwork, thereby proving beyond a shadow of doubt the veracity of this tale. Of course, the incontrovertible evidence has since vanished into thin air, as is usually the case.

Bisham Abbey is now owned by Sport England and is a national training centre for sporting excellence. It is said that in a panelled room the ghostly gnashing of teeth may be heard, caused by Lady Hoby's frustration at not being able to get her hands on failed tennis players, golfers and footballers.

J reminds us that it was at Bisham, while floating in a boat under the beech trees, that Shelley wrote his epic poem *The Revolt of Islam*. Meanwhile, Mary Shelley was busy scribbling away in their rented house in West Street, Marlow, at something more in the paperback line – *Frankenstein*.

★

To the west of Marlow, where the land slopes upwards to the Chiltern Hills, is Marlow Common. J moved there into a substantial house, Monk's Corner, before the First World War and moved out after his health was broken through working as an ambulance driver in France. A photograph shows him sitting in front of the fireplace, while over the mantelpiece hangs his portrait by the society painter De Laszlo[5]. J occupied two other houses nearby before ill health compelled him to return to London in 1923.

Attached to Monk's Corner was a tennis court: J was a keen player, his interest dating back to the days before the rules were properly formalised. Partners would turn up then with all manner of strangely shaped racquets. One of them, W S Gilbert, had his own ideas about how long a court should be, and would expound with true Gilbertian logic a theory to prove that everyone else's was too short.

J lavished attention on his tennis court. Rarely a day went by without his spending an hour on his knees tending it – or so he tells us. A Wimbledon champion once told him it was the best private grass court he had played on. Alas, it no longer exists, but a neighbour has a clay court, the descendant of the hard playing surface laid down by the art critic Alfred Baldry[6]. With a short woodland path connecting the two courts it was possible for J to enjoy tennis whatever the weather.

Baldry, a popular man-about-art in his day, was a close friend of J's. He inherited money just before the First World War and used it to build a house here, so it is probable that J moved to Marlow Common to be close to his friend.

Monk's Corner still stands in a clearing in the woods, and has its own interesting story to tell. For although Marlow is now a prosperous place, when the relatively well-off Three Men and their fellow tourists enjoyed themselves on the Thames, grinding rural poverty was never far away and was to continue to blight people's lives for many years to come.

Robert Hudson, son of the inventor of soap flakes, lived in the great mansion at Danesfield further up the river, and was involved in good works. He established a pottery to provide jobs, producing tiles of the highest quality in the style of the Arts and Crafts movement. To oversee the artistic side of the operation he brought a sculptor, Conrad Dressler, down from London and built Monk's Corner for him.

Medmenham Pottery, as it came to be known, lasted only a few years, but its surviving products are still prized among tile aficionados. Some can be seen in the walls of Monk's Corner, where they would have been familiar to J, and other remnants have been embedded in a concrete path leading up to Jerome Cottage, part of the old house that was hived off from the main building about 30 years ago.

The 25ft frieze along the front of the house was a trial for a ceramic panel entitled 'Industry' that was to adorn the soap company offices in Dublin. There are also some portrait roundels made for the same purpose.

At the time I went to see the house, it was owned by a distinguished oarsman, who was once stroke in the Cambridge reserve crew. It is a tradition that they compete with Oxford immediately before the Boat Race. He was kind enough to speak to me on the phone and told me that he took a delight in his home's connection with the author. In a lavatory, there hung a framed letter from the great man on the Monk's Corner letterhead.

Upstream from Marlow, Danesfield House still dominates the river, although it is now a hotel. It was given its name, J tells us, because invading Danes once stopped there on their march to Gloucester. Near to it, but not visible from the Thames, is Wittington House, built in 1908 for Ewbanke Kearley, later Viscount Devonport. As Hudson owed his fortune to soap, so Kearley made his money in tea, being owner of the International Stores. He was Minister of Food during the First World War and Chairman of the Port of London Authority.

For some reason these men of substance – soap and tea – did not get on together, a bitter rivalry having developed when they both lived at Medmenham a few miles upstream. Purely to spite Hudson, Kearley acquired land beside the Thames to deny his neighbour access to the river. Their rivalry even extended into good works, as Kearley also helped to alleviate the serious unemployment problem after the Boer War by using hundreds of men to create garden terraces below Wittington. The gardens became famous in cherry blossom time, and in 1931 Queen Mary came to visit them. The house, after serving for a time as a Salvation Army old people's home, has been sensitively restored, and is now the UK headquarters of SAS, an IT company. It is good news that they are re-instating the cherry trees so that blossom time will soon be famous here again.

It must have seemed that time had called a plague on both these great houses when in the 1950s a large caravan park appeared in unspoilt countryside on the opposite side of the river. It reminded one much-travelled boater of the slum hamlets of the Bedouin scattered among the pines around Beirut. The ramshackle caravans have now been replaced by luxurious static ones provided with all mod-cons and surrounded by neat little gardens – luxury camping which J could not have imagined.

Fortunately the area close to Hurley Lock and village retains its charm. It was by Hurley Weir that J thought he could stay a month without having sufficient time to drink in all the beauty of the scene. The hamlet itself has successfully hidden itself among the trees to escape marauding developers. At its centre is a little row of quaint dormer-roofed cottages that overlook the tiny church.

You might think that the place has been in a gentle decline since monastic times, but Hurley has had its glory days. There was once a great Elizabethan house called Lady Place, taking its name from the old monastery dedicated to Our Lady, on which its foundations rested. Beneath it was an ancient vault, and it is said that the Glorious Revolution of 1688 was hatched here by conspirators plotting to invite the Prince of Orange to come from Holland and take the English throne. William III is believed to have visited the place in gratitude, and it was graced with another royal visit when George III came in 1785. Nothing now remains of the house but some garden walls.

During the Second World War the American Office of Strategic Forces set up a secret communications centre here controlling foreign agents working in Nazi-occupied Europe.[7]

★

When Neil Armstrong, the first man on the Moon, came to Hurley, it was to visit the yard of Peter Freebody, whose reputation for building beautiful wooden boats had crossed the Atlantic. Neil was so impressed with what he saw that he stayed longer than he intended and was in danger of missing his train from Maidenhead. Peter, noted for his relaxed style of driving, offered to take him to the station. When he got out of the car the astronaut remarked: 'I have been to the Moon and back, but I've just had the scariest journey I ever made.'

★

Although picturesque, historic and remote from a major town, the river above Hurley Lock unexpectedly takes on a happy-go-lucky atmosphere due to the adjacent camping site. Inflatable boats buzz about, children paddle or float about on airbeds, and at the height of the summer you may find an ice-cream boat complete with outsize cornet on top. It's 'Appy 'Ampton revisited.

The Crown Hotel in Marlow in J's day. In more recent times it has been converted into shops.

9

Those Mad Monks

Danesfield to Henley: The truth about high jinks at Medmenham – Bread rolls sent post haste – A pointless victory commemorated – A lock tragedy – Pinafore Smith – Henley given the Windsor treatment.

AFTER Danesfield, the wooded banks close in and the river sweeps around in broad curves to Medmenham. J very poetically evokes the ancient Cistercian Abbey which once stood here:

> A grim fraternity, passing grim lives in that sweet spot that God had made so bright! Strange that Nature's voices all around them – the soft singing of the waters, the whispering of the river grass, the music of the rushing wind – should not have taught them a truer meaning of life than this. They listened there, through the long days in silence, waiting for a voice from heaven; and all day long and through the night it spoke to them in myriad tones, and they heard it not.

It is the Medmenham of the Hell Fire Club that most interests people now – the fraternity of 'monks' known as the Order of Knights of St Francis of Wickham that flourished between 1745 and 1760. It was founded by Sir Francis Dashwood, whose family bought West Wycombe Park after making their fortune trading in silk. Like Hudson and Viscount Davenport a century later, Dashwood was moved by the plight of poor agricultural workers and created jobs for them by enlarging the caves at West Wycombe in a fancy gothic style.

He bought Medmenham Abbey as a meeting place for his notorious club, one of many such Hell Fire Clubs that existed in the eighteenth century, although it never officially went by this name. Its twelve 'apostles' included the Earl of Sandwich, Thomas Potter (the son of the Archbishop of Canterbury), John Wilkes, William Hogarth, the Earl of Bute (Prime Minister), the Marquis of Granby, the Prince of Wales and Horace Walpole.

This was an extraordinary collection of people – radical and Tory – who seem to have been forever at each other's throats. The banter must have been blistering. When Sandwich said to Wilkes: 'Sir, I do not know if you will die on the gallows or of the pox', Wilkes famously replied: 'That, Sir, depends on whether I embrace your principles or your mistress.'

Sandwich got the last word, however. He read a scurrilous poem written by Wilkes and Potter called *An Essay on Women* to the House of Lords. One imagines those noble peers, slowly aroused from their torpor as a torrent of pornography assailed their ears. Rising to their feet, wigs awry they would have shouted that something must be done, and Wilkes fled to France. It is said that Sandwich was taking revenge for a prank played by Wilkes at Medmenham when he dressed a baboon as the devil, and his lordship fell for it – or perhaps was bitten by the baboon. One can never get to the truth behind these stories.

But one thing is sure. With so many enemies within there must have been huge numbers of ill-wishers without. So no doubt many of the allegations made against the club were exaggerated. The more extreme of these claimed that members celebrated black masses over the naked bodies of ladies of rank, and brought prostitutes by barge up from London.

Recent commentators play down the orgies saying that drink, dressing up and politics featured far more heavily than sex, and that there was no evidence worthy of the name for any black magic at Medmenham. No doubt the then fashionable elements of Druidism, Freemasonry and classical paganism were more to their tastes.

What later generations considered to be an orgy was probably little more than par for the times. As Dickens Jr put it: 'There seems to be no doubt that considerable 'high jinks' were indulged in by this fraternity, and that they were not altogether what is generally known as respectable society.'

Other writers on the Thames offer their own peculiar speculations about what went on. E Arnot Robertson was a well-known broadcaster in those prudish BBC days of the 40s and 50s. She pondered in *Thames Portrait,* published in 1937[1], over what a 'nameless' Medmenham orgy might be, and concluded: 'I have one not very helpful analogy to offer.

'My small cousin and myself once decided to start a Disgusting Club, just the two of us. "Let's be absolutely awful!" we said. …the set-back came in deciding what to do. We discussed this more and more desperately for a long time, while enthusiasm for the idea dwindled despite our efforts, and finally we got under a table and showed one another our bottoms, a spectacle which would make up in awfulness, we hoped, what it lacked in novelty ...'

Not very helpful indeed!

The Dashwood set may not have been respectable, but they were certainly distinguished. Dashwood himself became Chancellor of the Exchequer in later life, though he only survived for a year after introducing a disastrously unpopular tax on cider. Appropriately, he claimed to be drunk at the time. John Wilkes is remembered as a campaigner for civil liberties, parliamentary reform, freedom of the press and religious toleration. So J is not quite fair when he calls the club a group of irreverent jesters including the 'notorious' Wilkes'.

Medmenham still has a picturesque appearance though it is more of an eighteenth century gothic folly than the remnants of the thirteenth century abbey. The old stonework of the tower, which appealed so much to artists with its lichens of grey and gold and occasional draperies of ivy, has been painted white in recent times which almost makes it a ghost of its former self. The motto of Dashwood's disciples 'Fay ce que voudras' – do as you will – can still be seen over a doorway, so we are told.

When J and friends passed by, the lawns were a favourite spot for picnickers, and the motto took on a more benevolent meaning, as a large room there was kept to accommodate trippers. The ferry was still operating and there was a Ferry Inn in the village, particularly popular with 'bretheren of the brush'. The inn sign, painted by one of them who later became famous, was considered good enough to exhibit at the Royal Academy Summer Exhibition.

Neither ferry nor inn remains, but a large stone monument celebrates a somewhat pointless legal victory by Viscount Davenport. In 1899 he won an action in the Court of Appeal that decided the ferry could carry ordinary members of the public and not be restricted to men or horses used to draw barges. The landowner had claimed that it was an 'accommodation ferry' for the use of commercial traffic alone. No doubt the good Viscount believed his victory on behalf of the common man would stand for all time, but it can't have been so many years before the ferry ceased for economic reasons.

From Medmenham to Hambleden the river, as Jerome says, is full of peaceful beauty.

High up on the left-hand bank is Culham Court, a fine mansion of Georgian dolls-house symmetry. Tradition has it that when George III stayed here for a day and a night, his sycophantic host, the Hon Mr West, arranged to bring hot rolls from the King's favourite baker in Berkley Square the 40-odd miles, wrapped in hot flannel, by relays of horsemen. The king expressed no surprise, merely exclaiming. 'Ah! Gunter, Gunter. I am glad you deal with Gunter, West.'[2]

J describes Hambleden lock as 'sweet'. It was probably more picturesque in his day when the old clap-boarded paper mill was still working, but the buildings have been preserved as apartments, and there is a spectacular weir here specially designed for adventurous canoeists. The three friends were rebuffed by the churlish lockkeeper when they asked for their water supply to be topped up. They were referred to the river and told that the lockkeeper had drunk it himself for 15 years without any ill effect. J found this miserable old soul was hardly an advertisement for Thames water, and recalls an attempt at drinking tea made with river water some years previously which was abandoned after a dead dog floated past.

The Hambleden keeper at that time was Charles Phillis, and the poor fellow drank more than his fill of Thames water in 1890 when he fell into the lock and drowned.[3]

★

In a footnote J remarks on the lockkeepers of his day: 'The (Thames) Conservancy of late seems to have constituted itself into a society for the employment of idiots. A good many of the new lockkeepers, especially in the more crowded portions of the river, are excitable, nervous old men quite unfitted for their post.' Lockkeepers are cherished by those who use the river now, and boaters are among the first to protest when the Environment Agency (the Conservancy's successor) threatens to reduce their numbers, which it does regularly.

Greenlands, the Italianate country house with lawns leading down to the river, is described by J as the 'rather uninteresting looking river residence of my newsagent'. This was W H Smith junior, who built up the family business by ensuring every railway station sold his books and newspapers. He would have been close to the end of his life when J observed him as a 'quiet, unassuming old gentleman, who may often be met about these regions, during the summer months, sculling himself along in easy vigorous style.'

Apart from the family business, Smith had also gone into politics, and it seems strange that someone whose sole nautical experience was gained from messing about in boats on the Thames should end up as First Lord of the Admiralty under Disraeli.

W S Gilbert parodied his career in the character of Sir Joseph Porter in *HMS Pinafore,* first performed in 1878.

> 'I grew so rich that I was sent
> By a pocket borough into Parliament.
> I always voted at my party's call,
> And I never thought of thinking for myself at all.
> I thought so little, they rewarded me
> By making me the ruler of the Queen's Navee!'

From then on he was known as Pinafore Smith.

Greenlands has, since 1948, been the home of the Henley Business School, which has the goal of improving industry through high-quality management. It is situated only a few hundred yards from the start of the Regatta, so how do its international students view the extra-curricular corporate junketing taking place on their doorstep? Professor John Board, the Dean, told me it was with 'a mixture of admiration and bemusement. Whatever their views, the Regatta certainly shows a different side of the river than the air of calm and relaxation that it brings during the rest of the year.'

★

They would probably not share the sentiments of J when he declares – but surely with tongue in cheek – that the river from Greenlands to beyond Henley is 'somewhat bare and dull'. He is giving it the dismissive 'Windsor snub', no doubt because he believed too much had already been written about it.

Here lies Temple Island with its perfect little classical fishing lodge designed by James Wyatt. Then there is the magnificent up-river view with the tower of Henley Church in the distance, a favourite subject for many artists. Henley itself spills down to the river with its picturesque buildings, bridge and streets. Bare and dull it is certainly not – a joke that must have been enjoyed by many of J's original readers.

At the time the Three Men were passing though Henley it was 'just before Henley week', and I suggested earlier that J and Harris left Tavistock Place on Saturday June 23rd, 1888, and rowed from Kingston to Picnic

Point at Ankerwycke, near Runnymede, camping out there after picking up George on the way. We may then assume the following timetable: On Sunday, June 24th, they had lunch just below Monkey Island at Bray before spending the night at The Crown, Marlow. After shopping in Marlow on Monday June 25th, they passed through Henley and reached Wargrave for lunch, spending the night on Buck Ait downstream of Sonning. Tuesday took them through Reading and on to Streatley, where they had lunch.

At this point their holiday took on a more leisurely pace. Perhaps they had planned to pass through Henley as quickly as possible to avoid the worst of the frantic Regatta preparations.

A lucky tow from a steam launch gave them an easy journey to within a mile of Streatley, where they could relax, and they remained there on Wednesday and Thursday, moving off on Friday to spend the night at Clifton Hampden.

Saturday saw the Three arrive in Oxford, where they spent two mysteriously unaccounted for days, before leaving on Monday July 2nd and spending the night just below Day's Lock. They had to endure incessant rain on the return trip, and by the time they reached Pangbourne late on Tuesday afternoon, July 3rd, they had decided to call it a day and slipped off by train back to London. After a celebratory night out at the Alhambra they would have returned home, having cut short their two-week holiday by three or four days, perhaps a little shamefaced at having to tell their landlady and friends that they had not stayed the course. They had also avoided passing through the Henley Royal Regatta. It was a leisurely journey and they only spent seven of the projected fourteen days actually rowing, towing or sailing the boat. It would have been considered by serious rowing men as rather a relaxed trip.

But to return to Henley, such a curious reticence about the place belies the fact that J was an enthusiastic Regatta goer. Having passed through by boat, he couldn't stay away, and together with George took the trouble to walk back in the rain from Bucks Eyot below Sonning to the town, which was about five miles there and back, in order to meet up with some friends.

The river at Henley before the Regatta was a hazardous place. *The Times* reported in July 1890 that crews practising for the races were complaining of lubberly rowboats, unwieldy houseboats being marshalled by their tugs along the Oxford bank and the usual 'reckless' steam launches. It said that on the Saturday before the Regatta a Leander four-oared crew rowed right through the side of a skiff occupied by a man and two women who obstructed the racecourse, resulting in the racing boat being smashed up. We don't know what happened to the lesser mortals in the skiff.

Looking at old photographs of the vast array of small boats on the course during the actual Regatta, it is a wonder that any races were run at all. By the late 1880s things were improved by the introduction of piling to separate the course from the spectators. This was the start of the Golden Age of the Regatta. All the wealth of empire and industry enabled the well-off to provide lavish entertainment, while the railway brought the 'Arrys and 'Arriets in droves. Toffs and the hoi polloi mingled among the boats and houseboats. It was like Derby Day on water.

Of course there was tension between the serious oarsmen and those who saw it, in the words of *The Times,* as the 'champion picnic of the season'. For sightseers on the water, the most exciting part was when the latest product of Mr Des Vignes's 'torpedo boat manufactory', performing the task of umpire boat, raced down the course sending out an enormous wash.

While the rich entertained their friends in magnificent houseboats with the food sent down from London, the plebs made do with camping on the banks, or even living on the skiffs themselves, as many were provided, like the boat of the Three Men, with a covering supported on iron hoops. The practice of living on a skiff at the Regatta was carried on until the 1970s by an eccentric lady who, in her late 70s, regularly rowed her 14ft camping dinghy up to Henley from Cookham, and lived on it during the Regatta, spending a further two weeks at Marsh Lock entertaining her friends. A baler served all hygienic and culinary needs. Miss Meadows became such a well-known figure on the river that the Environment Agency granted her a free boating licence. She was the only person to have been granted this favour, but alas, she died a year later.

The hygienic implications of all this are horrible to contemplate, and I suppose the residents of Henley could console themselves with the thought that all the noisome material thrown in the river was washed down to Marlow. It was, of course, for the social side of the Regatta rather than the serious rowing that the cream of Society came to Henley. This was to be experienced after the races had ended and the focus of attention moved to those resplendent houseboats, gaily painted, adorned with flowers and beautifully illuminated at night with paper lanterns. Their wealthy owners or tenants would commission concert parties to perform on a punt or mooring platform in front of their boat. A multitude of skiffs would gather round to share in the entertainment while a man with a net on a long pole would solicit tips. One cannot write about those floating palaces without a pang of regret that the Thames will never see their like again. They had become unfashionable by the end of the century, and died out with the coming of the First World War. Foremost among them was 'The Golden Grasshopper' owned by the magazine proprietor Raymond Radcliffe. She was painted all in yellow – a novelty – and as he let the boat out for profit, it paid him well.

One of his tenants was perhaps the most colourful show-off of all the Regatta goers. Colonel North had gone out to South America as a riveter of boilers and taken advantage of political developments there to corner the world market in nitrates. He wasn't a real 'colonel', it was just an honorary title in a part-time regiment.

On the final night of the Regatta, Pierrots gave a performance from his houseboat, and at the conclusion he was called upon to make a speech by the appreciative occupants of the 300 to 400 punts, skiffs and canoes who had been enjoying the show. He mounted to the roof and invited them all in to supper – he had a reputation for hospitality. When as an afterthought he added that he was not sure if there was supper enough for all, but he was quite certain there was enough to drink, voices from the crowd shouted: 'We're quite sure of that, Colonel!' This was never put to the test, for the Colonel then began to dance a hornpipe and ended up falling on the floor.

Another Henley visitor of humble origins who had made his fortune in South America was Charles Jewell. He had amassed great wealth as a grain broker in Argentina, and in 1890 he hired the 'Rouge-et-Noir' on which he held a large luncheon party, captured for posterity in oil on canvas by the artist Herbert Sidney. [4]

There was the soap magnate Benjamin Brooke, who made a memorable appearance with his houseboat named 'Monkey Brand' after his 'miracle' cleanser. He had a band of about 20 performers on board who played beautifully every night for the two weeks of his residence. Everything was done in the most elaborate style, but he only came to Henley once: it had cost him too much money.[5]

The *Lock to Lock Times* reported in 1890 that over 240 applications were received from owners of houseboats … double the number for which there was room. The owners of the boats were expected to make a voluntary contribution towards the Conservancy's costs, but they were a mean lot. In 1888 the 86 houseboats present contributed a derisory £18.

★

Ostentation there was aplenty, so it seems strange that J should blame the visit of King Edward VII in the early 1900s for 'spoiling' the Regatta. Perhaps he preferred the uninhibited fun of the parvenus and lower orders to the stuffier fashions of the noblesse. Or perhaps his memory was mellowed by the years when he wrote in his autobiography in 1927 that the King's coming turned it into a Society function and brought down the swell mob. It was also a little ungrateful to the King. Edward had come to see J's play, *The Passing of the Third Floor Back,* which caused the 'swell mob' to boost his audience.[6]

'Before that, it had been a happy, gay affair, simple and quiet. (Come on J, pull the other one!) People came in craft of all sorts, and took an interest in the racing. One could count the people on the tow-path: old blues, the townsfolk, with the farmers and their families from round about.'[7]

He even had a foot in the houseboat camp.

My nephew, Harry Shorland, brought his houseboat up from Staines by easy stages one year. A pair of swallows had started building on it, and came with him all the way. They finished the nest just in time to take a day off and watch the finals.'

Truly idyllic, but birds of a very different feather compared to Messrs Jewell, North and Brooke.

Medmenham Abbey, once the meeting place of the 'Hellfire Club', as it is today.

10

Holed Up at Henley

*Henley to Shiplake: Extreme weather affecting today's boaters – Why it took
five weeks to cover a journey of 100 miles – A welcoming backwater – The great
waxworks mystery – Perils of writing poetry on your wedding morning.*

J WAS lucky that he was spared the kind of extreme weather we are
experiencing at the beginning of the twenty-first century. He suffered
only the traditional British rain, Henley for him was just wet.

It was a different story when my wife and I brought our cabin cruiser
down from Oxford for the Thames Traditional Boat Rally in July 2007.[1]
We had moored up above the lock at Sonning the night before, and were
woken up by rain drumming on the roof. Not any old rain but what
sounded like a cloudburst; and expecting it to behave as such we lay awake
waiting for it to stop. But it didn't. We felt we were inside a big bass drum
until 11am the following morning. Then, when we looked out of the
window, we could see the water level slowly creeping up the bank. The
rain still came down, but it was of the ordinary kind.

We decided to cut and run for Henley where there would be help if
the river got out of hand. As we passed through the locks, the 'lockies'
shook their heads and said there would be no activity on the water that
weekend. We arrived at Henley and tied up on our usual moorings. All
seemed as it should be and even the sun came out. On Saturday morning
an intrepid party of gondoliers from Venice demonstrated their skill in
some of the worst conditions the Thames could throw at them.

But by lunchtime it became clear that something nasty was going to
happen. The speed of the river increased so much that it was unsafe to go out
on the water. By mid-afternoon the booms that mark the racing course for
the Regatta (which had taken place two weeks previously) were lifted off their

metal brackets and were whizzing downstream like javelins. The judges' box at the end of the course was swept off its stilts and sent down river after them before it could be lassoed by a high-powered inflatable boat.

The river was creeping inexorably up its banks. Red boards had appeared at locks warning of a strong stream – if you navigate in those conditions you are not covered by insurance. Lockkeepers were moving their furniture out of the ground floors of their cottages.

Boat owners, afraid their craft might be lifted on to the bank and capsize when the water went down, were sending out for scaffolding poles and planks to fend them off. By Sunday afternoon the water overflowed the banks, flooding the marquees and stands, and the event had to be abandoned.

And that is how we came to be stranded for three weeks at Henley. An uncomfortable situation, as the pontoons to which we had been attached had been hired for the weekend and needed to be taken back by road to the hirers. This left us standing at right angles to the bank with nothing to moor the stern to, so I had to buy some additional chain to which we could attach our anchor. Other boats were tied up alongside us. We had a sturdy bush to tie our bow line to, and the bank, fortunately, was relatively high. With the help of an old pallet and a plastic stool from Woolworths, I could just about crawl up on the bow to get inside.

That night I stayed on board to make sure nothing could come adrift. Radio and television news were full of stories that a great 'surge' was on its way down river – just to scare us – because nothing happened.

I spent two more days on board just in case the boat should be put at risk, then went home by train and brought the car down. I was no longer marooned, but the boat was. It was three weeks before the Red Boards were taken down and we could move her.

Being marooned at Henley is not the traditional desert island experience, of course. There are no great deprivations in this well-off little corner of England. Rather the reverse, you can find what you need, but it's expensive. If you want a spare pair of underpants, for example, they have to be Calvin Klein. The only wellingtons I could find were in a shop serving the needs of horse riders and were green. They did not fit very well, either.

After we escaped from Henley we cruised down to Windsor and back to allow the river to settle before we returned to Oxford. But two locks away from the city we were advised that Osney Lock was too dangerous to navigate, and we had to abandon ship again and leave the boat for a few days at Sandford Lock under the watchful eye of the lockkeeper.

So we returned to Oxford five weeks after our departure, a horrendously long time for the planned 85 miles to Henley and back. We thought such a summer flood must be a once in a lifetime experience, but in 2012 the rains returned and the Traditional Boat Rally had to be abandoned because the river was unsafe. Then in 2014 the phenomenal winter rains meant the site was too waterlogged to be used. Can we ever trust Old Father Thames again?

★

After leaving the hustle of Henley and passing through Marsh Lock a scene of tranquillity opened up before the Three Men. This is where the estate of Park Place, the grand house called Crochet Castle by Thomas Love Peacock and referred to earlier, sweeps down through wooded hills to the river.

Its most famous owner was The Prince Regent, father of George III, who bought the house in 1738 making it a mecca for fashionable society. After the prince died of lung disease the estate was acquired in 1752 by Henry Seymour Conway who transformed the grounds. In addition to the usual grotto there were underground passages, a classical temple and a menagerie. He built a rustic bridge using stones from the ruins of Reading Abbey which still carries the road from Henley to Wargrave over a swathe of lawn known as the Happy Valley. But the *pièce de résistance* was a genuine prehistoric stone circle brought over from Jersey as a gift from the islanders to commemorate his governorship there.

The house is not visible from the river, and some would say this is no great loss as it was rebuilt in a rather overblown French Renaissance style after being burnt down in 1870. Nicholas Pevsner, the architectural historian, wrote in the mid-twentieth century that the interest of the place was in its grounds as designed by Conway. The estate has since been reduced after sale to a property developer who used part of the land to build luxury homes.

On the riverbank the 'charming' gothic boathouse noted by the Halls can still be seen, although the trees that once shaded it have all been cut down. Over the past few years the addition of outbuildings and grey walls have given it a rather bleak appearance. This was a more welcoming place in Victorian times. Visitors then had easy access to the grounds on fixed days after obtaining admission from the boathouse, which was itself worth a half-hour visit according to George Dunlop Leslie RA, because of the remarkable works of art and foreign curiosities it contained.

It would be folly for any boater to attempt to land here today as the current owner is extremely security-conscious. In 2011 Park Place became the most expensive house in Britain when it was bought by a former Russian banker for £140m. He was granted asylum in Britain after claiming political persecution by the Kremlin. The Russian establishment continues to breath heavily down his neck, however, and this piece of English heritage has been the subject of legal wrangling in Russia.

★

The broad, lake-like stretch of the river here gives access to a peaceful backwater on the left-hand side that leads to the village of Wargrave. J reckoned he could save half a mile by using this 'shady little piece of stream'. Boaters who wish to follow his example today will have to negotiate the same low arch, known as Fidlers Bridge, by lying flat on the bottom of their craft.

In Victorian days the entrance to the backwater was studded with posts and chains and surrounded by menacing notice boards, but this did not deter the intrepid three, and J suggested that anyone with five minutes to spare here might spend it tearing down the forbidding boards and throwing them into the river. This sounds rather like manufactured anger as Leslie RA writing about the same backwater in 1881 noted:

> You need not mind the notice-boards about private waters &c, if you wish to explore this stream. These boards are generally put up at backwaters; but as long as the stream is navigable and no landing attempted, the right of way cannot be disputed.

However, it must be said that J and friends *did* make a landing here.

Hennerton Backwater, as it is called, is positively welcoming these days. Far from warning people away, the riparian owners have formed a working party to keep it navigable, and they are proud to tell you that this is the place where Harris and the pork pie miraculously disappeared, having apparently been swallowed up by the earth. Of course it was only Harris tumbling backwards into a hidden ditch when the Three stopped half-way down the stream for lunch, thereby providing one of the great comic moments in the book. Harris bitterly insisted that it had all been carefully choreographed by his two companions.

J must be teasing us with his chapter sub-heading '*Wargrave – Waxworks – Sonning*'. This would have created the expectation among impetuous Victorian visitors using his book as a guide that a wax-works was imminent.

They would have eagerly jumped off their skiffs, hailed the boatman of the George and Dragon, and asked to be directed to the main attraction. The old man would have stroked his beard with his one good hand – for it was old Charles Avery who lost an arm in the Indian Mutiny[2] – perhaps bewildered by this strange but oft-repeated request.

When visitors actually troubled to read the book and came to the word wax-works, it was a bit of a let-down. We learn that generous old Sarah Hill bequeathed £1 a year to be divided between two boys and two girls who 'had never been undutiful to their parents; who had never been known to swear or to tell untruths, to steal or break windows.' J jokes that when such a boy was found, many years ago he was exhibited for three weeks afterwards in the Town Hall under a glass case. 'What had become of the money since no one knows. They say it is always handed over to the nearest wax-works show.' So there you have the wax-works!

Those with a serious interest in this form of entertainment need not think they have wasted their time at Wargrave, however, for they can visit the tomb of *a* Madame Tussaud in the local churchyard – although it is not that of the famous wax-works owner but of her granddaughter-in-law.[3] It was tempting for local people to blur this distinction and it is said that young men would punt their girls up river to the churchyard in J's time and show them 'old Tussaud' and ghoulishly explain how during the French Revolution she peeled death masks off the faces of the recently guillotined.

★

Wargrave, being such a pretty little place, attracted many artists. Two of them left a record of their visit by painting the inn sign for the George and Dragon. On one side our old friend Leslie RA pictured the fight, on the other, Hodgson, also a Royal Academician, painted St George downing a pint after a job well done.

In recent times, when the sign became too dilapidated to be left hanging, it was brought into the pub and put on display over a mantelpiece while a copy was made to do service outside. There the copy remained until about ten years ago when a 'pub grub' chain took over the George and decided to have a new sign more in keeping with its happy family image.

The 'dumbed-down' cartoon version that resulted caused a great furore in the village over the destruction of a piece of English heritage mentioned in *Three Men in a Boat*. But a year later another pub chain took over. This time it was going up-market, so the cartoon sign was replaced by one simply showing the name in staid lettering. I am happy to report that the pub now sports a copy of the famous old sign, the original still being on display inside. It is pleasing to see genuine painted signs on Thameside inns these days. There is a tendency to use banal photographs instead.

J considered it to the credit of the place that Thomas Day was killed at Wargrave, for he wrote a book in 1789 much hated by Victorian school boys. It is called *The History of Sandford and Merton* and Dickens Junior drily notes that if ever a blameless boy was found in Wargrave deserving of Sarah Hill's bounty, then he would have been a lineal descendant of that exasperating Master Sandford, hero of the book.

Early on in *Three Men,* J assumes we are familiar with this character when he says a pupil at his old school who really liked to study was given the nickname of Sandford and Merton. J would be amazed to know that Day's work is still very much alive and flying around the world on the internet, for such is his esteem among American academics that his book has been digitised.

When I first came across J's reference, I thought it might be interesting to follow it up, so I went to my local library, which retrieved a dusty old volume out of a depository, the whole process taking a few weeks. Now anyone can simply sit in their armchair and have *The History* of *Sandford and Merton* delivered to their tablet free of charge within seconds, although without the rather quaint illustrations.

The story concerns Tommy Merton, son of a rich Jamaican planter, who had two black servants to accompany him everywhere – one to carry his umbrella and the other to carry *him* when he was tired. He also had a golden carriage borne on men's shoulders when he went to visit his little friends. His mother refused to allow him to read because it might give him a headache.

At the age of six, this thoroughly spoiled little brat is brought to England, where he lives in a large country house close to the home of virtuous Farmer Sandford, whose son, Harry, is a prodigy of goodness and a terrible prig. The boys meet when Harry rescues Tommy from a large snake that has entwined itself around his ankle. Harry is taken to meet the grateful Merton family and impresses the father so much that he gasps 'Upon my soul, the little man is a great philosopher.' He is later awed into saying: 'that little boy has the noblest mind that ever adorned a human being'.

It is decided that the two boys should be educated together by the local clergyman. The rest of the book consists of moral tales, fables and yarns of derring-do that the boys are made to read between practical instruction in gardening and carrying out good works.

Curiously, considering his dislike of Day's work, J considered using it as a model for his book about the river. Once he had collected a pile of notes from the Victorian guide books, some memoirs and some poetry, he had a 'vague idea' of making it a modern *Sandford and Merton*.

> I thought George would ask questions, and Harry (Harris) intersperse philosophical remarks. But George and Harry would not; I could not see them sitting there and doing it. So gradually they came to have their own way, and the book as a guide to the Thames is, I suppose, the least satisfactory work on the market.[4]

Note that J refers to Harris as Harry. Can Harry Sandford be the reason why Carl Henschel, sometimes called Charles, became Harry and then Harris? J seems to have imagined this character at first as someone providing elevating sentiments and tedious facts about the river. Harry was a much over-used name in his day – 'Arries and 'Arrietts again – but change the name to a surname, Harris, and an entirely different chap is conjured up. Comically pompous, he is the only one of the Three to be referred to formally, and to use a Jeromean expression, 'wouldn't elevate a cow.'[5]

Day met his death, not in Wargrave itself, but at a place nearby called Barehill, where, on a visit to his mother from his home in Surrey, he was thrown from his horse and killed instantly by a kick to the head. This was a particularly cruel twist of fate as the horse that threw him was one he had trained himself according to his own humane principles.

Day was a true product of the Age of Enlightenment and an early advocate of the abolition of slavery. But he did have one blemish in his character – he treated horses rather better than women. He took two girls from an orphanage over to France with the idea of bringing them up under a strict educational regime based on the principles of Jean Jacques Rousseau. He wanted to see if one of them could be trained to become his ideal wife. To test the nerve of the most likely contender, he poured hot wax on her arm and fired a bullet at close range. Unsurprisingly neither was found worthy of his high ambitions.[6]

Long after his death at the age of 41, his best known book was used by lesser minds as an instrument of torture in schools

J could never resist a good melodramatic story and would have been interested in this one. When Mrs Day heard of her husband's death she took to her bed, closed her bed curtains, and never allowed the light of the sun to visit her. She spent two years thus, and was then re-united in the grave with him she had so tenderly loved.[7]

A fine monument was erected to Day's memory in Wargrave Church. But fate dealt him another blow here – it was destroyed when suffragettes set fire to the building in 1914. This was most unfair as Day, despite his experiments, was all in favour of the advancement of women.

Some say that Wargrave Church was chosen to be set ablaze because the suffragettes believed the vicar had refused to drop the word 'obey' from the marriage service. If so, they were wrong, and confused him with a clergyman at another church. You can image the reaction of male chauvinists in their London club: 'Women! How can you trust 'em with the vote when they can't even burn down the right church!'

J was not a supporter of votes for women, believing that it would simply give their husbands a second vote.[8]

★

A gentle breeze gave the boating party a respite from rowing as they sailed up past Shiplake, and J notes the little church on the hill where Tennyson was married.

It is not a good idea to write a poem on your wedding day, as Tennyson did – emotion is likely to get the better of you – and I put this forward as an excuse as to why the future poet laureate came to pen what is possibly one of the worst poems in the English language. The last of the three verses of *Marriage Morning* runs:

Heart, are you great enough
For a love that never tires?
O heart, are you great enough for love?
I have heard of thorns and briers,
Over the meadow and stiles,
Over the world to the end of it
Flash for a million miles.

Surprisingly, these words are still treasured by the undiscriminating few. For £8.50 an online shop will arrange to have them delivered to your beloved in a tasteful little gift box.

Shiplake is a much swankier place now. The river bank where houseboats moored in J's time is lined by large houses whose residents include a pop-singer from the 60s and 70s and a banker in the *Sunday Times* rich list. Alan Wykes, who visited it in the 1960s, described the place as 'twee'. His guide, who was a rich, dark City man, showed him the ultimate in 'tweeness' – what he called his jewel set in a silver sea of the Thames.

In the cabin of his cruiser he opened a panel of rich wood to reveal a safe. From the safe he took a smaller casket of black crocodile, and from this he took a small box that he explained was fireproof. Another key opened the innermost casket which contained a tiny tube of the type attached to dogs or umbrellas. In it was what he described as the most beautiful poem in the English language. You've guessed it – *Marriage Morning*. Wykes, rather unkindly, I think, said this gimmickry 'just about summed up Shiplake and all who lived in her'.[9]

J, on the other hand, found it placid, hushed and lonely.

Few folk, except at twilight, a pair or two of rustic lovers, walk along its banks. 'Arry and Lord Fitznoodle have been left behind at Henley, and dismal, dirty Reading has not yet been reached.

Harris disappears with the pie in a ditch beside
Hennerton Water, Wargrave.

11

Harris Hits the Bottle

Sonning to Caversham: The despicable practice of spitting over bridges – Hurrying past Reading – Finding the island where Harris was left alone – The aggressive nature of swans – Hard work involved in sleeping in an open boat – The terrible secret of Caversham weir.

WHEN the venerable red-brick arches of Sonning Bridge came into view the Three Men pulled to the bank and explored the village, which they found the 'most fairytale-like little nook' on the whole river. Every house was covered in roses in bloom 'as it was early June', – clearly J is playing tricks with the calendar here. It was almost July when they left Henley as the town was getting ready for the Regatta. He wanted to describe Sonning at its best and no doubt was recalling a visit on a more floriferous occasion.

There are fewer rose trees in Sonning these days as it is a place of commuter and holiday homes. It has no village shop, and the small tearoom we used to enjoy on winter days when returning from checking on the boat is now an Indian restaurant. At rush hours the beautiful eighteenth century brick bridge causes gridlock on the surrounding roads.

One thing that has not changed is The Bull Inn, still very much 'the picture of an old country inn', and the wisteria growing over its walls looks as if it must have been there since J's time. But the green, square courtyard, where on seats beneath the trees the old men grouped of an evening to gossip, has become a car park and the tables jostle for place with four-by-fours. The gossip most probably concerns work in one of the many offices found in this stretch of England's 'silicon valley', and mobiles and laptops are much in evidence. The choice of food includes Spanish or Thai. In a cosy nook, celebrity spotters hope to glimpse George and Amal Clooney, who bought a home in the village in 2014. The village is no stranger to celebrities. Theresa May, the Prime Minister, has a weekend home here. Uri Geller, the famous cutlery bender, lived here for 35 years. As a parting gift he left a huge red bent spoon bolted to a tree stump on the riverbank and it was hardly surprising that it quickly disappeared since it had not been given planning permission. However, a new artefact has appeared in its place, a length of railway line bent into a U. Inscribed on it is: 'Bent by the power of the mind by the Ehrlich Brothers[1] inspired by Uri Geller 09.02.2012.' A plaque describes it as a gift to the village. A greater gift would have been to have left this sylvan scene unsullied.

Once, when passing under the picturesque old bridge, resplendent in our slipper-stern launch, we were spat on by a group of youths. We carried an umbrella with us for a while as a precaution, but we never experienced such a 'spit-head' review again. We put it down to the deplorable decline in the behaviour of modern youth until I discovered that it was something of a Thames tradition. Even the children of quite respectable parents indulged in the despicable practice.

E Arnot Robertson, whose interesting views on orgies I quoted earlier, wrote in 1937 about a voyage down the London tideway. She said she kept the canopy on the boat as long as possible because of the keen competition among messenger boys to see who could spit with greatest accuracy into open boats from bridges. She wrote that as a child she spent countless hours practising this accomplishment, furious because being a girl prevented her from being taken seriously by the 'experts'. She was very nearly in their class: a hit on the boat counted as one point and a passenger two. To hit a policeman counted as three – there were open police boats about in her childhood. She noted that the standard seemed to have fallen since her day, possibly because middle age was creeping up on her, and she had become more critical of the skills of current hoodlums.

The great John Ruskin witnessed such an outrage at Clifton Hampden Bridge. While contemplating the setting sun reflected in the water as it flowed beneath the brick arches, he saw a small boy run from one side of the bridge and lean far out over the parapet. The heart of the great Victorian arbiter on taste warmed to this youth. Had the beauty of the river awakened in him higher thoughts? As a boat drifted through the arch, the boy leant down lower, spat on the oarsman and ran away. The great aesthete went on his way, 'a sadder but a wiser man'.[2]

There was a bizarre occurrence at Sonning Bridge in 2013. A red letter-box suddenly appeared on one of the piers, totally inaccessible to anyone without waders – unless they were in a very small boat. It turned out to be the work of a local joker or performance artist. News of it spread far and wide. A Dutch television station reported that it had been placed there for the convenience of boaters, while a Radio 4 news bulletin solemnly declared that the Post Office had installed it without planning permission and it would have to be removed. It was taken away shortly afterwards when repairs were being made to the bridge, and auctioned for charity. But this was not the end of the story, in 2016 I spotted it attached high up on the retaining wall that protects the mainline railway near Mapledurham.

★

Such were the delights of Sonning that the Three Men left it too late to row on to Reading, and decided to spend the night on one of the islands between the village and Shiplake. But the siren call of Henley beckoned J back, and he decided to walk there in the rain with George to meet some friends. Harris was left alone with the boat.

It was midnight and pouring with rain when J and George returned to Shiplake Lock and started to stumble around in the dark looking for the last of four islands. Tiny as they are, these islands, like all the others on the Thames. have names – Phillimore Ait, The Lynch Ait, Hallsmead Ait, and Buck Ait. You can sail happily around the first three of these today on the towpath side, but when you think you have come to the fourth you suddenly find yourself heading into a bog and will have difficulty reversing your boat out of the clinging mud; for Buck Ait has, over the years, joined itself to the riverbank.

R R Bolland recalls that at a London Livery Dinner he was asked by the then director of the National Maritime Museum, 'Do you know which of the islands at Shiplake Jerome's party moored to?'

'This', he says, 'was enough to start a lengthy discussion. As it happened I had spent some time at Shiplake during the previous summer trying to identify the island.' Bolland dismisses Buck Ait because, he says, it can scarcely be considered as an island at all. Even in the 1880s he believed it doubtful whether it would have been possible to float a skiff on the channel on the towpath side. He plumps for the third island, Hallsmead.[3]

I think he is wrong here. *The Oarsman's and Angler's Map of the River Thames,* published in 1893, has the following note: 'There is usually a very strong stream past the islands above Shiplake. The course is between the islands and the *left* bank (i.e. towpath side, facing down-stream) to avoid the eel-bucks.' Boats were still being towed from the towpath in J's day, and it would have been impossible for a tow rope to sweep the wooded Buck Ait. There must have been a navigable channel.

Furthermore, the 1893 map clearly shows some kind of obstruction between the ait and the right-hand bank, presumably the eel-bucks which gave their name to the island. Eel-bucks consisted of a row of phallic-shaped baskets which could be raised or lowered into the river on a wooden frame to trap this Thames delicacy.

In 1892, after *Three Men* had been written, the eel-bucks were removed. River traffic then found it more convenient to pass on this side, and the old channel next to the tow path was left to silt up with the decline of commercial traffic.[4]

It would seem to us a rather curious arrangement that Harris had to stay alone on the skiff moored to the island, instead of the boat being prepared for the night and left against the tow path so that he could take his ease under cover and all would be ready for his chums' return. But they were obeying the golden rule of Victorian boating – never moor alongside the tow path. You wouldn't want to be woken up in the middle of night by a group of rough hauliers pulling a barge and finding your skiff in the way of their rope. The island also provided security from wandering vagabonds.

It is hardly surprising that a chap left alone in such a miserable spot on a wet night should resort to the bottle, and Harris's tipple provides us with the marvellously funny story of how he claimed to have done battle with a legion of swans. These are Victorian times, and getting drunk has to be implied very gently. So Harris is described as keeping his friends up all night wandering about the boat with a strange obsession about losing his clothes, and later the whisky bottle could not be found. In the morning he has forgotten all about the swans.

As for these regal birds, most people have a sentimental regard for them – *Swan Lake* and all that. Harris's fantasy was perhaps closer to the truth in that it showed them in an aggressive light. They are fiercely territorial. Moor up for the night and the Swan General will soon be on the scene to inspect your boat and demand the usual fee payable in tasty snacks. If you ignore him he will start to nibble your immaculate varnish. On the other hand, if you start to feed him, he will persist in pestering you for more, wagging his tail, not in friendliness but anger. And when you stop, he is not above reaching into the boat with his long neck and giving you a peck on the arm. Charming behaviour from something that was once just an innocent egg.

The swans on the Thames are well looked after now. They are given an annual health check by the Queen's Swan Warden from the University of Oxford's Department of Zoology. This takes place during the annual Royal Swan Upping in July, a colourful ceremony dating back to the twelfth century when the Crown claimed ownership of all mute swans. They were considered a great delicacy then, and only royalty or their favoured subjects were considered worthy of this delicacy.

On the Thames the royal privilege was shared with two great London guilds, the Dyers and Vintners companies – useful people to have on board if you wanted your banquet to go with a swing with fine wines and colourful outfits. The aim of the Upping was to work out which proportion of the swans belonged to the two city companies and which to the Crown.

This would seem to be an extremely tedious, if not impossible, task, and Upping these days is confined to an area of the Thames above Sunbury Lock and below Abingdon Bridge so that its work can be completed conveniently in the course of a five-day week. In Victorian times it was considered a jolly holiday for selected London Watermen who manned the six skiffs required for the operation. It did not have a good reputation then. Swans were seized round the neck with long iron hooks and their beaks cut with notches to indicate who they belonged to. On one occasion the royal uppers were reported to the Royal Society for the Prevention of Cruelty to Animals.

It is much more humane these days, and the health of the birds is paramount. When a brood of cygnets is spotted the cry goes out 'All up!' and the skiffs glide in together to pen the swans in. The cygnets are gently lifted up and held under a man's arm, put in a canvas sling to be weighed, and identifying rings are attached to their legs before they are returned to the water none the worse for their experience. A report from this swan health service is sent to the Queen every year.

The skiffs of the Uppers are still largely manned by former London dockers and working watermen and lightermen, dying breeds, and it is still something of a holiday for them. In 2007 there was near-mutiny and resignations among the Queen's men when Buckingham Palace decreed that, on health and safety grounds, no alcohol should be consumed while they were in uniform. It had been their custom to swig a mixture of rum and milk from bottles kept in the bottom of the boats – hoochy-coochy it was called.

The work of the oarsmen in the skiffs has been made less arduous by providing them with a tow. Some of the best-looking boats on the river, recruited from the Thames Vintage Boat Club carry out this task. The

Uppers – dressed in their bright red and blue blazers with swans' feathers in their caps – are a striking sight which draws crowds to the banks, and more affluent sightseers in boats hired for corporate entertainment. If you want to see them, the best place is on Abingdon Bridge at about teatime on the Friday of the third week in July. Chatter among the bystanders following progress on mobile 'phones will tell you of their approach, and looking over the parapet you may see them stand in their skiffs and toast the Queen.

Swans, of course, are not eaten today, and are prized only for the beauty they add to the river scene. It is a shame that their place on the menu cannot be taken by Canada Geese, a noisy black-necked horde which is multiplying at a rapid rate and polluting the river banks with its mess. They are highly organized, not only in their formation flying, but also in their child-care. They organize crèches, and you may come across a sheltered spot where two or three adults are looking after a vast number of goslings. One should not be too sentimental about this. Unless large numbers of these endearing chicks suffer a dreadful fate, the whole of the Thames Valley would be carpeted with black and white feathers in no time.

These geese are beginning to spawn their own urban myth, alcohol fuelled or otherwise. It runs thus: a Canada Goose is seen swimming on the water when, suddenly, it disappears vertically. The hunt is then on for 'the terror of the Thames' variously described as a giant pike or escaped crocodile. Local media are then kept busy reporting Loch Ness Monster-type stories of phenomena that might, or might not, be related to the occurrence.[5]

★

With a hung-over Harris, and George and J feeling the effects of their late-night walk in the rain, it was not a happy trio that awoke the following morning. Harris only wanted a simple breakfast of 'non-dainties', and putting everything back into the boat and cleaning it up seemed to take longer than usual. J remarked that it was beginning to give him insight into how a woman with only one house on her hands managed to pass away her time.

There was a certain amount of ill-temper as each of the three accused the others of shirking their fair share of the work. An indignant J, beginning to feel strongly on the subject, makes the famous observation that 'I like work; it fascinates me, I can sit and look at it for hours.' He seems to have come off best in the argument, however, as it is agreed that George and Harris should row up past Reading and J tow the boat from there on.

The first sight of Reading was not an attractive one, with the gas works, a canal entrance and the noise of a constantly busy main line to the West Country. It has not improved much since. A variety of modernistic 'pavilions' can be spotted as you approach the town, which are part of a high-tech business park. Shortly after they were built, a clumsy metal sign was put up on the river bank further up-stream welcoming you to Reading, and stating that the town was keen to protect the environment. We thought dirty work must be afoot and, sure enough, a Tesco hypermarket was built beside the river a few hundred yards away.

I have to say it is well screened by trees, and the long pontoon it provides is a handy place to stop and seek provisions. It is also one of the few places on the river where you can fill a can of petrol for your motor launch. But on the downside it was too useful for that curse of the river, itinerants living on clapped-out old boats. They have been chased off to a large extent, but the riverbank opposite Tesco's has become their capital city on the Royal river, with tiny broken-down boats moored up, and through the trees a prospect of improvised bivouacs. There is, however, one thing I would not change. A derelict wooden Dutch barge has been colonized and is covered with flowers in summer, a cross between the hanging gardens of Babylon and Noah's Ark.

After passing a bend in the river it is possible to spot the roof of Reading Gaol, where Oscar Wilde glimpsed 'that little tent of blue which prisoners call the sky' when imprisoned there in 1898. After being found guilty of sodomy he was sentenced to two years 'first-class' hard labour which involved spells on the treadmill and sewing mailbags. It seems J did not approve of Wilde, who met him later on in his life at a cosy little restaurant they both frequented. J wrote that there were rumours going around which his company did nothing to dispel, so he pretended not to see him. Wilde, on the other hand, thought *Three Men in a Boat* 'funny without being vulgar'.[6]

It is at 'Reading lock', actually Caversham Lock, that the Three met up with a steam boat driven by a friend of J's who offered to give them a tow. This was very handy for J, as it excused him from the bargain he had made to tow the others up to Pangbourne.

Being towed by a steam boat gives J cause to eat his words about what he had regarded as a menace on the river, and we enjoy the playful hypocrisy with which he condemns small boats for getting in their way. I must say that this is a double standard I share when applied to today's big white plastic boats. I agree that they spoil the look of the river, but if my engine breaks down and they generously agree to take me in tow, perhaps providing a mug of coffee and a slice of cake, my heart warms to them, and I feel guilty about my mean thoughts of 'gin palaces'. They also contribute – by means of licence fees – a relatively high proportion of the cost of keeping the river navigable.

★

The Thames holds a dark secret here. On the other side of Caversham Lock Island is a weir whose roar makes known its sinister presence, although it cannot be seen from the main channel. In J's time it was a wooden structure crossed by a rickety bridge known as the Clappers. On a March day in 1896 a tall, well-built, middle-aged woman could be seen crossing the bridge. Beneath her dark cloak she was carrying a brown paper parcel. This was the notorious 'baby farmer' Amelia Dyer, probably the most prolific mass killer in British criminal history. She is believed to have killed about 400 babies entrusted to her care, and the river here is the place most associated with her activities.

Shortly after Dyer was seen walking along the river bank, the parcel was fished out of the water by a passing bargeman hoping to find something valuable in it. Instead, he saw the corpse of a 12-month-old baby girl who had been strangled. There was writing on the paper that had been wrapped around the child, and this enabled the police to bring Dyer to justice, when a terrible story unfolded. In the nineteenth century the plight of unmarried mothers was dire. The Poor Law Amendment Act of 1834 ended a father's financial responsibility for an illegitimate child, Victorian logic dictating that young women would be less inclined to immorality if it led to certain financial ruin. We have already met one such 'fallen woman' in the form of Harriet Buswell. We shall soon meet another whose desperate state was described by J in his book.

Exploiting this helpless and hopeless multitude became a profitable business for Amelia Dyer. She advertised in local newspapers that she would take in unwanted children. For a 'premium' of £5 she would take full responsibility for the baby and 'find it a good home.' A mother could walk away from the responsibility, and many no doubt did. But Dyer had no intention of looking after the child. She simply strangled it with a length of white tape and disposed of the body. The clothing provided was exchanged for money at a pawn shop.

This terrible trade went on for over 30 years, with Dyer changing her name and moving to different parts of the country. She ended up in Reading, and babies' bodies began appearing in the Thames wrapped up in parcels and weighted with bricks. In a letter leaked to a newspaper after her arrest, Dyer said that she could not remember how many dead babies she had thrown over the weir, but hers could be recognised by the white tape around their necks.

It was the parcel thrown over the Clappers on that day in March 1896 that led to her downfall. The brown paper wrapping carried her name and address in Reading, and she was soon traced and the river below the weir dragged. Among the horrors brought to light was a carpet bag with two babies inside. Other packages provided circumstantial evidence incriminating Dyer, and she was hanged at Newgate Prison on June 10 1896.[7]

The trial was a sensation, Dyer's pram ended up in the Chamber of Horrors at Madame Tussaud's, and Reading mothers told their children that they would be sent to Mrs Dyer if they misbehaved. It is shocking that such a cold-blood massacre of the innocents could have occurred on the threshold of the twentieth century, but its memory seems to have passed from public consciousness, while Jack the Ripper, another devilish predator on 'fallen' women, is firmly fixed in the public imagination even though he had far fewer victims. Dead babies were always turning up in Victorian times, abandoned by helpless and desperate women, so people were probably much less sensitive about it. This is illustrated by J's funny story early on in his book about the man who was given a very smelly cheese and was thwarted whenever he tried to get rid of it. An undertaker told him it smelt like a dead baby.

Harris battles sawns at Bucks Alt, near Sonning

105

12

The Journey Speeds Up

Reading to Pangbourne: A festival that really rocks your boat – A millionaire's own Thunderbirds island – Prospects of Alpacas and Vineyards – Mapledurham, a place of literary pilgrimage – Surreptitious milking of cows at unholy hours – A most welcome spot on the River slowly disappearing – How D H Evans brought Vanity Fair to Pangbourne.

I T IS not only the Three Men who speed up their journey when taken in tow by the steam launch at Reading. The whole book quickens its pace. We are half way to Oxford, and the 47 miles will be covered in just 28 pages compared with the 216 (in my edition of the book) it has taken us so far. One senses that – having nearly completed the very successful serial version for the magazine *Home Chimes* – J was anxious to publish the book as soon as possible and get his hands on the royalties.

But one does not linger in the neighbourhood of Reading in any case, as J remarks. At least Father Thames has managed to keep Berkshire's county town at bay over the years by flooding its low-lying outskirts occasionally, so it is not long before we bid the urban landscape farewell, and after passing a restaurant, appropriately called The Three Men in a Boat, we find ourselves in public parkland, although of an unexceptional nature.

Unexceptional, that is, unless you happen to pass through on the August Bank Holiday weekend, when the Reading Music Festival takes place. Boaters are advised at the lock to take their fenders up in case swimmers grab them and give the boat a really violent rocking. Residents on the opposite bank protect their lawns with barbed wire. That said, the vast majority of young people are well behaved, and I think J would have found this classless jamboree rather more agreeable than the Henley Regattas after they became major social events, though he probably would not have enjoyed the music.

There was once a little old boathouse on the Caversham bank here. We admired it whenever we passed. It was a survivor from the last of the golden days of the river. The story of its destruction and replacement is bizarre. A picture book of the river published in 1998[1] described it as 'a rare example of what today is an endangered species'. It had a living area above the boat dock, and a balcony over the water.

I had kept an eye on it for about ten years, noting a few more panes of glass broken by vandals, a few more tiles missing from the roof. Then in the summer of 1998 some drop-outs moved in. They sat on the balcony playing bongo drums and blowing down a long hollow instrument. Bits of the balustrade and weather-boarding had disappeared, possibly to fuel their cooking fire. The next time we passed the whole of the roof had been removed, no doubt with the intention of making the building uninhabitable by the squatters.

Again we passed by, but this time all that remained was a hole in the bank. The surrounding shrubbery had been removed and six pairs of massive brick piers arose. The site had been bought by a property developer who was building a six-bedroom house for himself. For good measure, a double garage with games room above was added, and a swimming pool. It seems that established residential use existed because an inhabited boat house had stood on the site for 30 years. A magazine called *Brick Bulletin* described it in 2000 as 'an assertive and dramatic new presence', and 'in the Reading brickwork tradition.' Architectural and brick trade awards for the new house followed.

It goes without saying that we much preferred the old boathouse. But the story did not stop there. I casually picked up a copy of *Metro* on the London Underground in April 2005, and my eye was caught by the following rather convoluted headline: 'My own Tracy Island, well perhaps not, but you get the idea (don't you)'. There was a picture of the new boathouse. Its owner, apparently, was a fan of *Thunderbirds*, and had built a landing pad for his helicopter over his swimming pool.

He told the reporter: 'I wanted it to be made so the pool opened up with the waters draining out so I could land like they did in the series. Then the pool closed over again and filled up with water. It was something I seriously considered but the costs of replicating it were in excess of £1 million.'

So he didn't, and the Thames was deprived of such a marvel. But it is, perhaps, an interesting reflection on planning laws. The owner has since died and the helicopter has disappeared.

A large brick-built canoe club further spoils what should be a pleasant rural scene. But the twentieth century has added some pleasant traditional houses and gardens on the Oxford bank here. Right on the end is an Edwardian fantasy with a 'pepperpot' tower.

★

The Three Men passing through this stretch were under tow and at liberty to enjoy the view which a little further on is 'very lovely', as J observes. The railway rather spoils it near Tilehurst, he says, 'but from Mapledurham up to Streatley it becomes glorious.'

Glorious it remains, although the scenery around Tilehurst has been blighted by the monstrous gantries necessary for the electrification of the mainline to the West Country.

The name of Mapledurham will ring a bell among those who have read John Galsworthy's *Forsyte Saga*. But it is difficult to pin down his attachment to the river here. Mapledurham House is popularly associated with Soames Forsyte's country house. But it was never used as a location for either of the two TV versions of the saga – for good reason. The Jacobean manor house was well known at the time the books were written as the ancestral home of the Blount family. Soames's house is described as a typical Victorian gentleman's villa, with a veranda and billiard room, and lawns sloping down to the river where there was a boat house. It is the kind of house you would expect to find in a place with good rail connections, such as Maidenhead or Pangbourne.

So there is a bit of a mystery here.

Why did Galsworthy choose Mapledurham? If you put together the various descriptions of this spot scattered through the novels, it is obvious that he was familiar with the place. Yet, after reading biographies of the author, I can find no indication that he ever stayed in the area for any length of time.

Perhaps an important clue to the solution of this puzzle lies in a passage from *To Let,* the third part of the saga. The year is, I think, 1920. The story has reached the point where the family is divided into two antagonistic branches and Fleur, the daughter of Soames, falls in love with Jon, the son of Young Jolyon. It is a Romeo and Juliet situation.

How can they meet without their respective parents suspecting anything? They contrive to take a train from Paddington to Reading together, and then prolong their fleeting tryst by walking along the river bank from Caversham Lock to Mapledurham, a distance of more than four miles. A car has been sent to Reading to pick up Fleur, but she says she is 'train giddy' and prefers to walk home. Jon, meanwhile, has cut across a field to Caversham Lock to wait for her, and the couple walk along the 'towing path'. This would have been kept well clear of undergrowth in those days so that towing lines were not obstructed. That meant Jon had to return to Reading after reaching the bend in the river before Mapledurham, because it 'all gets open' and he is afraid he might be seen.

After the couple parted, the novel describes how 'Fleur sped on … she passed the islands (Apple Tree and Poplar), the station (Tilehurst) and hotel (The Roebuck) and was about to take the ferry.' This was known as the Roebuck Ferry after the hotel, and the little hut that once served the ferryman can still be seen, although it has been converted into a holiday home. There were once two ferries here known as the Purley ferries. They were established in the late eighteenth century to by-pass land on the Berkshire bank where a farmer refused to allow a towpath.

As it turns out, she has no need of the ferry, for she finds a skiff with a young man standing in it. He has been visiting her father and been sent out to meet her.

The approach to the fictional Mapledurham accords with the real Mapledurham at this point, and this is reinforced by other descriptions given by Galsworthy. There were poplar trees lining the banks. You do not see them today, but landscapes taken by the Victorian photographer Henry Taunt show them to have been much in evidence.

But where exactly did Galsworthy imagine Soames's villa to stand? Later on in the story Soames buys land on which to graze cows – a rich man's whim to provide something to look at. This would suggest the water meadows on the Berkshire bank above Mapledurham Lock, so the villa would have to be on the opposite side, on what is now an events showground for Mapledurham House.

Galsworthy himself was involved in a passionate and agonising secret love affair. When he was in his late twenties, towards the end of the 1890s, he fell in love with Ada, the wife of his cousin, Arthur Galsworthy. It eventually led to divorce, which allowed the couple to marry, but not without scandal. After John had become a celebrated literary figure they destroyed all letters and documents relating to their affair.

In those strict Victorian days the Thames provided an ideal place to carry on illicit relationships. There was ample accommodation in camping skiffs, summer lettings of cottages and inns, or houseboats where not too many questions might have been asked. Between them all, the river provided a discreet means of communication. But the couple would not have been welcome in Mapledurham itself. The Blounts of the time did their best to discourage tourism, refusing to allow an inn to be built on the estate. But there was, unusually, a houseboat stationed there throughout the year. Could this have provided a haven?

On the now overgrown towpath that leads back to Reading, it is not difficult to imagine the shades of John and Ada strolling hand in hand in the dusk.

The house was a great draw, in all senses of the world, for the 'brethren of the brush' as Leslie called them. The old watermill and manor house, with its tall barley-sugar twist chimneys emerging from the surrounding woodland, would have been a familiar sight at the Royal Academy summer exhibitions. It remains an attractive and historic spot in possession of a Blount family descendant. The Blounts were Catholics, and Mapledurham is believed to be the only English manor with purpose-built secret hidey-holes for priests. A gable facing the river is covered with scallop shells, the symbol of pilgrims, and a sign that co-religionists could seek haven here.

As J notes, Reading was besieged by the Earl of Essex during the English Civil War, and it was not long before the Roundheads turned their attention to Mapledurham, where Sir Charles Blount was a supporter of the King. The place was sacked, but since Blount was a spendthrift there probably wasn't much left to be pillaged. He also seems to have been rather an arrogant man. The story goes that at the siege of Oxford he was challenged by a cavalier sentry to identify himself. He gave a brusque answer, saying everybody knew who he was. But the sentry took no chances and shot him dead.

Kenneth Graham rowed about the river here while working in London as Secretary to the Bank of England, but it was not until he had written *Toad of Toad Hall* that he moved to Pangbourne, a short distance from Mapledurham. He must have heard its story, for Charles Blount's Mapledurham seems to me a strong candidate for the inspiration for Toad Hall in *The Wind in the Willows*. It is certain that it was used by Ernest Shepard as the model for his illustrations.

There is evidence that the classic children's book was a parable designed to warn young Edwardians of the risk of social revolution, a very real fear at the time. Toad is an effete member of the upper class who ignores his social responsibilities. Badger and Ratty represent upper middle class practicality and solid morals. Mole is a well-intentioned, though ineffective, member of the lower middle class.

This Edwardian paranoia is tellingly expressed early on in the book

when Graham equates weasels, stoats and foxes with the working class
and their revolutionary potential. The Rat says: 'They're all right in a way
– I'm very good friends with them – pass the time of day with them, and
all that – but they break out sometimes, there's no denying it, and then –
well you can't really trust them, and that's the fact.'

A short distance up river we come to Hardwick House, another
sixteenth century manor house. J falls into the trap of quoting from one
of young Dickens's rambling erroneous asides when he says Charles I
played bowls here. Dickens wrote:

> It is said Charles I frequently indulged in his favourite pastime of bowls, and
> if the royal martyr had been as judicious in all matters as he undoubtedly
> was when he selected Hardwick for a playground, the course of English
> history might have been considerably changed.

In fact Charles had no choice in the matter. He was brought here as a
prisoner of the Parliamentarians and was held in a lodge to the north
of the house, which by then had been knocked about a bit in the usual
Cromwellian manner. He whiled away his time in captivity on the bowling
alley of an adjoining inn, probably because there was nothing else to do.

Opposite the house you will find a scruffy little island of just a few
shrubs and trees poking out of the river. It has been much eroded by floods
and fast streams, since in Victorian times it was a favourite stopping off point
for the river-going public. The then master of Hardwick, a Mr Rose, built
a small summerhouse on the island with flower beds and a tiled pavement.
Boaters were welcome to eat their picnics there and sign a visitors' book.

Sir Walter Armstrong, writing a couple of years before J's trip, said
that the little wooded islet had lately become the most welcome spot on
the river to the boat voyager, thanks to the generosity of Mr Rose, who
even provided sticks for picnic fires and flowers for the table.

The Rev Paul Gedge[2], who took underprivileged children from
Lambeth on camping skiff holidays up and down the river in the thirties
and forties, sorrowfully chronicled its demise. He regarded Pavement
Island, as he called it, to be one of the features of the whole river. He
blamed the public for failing to appreciate it and for destroying the
flower beds, consigning the log book to a watery grave and vandalising
the summerhouse. By 1938 all that was left was a pavement of alternate
coloured square tiles. Even this was torn up, leaving only the bare concrete

foundation. He was right to suppose it would all disappear one day, for in the matter of islands the river itself is the greatest vandal of them all.

Every time we pass this spot the islet seems to have shrunk a little. Someday soon it will have completely vanished and become a mysterious lost place like Atlantis or Lyonesse. A legend will grow up that if you listen quietly in the moonlight, you might hear the tinkling of teacups above the gentle rippling of the water.

It was at Kempton Park that J vented his spleen on the selfishness of landowners along the river, which he said grew every year. He deplored their unwelcoming attitude to boaters. But here the boot seems to have been on the other foot, and indeed at many popular spots along the Thames it was the riparian proprietor who was abused.

Dickens, giving advice to campers in his *Dictionary*, cautions that a good deal of the land on the banks is private property and that trespassing in private paddocks and gardens occurs too often.

> The owner of one well-known and extremely comfortable camping ground has been, we regret to say, compelled to close it against campers owing to the ill return so often made to him for his courtesy. This gentleman is a man of the world, and not at all of a fidgety or touchy disposition; but when it came to cutting down valuable ornamental shrubs, climbing over garden walls, stealing fruit and eggs, and surreptitiously milking cows at unholy hours, it was felt that the line must be drawn.'

Superficially, the Thames seems to wear a timeless air here. But look more closely and you will see some changes that would have amazed J. Those rather long-legged sheep you thought you saw turn out to have very long necks as well, for they are Alpacas, more at home in Peru than in our riverside meadows. And the gentle slopes of the Chilterns are patterned with rows of vines – you can buy Chiltern wine from a winery a little way over the hill. Of course, you cannot satisfy everybody, and critics have thought some of the scenery almost too picture perfect. The village of Whitchurch was described by Charles G Harper in 1910[3] as having a kind of theatrical prettiness and pettiness – a stage set rather than somewhere lived in 365 days of the year. Over time, trees and shrubs have drawn a curtain across this scene, and you have to be quick to spot it as you pass down Whitchurch Lock cut.

J notes that Pangbourne, where the 'quaint little' Swan Inn stands, was another spot that would have been as familiar to those attending art exhibitions as it was to its own inhabitants. In those days it had not yet become a suburb of Reading, but the fashion for boating had swept through the small Thames-side towns like a summer storm, transforming their economy. In place of the little village shop selling bare necessities was the 'Store' profiting from the infant tourist industry, its windows filled with pyramids of tinned food, camp kettles, enameled cups and saucers and all manner of baskets fashioned from osier and willow harvested along the river.

All this was a cause for lamentation by Harper, wistfully looking back just over a generation to when those first tourists – 'something of the Ancient Mariner sort' – deserted the 'seaside lounge' for a cruise along the placid bosom of the Thames. Unspoiled it might have been in those days, but one man's picturesque scene is another man's picture of poverty. The bloom had been brushed off the peach by the rude hands of later visitors, as Harper put it, but at least the great wave of affluence that the twentieth century brought would ensure that more people could afford to eat peaches. Harper described the advent of the motor car as the final desecration of Pangbourne. 'Pah' as he so eloquently put it.

Pangbourne is now such a prosperous suburb that it boasts a Lamborghini showroom, up-market estate agents, and tourists of the modern sort are catered for by a travel agent offering exotic destinations. With a well-known public school and an independent co-educational prep school that Kate Middleton attended, Pangbourne has done very well for itself. The Swan Inn is still popular, offering a choice of pub fare, but its boathouse where the Three Men left their skiff before sneaking back to London was sold off to become a private residence in 1957. Ten years later it was bought by the guitarist Jimmy Page, who formed the band Led Zeppelin there. Its broad black and white gable gives it a distinctive appearance when viewed from the river, and in 2012 it was on the market for £1.1 million.

A little further up river we come to Pangbourne Reach overlooked by Shooters Hill, which in J's day formed a tall chalk cliff. This was another artists' delight. It formed a natural canvas bespangled with the bright colours of wild flowers, its whiteness reflected in the water. However, in the 1890s a speculative builder came along and put up, in Harper's words, 'detestable so-styled villas' This was a man he pompously called a highly successful trader in the 'rag trade'. 'Why is it that the drapery trade is so greatly affected by Welshmen?' he asked. We may include J's maternal grandfather in their company.

The guilty man was Dan Harries Evans, a farmer's son from South Wales, who made his fortune with a store in London's Oxford Street.

D H Evans became a household name, but in 1999 the famous shop signs came down as part of a rebranding by House of Fraser. Evans wanted to live like a country gentleman here, and scooped away some of the cliff to build an ornate house with picture gallery and gardens, including glass houses (something to the taste of Soames Forsyte.)[4]. But he was not averse to having close neighbours, so he turned his Arcadia into a business speculation and excavated further along the cliff to build six more houses.

His architect[5] chose a rather extravagant version of Jacobethan, with elaborate timbering over a red brick ground floor. The decorated gables, belfries and porches were a novelty for Pangbourne. They looked as if they had been transported from a fashionable seaside resort, and such pretension did not go down well with the local folk, who dubbed them the Seven Deadly Sins.

The draw-back to these houses is that they are sandwiched between the main road from Reading to Wallingford at the front, and a railway embankment at the back. No long lawns slope down to the water's edge here, but they enjoy a splendid view over the river and across the fields. Those of us familiar with modern utilitarian developments along the Thames can look upon them in a more sympathetic light than those old villagers, and the sin of envy must be the prevalent one among today's passing boaters.

The Three are towed by steamboat upstream beyond Reading.

13

Dark Side of Victorian Boating

Beale Park to Streatley: Unusual colonists from the Deep South – The sleep test for creating a new golf course – Holy birds invade a church porch – Spooky occurrences in the Grotto – Two tragic accidents and a 'suicide'.

L YING back on the cushions of their skiff while still under tow, the Three Men were in the fortunate position of being able to relax and enjoy what is, for my money, the most beautiful stretch on the whole Thames. Hanging woods overarch the Oxfordshire bank of the river surmounted by smooth downs close-cropped by sheep. On the other side, across the riverside meadows, is a wooded ridge. No doubt they would have been shocked out of their reverie if they had seen what I have spotted there more than once – a red-eared terrapin sunning itself on a fallen tree. These little amphibians became popular in the 1990s after the Hollywood blockbuster *Teenage Mutant Ninja Turtles*. Owners abandoned them in the river when they grew large and inconvenient. Although native to the southern United States, they are capable of surviving in our rivers, although unable to breed because the climate is not hot enough to hatch their eggs. With regard to the disappearing goose phenomenon mentioned earlier, it is not a great leap of imagination from turtle to crocodile for those susceptible to 'seeing things.'

I noted in the previous chapter how the generosity of riparian owners was frequently ill-paid. Fortunately there are still generous landlords to be found, and boaters navigating this reach have cause to bless Gilbert Beale. He made his fortune with Carter's seeds, being one of the first to bring seeds to a mass market between the wars with the help of colourful pictures on the packets. He bought Church Farm at Basildon in the 1940s, and in 1956 set up a trust to preserve this beautiful stretch of the Thames Valley for the public to enjoy. Signs here welcome passing boats with the offer of 24 hours' free mooring. It must be the best spot on the river where you can over-night free of charge.

Gilbert, an eccentric, was also a pioneer golf-course builder with an original method of site selection. He and his brother would take different trains out of London and fall asleep. They would then get off the train at the next station after they had woken up. A short nap, they believed, measured the ideal distance from London for a golf course, as opposed to those who believe that a short nap is preferable to a round of golf.

Beale Park started off with a small pond, some peacocks and garden statues rescued from stately piles under demolition. It now extends to 350 acres with several lakes and many exotic birds and animals.[1]

No doubt the Three Men would have noted the classical pile of Basildon Park nestling in the woods above the water meadows. The manor was bought from the Fane family by Sir Francis Sykes in 1771. He had made his fortune in India, and could afford a lavish rebuild in the new style, but he did not live to see the interior completed.

The house was there for the Three Men but we are very lucky that it is still there for us. In the 1950s the then owner planned to demolish it and take it to the United States. Lord Iliffe, whose family made their fortune in provincial newspapers, rescued it. His wife had a flair for interior design and a hands-on approach. At a time when money and materials were scarce, the couple scoured the country for architectural salvage and furniture. In the garden room she improvised silk hangings from old curtains which she hung on the walls with the help of her cook.

Before she came on the scene, one Adam fireplace, some ceiling paintings and plaster cornices did escape across the Atlantic. They can be found in a reconstruction of the dining room called the Basildon Room in the Waldorf Astoria Hotel in New York.[2]

The house is now happily in the care of the National Trust, but the fifties still haunt the building. This is Basildon's contribution to our social history – it has not been subjected to the grand design of some celebrity or oligarch. The guests' *en suite* bathrooms converted from dressing rooms look a bit tacky now, as does the kitchen moved in among the grand state rooms, so that it has an elaborate plaster ceiling at odds with a giant Westinghouse electric cooker. In spite of this, the house will be remembered as the glamorous setting for the ballroom scene in the 2005 film of Jane Austen's *Pride and Prejudice* starring Keira Knightley.

Between the wars a weekend shooting party included the directors of a paper-making company. They were trying to think of a name for a new

The departure of Jerome and Harris for their holiday as depicted by A Frederics in the first edition of Three Men superimposed on a photograph of 19 Tavistock Place, since renumbered as 32. JKJ lived for a year here in 1885 sharing his lodgings with George, and a Blue Plaque was attached to the house in 2015 recording his stay. However he moved across the road to live at No 33, since demolished, before taking up residence in Chelsea after his marriage in 1889, where his masterpiece was written. Frederics was acquainted with the author and Jerome is recognisable on the right. Even for the short journey to Waterloo convention dictated they should wear city clothes, hence the brown soft felt "Billycock" hats. The addition of two fishing rods is not supported by the text.

J was enchanted by the "mellow bright and sweet" wall between Hampton Court and the River and presciently described it has having "fifty shades" of tints and hues in every ten yards.

The ancient oak staircase at Kingston upon Thames now leads from a Next store to a Costa coffee shop.

SACRED to the Memory of M.ᴿˢ SUSANNAH THOMAS, Sole Daughter and Heiress of S.ᵗ DALBY
THOMAS K.ⁿᵗ Govern.ᵗ of all the African Comp.ˢ Settlem.ᵗˢ descended from an Antient Family in WALES.
and of DAME DOROTHY his wife, Daughter of J.⁰ CHETTLE, of S.ᵗ Mary Blandford in Dorsetts Esq.ʳ

*The monuments in Hampton Church to Mrs Thomas, above, and Sibel Penn, whose feet
and petticoat are shown inset. Sibel's tomb is in such a confined space that it is only possible
to see her head and feet through stategically placed mirrors. In this sense it is a "funny"
tomb. Did J get the two mixed up?*

The still venerated yew believed to be 2,500 years old at Ankerwycke Park near
Runnymede, with a votive wreath attached (inset). Below, the statue to the lino makers of
Staines-upon-Thames erected in the High Street in 2004. Frederick Walton, who invented
linoleum, opened his factory here in 1864.

"Boulter's Lock, Sunday Afternoon" (left), painted by John Gregory, which caused a sensation when first exhibited at the Royal Academy of Arts in London in 1897. The critics may have been divided, but the painting has enjoyed lasting popularity. It was bought in 1905 by Lord Lever, the soap manufacturer who used it in an advertising campaign. Compare it with boats taking part in a reconstruction of the scene in June 1995 (above). Note the dog in the foreground, the woman with the red umbrella and girl in a canoe. Of course, the hats and dresses could never be so elaborate.

Reproduction of John Gregory's painting by permission of National Museums Liverpool.
Photograph by Dieter Jebens.

The drinking fountain commemorating Charles Frohman near the church at Marlow. Frohman was J's friend and theatrical agent in America. He loved the town and wanted to be buried in the churchyard here, but he was drowned on the Lusitania when she was torpedoed in 1915.

Below: Monk's Corner, Marlow Common, where J lived from c1910 to 1917. It was originally built in 1900 by Henry Hudson, the soap magnate, to house Conrad Dressler, a sculptor, who was to oversee Medmenham Pottery which Hudson established here to provide work for the local unemployed. The ceramic frieze along the front (inset) was a trial for a panel called "Industry" intended to adorn the soap company's offices in Dublin. The house is about two miles from the centre of Marlow and is Grade II listed.

The modest little Edwardian boathouse at Caversham which was demolished to make way for a luxury home with swimming pool and helipad inspired by Tracy Island.

Photo above by permission of Orion Books. Photo from *Metro* newspaper below by permission of Citrus Studio Wokingham.

The rather austere house called The Grotto above Gatehampton bridge which is said to be haunted by the ghost of Lady Fane, who threw herself down a well. In J's time it was covered in ivy which would have made it even more forbidding.
Below: The poignant monument in Lower Basildon churchyard to two schoolboys drowned while bathing in a backwater near the house on a summer day in 1886.

kind of stationery they were about to market. Eureka! It must be Basildon Bond – eat your heart out, Basildon, Essex.

The little church of St Bartholomew, Lower Basildon, stands in isolation from the rest of the village, which gradually migrated north away from the river and closer to the Reading-to-Oxford road. When I visited it, a family of white doves had made their home in the porch, and the apologetic lady minding the place said nothing could be done as nets were not permitted on a listed building. We trod carefully over the newspapers laid out to protect the floor against their mess. It seemed appropriate for such holy birds of peace to make their home here, but the Bible contains no advice to Noah about the advisability of putting newspapers over the floor of the Ark.

The churchyard at Lower Basildon has a touching life-size marble statue of two schoolboys aged 15 and 16 who drowned in a backwater of the Thames. (Harris had lost his interest in tombs by this point.) Harold and Ernest were the sons of Edward Deverell of Church Farm. One sunny afternoon in June 1886, they rowed with a friend the few yards up river to a backwater behind an island near a large house called The Grotto. They had bathed there many times during the previous year, but unknown to them the Thames Conservancy had been dredging to allow for sheep dipping and the two boys, neither of whom could swim, soon found themselves out of their depth. Despite frantic attempts by their friend to bring the boat close to them, they drowned.[3]

Jethro Tull, a pioneer of agricultural revolution in the eighteenth century, was born and buried here although his experiments were carried out elsewhere. His great invention was the horse-drawn seed drill. In 1741 he was buried in the crypt, which is now inaccessible to visitors, so the beneficent Gilbert Childe-Beale arranged for a stone tablet to be placed against the church wall to his memory. Appropriate for a man who made his fortune in seeds to salute one whose fame resides in the sowing of them.

Passing under the gloomy vaults of Gatehampton Railway Bridge, the Thames takes on a sinister aspect. Death seems to have visited this shady tree-lined stretch more than most other parts of the river, and shortly before J's book was published the Oxfordshire Coroner, Dr Cox, was called to enquire into two other tragic events at this spot in addition to the deaths of the two boys.

The Three Men were cast off from a friendly towing boat here just below The Grotto. This is a house of austere Georgian design often referred to in the writings of Victorian boaters, and it remains a landmark for river users today. It was built as a dower house for Lady Mary Fane in 1720 when the Fanes owned Basildon Park. She followed the fashion of the day by building a grotto, although it was not quite on the lavish scale of the Duke of York's folly at Oatlands described earlier. The centerpiece was a room with shells arranged in the most elaborate patterns to suggest flowers and ribbons. There was a bed for a hermit (perhaps the under-gardener played this role), and an oval room built from large rustic blocks which housed a cascade falling into a cold bath.

When this fad went out of fashion the grotto disappeared. But the little octagonal room and half the oval room still survive. Various attempts were made to call the house by different names, but they all failed. In J's day it was clad in a gloomy vesture of ivy. Then in the early 1950s it became the headquarters of the Institute of Leisure and Amenity Management, which sounds like nice work if you can get it. Those who looked after the interests of the custodians of our parks and sports facilities must have got tired of being asked: 'How can you work in such a beautiful setting?' But even Arcadia has its drawbacks and the place is definitely spooky. The ghost of Lady Fane, who drowned herself in a well in the garden, is said to manifest itself on the hearthrug of one room and occasionally pass in and out of the walls of a corridor. Such stories were rife in Victorian times, but more recently Lady Fane took to meddling with the electricity supply. Unexplained power cuts bedeviled the deliberations of those worthy toilers facilitating our leisure. Then there was the paper-punch which took flight across an office all on its own, witnessed by three of the staff.

Privatisation of council leisure facilities created a harsher economic environment for the institute, and they had to move out of their Eden. At the beginning of the present century the house was sold, with the intention of converting it back into a family home.[4]

The Grotto figures in a fatal accident that occurred on the August Bank Holiday of 1879. The Stewart family from Reading had planned to take a trip up river to the picturesque little village of Streatley. Mr and Mrs Stewart took the train there, but their sons William and Thomas, daughters Annie White and Harriet Stewart, together with their son-in-law Thomas White, were going by boat. They borrowed a gig with a pair of oars from Reading Rowing Club. It was a narrow, unstable boat with iron brackets extending over the sides to support the oars – similar to the boat involved in the accident at Dockett Point.

The river was in spate after heavy summer rain and the party chose to tow the boat wherever possible, as this was the most efficient way of moving it against a strong current. They had taken a ten-foot pole from the club and set it up in the gig, attaching the towing rope a few inches from the top of it.

They proceeded up river from below Caversham Bridge without incident, the men taking it in turns to tow, and the younger sister Harriet steering all the way. When they reached the Gatehampton Ferry, where the towpath changed sides of the river, William got into the boat and Thomas Stewart and Thomas White took up the tow rope when they reached the opposite side. A few hundred yards on, the river curves to the right, and a reed bed caused the two men to make a slight detour inland, where they lost sight of the boat. As the gig was turning, William, who was lying on the floor, felt it rolling over to the side nearest the shore, while the bow moved out to the centre of the stream. He immediately got up and told his sister to pull on the inside rudder line. He intended to take the lines over himself but found they had been crossed over, and before he could uncross them, the boat overturned.

The two men who had been towing the boat heard screams and, through a gap in the reeds, saw that it had capsized and their companions were in the water. Unaccountably, they let go of the rope, the surest means of rescue, and ran along the river bank to get nearer to the scene of the accident a hundred yards away. At this point Thomas White was overcome by shock and suffered some kind of fit. Meanwhile William struggled to rescue his two sisters. Twice he dragged them on to the overturned boat but twice the current caused it to turn over, and the women sank in the water and did not come up again. Only their two waterproof cloaks rose to the surface. William was plucked to safety by the occupants of a passing punt and put ashore at The Grotto, then occupied by Arthur Smith, the High Sheriff of Berkshire, who took him in and looked after him until he was fit enough to leave for home that evening.

The bodies of the two women were not recovered until the following Sunday when they were found floating three-quarters of a mile downstream.

At the inquest the jury found that the boat had been upset through the pulling of the wrong steering line by accident, and the towing rope being too short.

The coroner praised William Stewart for the gallant way he had attempted to save his sisters. He said the accident should serve as a warning to pleasure parties to take care how they ventured on the Thames in flood time, particularly in such a dangerous spot.[5]

But I believe using a ten-foot pole attached to the towing line must have been a contributing factor. William Stewart hesitated in his evidence when he was asked to give the height of the pole and had to be prompted by a juror who had read 'in the paper' that it was 10 feet.

★

It was just after J and Harris started to wrangle again over who should row the boat that 'the grotto', spelt in the book with a lower case 'g', again casts its macabre spell. 'Something black floating in the water' which George is about to grab turns out to be the body of a drowned woman.

Assiduous work by R R Bolland, poring through local newspapers, has shown that this incident is based on reality. A young woman *was* drowned here a year before the book was written. It was a very sad and moving tale which J must have heard about through local gossip or from local newspaper reports, and decided to include it as a melodramatic set piece in stark contrast to the prevailing jollity.

Artistic licence is taken with the facts. The body lies 'very lightly on the water', the face, though too prematurely aged, was 'sweet and calm like the face of the sick sometimes when at last the pain has left them.'

Normally the bodies of the drowned do not float lightly on the water like Ophelia in Sir John Millais's famous painting. They sink, and when they rise to the surface again, are horribly disfigured. In this case the body was found still submerged, the face and hands purple. Alice Douglass, a Gaiety Girl, who was the victim, had no daughter to kiss goodbye in a 'dull weary way' after she had put into the girl's hands a penny box of chocolate, as J would have us believe. But her story is no less pathetic and has the power to move us still. This is because she kept a diary as she wandered about Hartslock Wood for three days telling of her hunger and weariness.

Alice, or to give her stage name, Alicia, was described at the inquest as a tall, good looking young woman aged 30. She came from a respectable family in Brighton and worked at The Gaiety Theatre at the Aldwych. That was at the time when it was managed by John Hollingshead, who described himself in those prim old days as a licensed dealer in legs and short skirts.

Alice's family would have been horrified. Her father was a skilled machinist with a railway company, and had given her a good education. She was clearly leading a rackety life, and to make ends meet had taken a lover and 'put herself under the protection', as the phrase was in those days, of a soldier. Alas for her, after four years he was posted overseas and killed in the Egyptian campaign.

Alice's position was now very precarious. To add to her difficulties she had injured her foot and was in danger of losing a toe, which would put an end to her dancing career. But there was a ray of hope. She was attracting the attention of a man of substance, Charles Jewell, who gave as his address a club in Hanover Square in the West End. On Saturday June 23 he took Alice down to Goring by train, having met her some weeks previously in a London park. She had confided her troubles to him, including the fact that she now lived in a 'wretched hole' in Soho. The pair rented a cottage in this popular and attractive village, where they lived as husband and wife.

The arrangement does not seem to have been particularly successful. The cottage had been booked for a month, but after a few days Jewell returned to London. He came back on July 2 and three days later they travelled to London together, where he found her some more salubrious lodgings in Osnaburgh Street near Regent's Park.

On the following Friday, July 8, Jewell called for her at her new digs only to be told by the landlady that Miss Douglass had gone to the country for a few days. He did not see her alive again.

Alice had returned to Goring to enjoy for one last time the beauty of the Thames where she had spent a few days in a relationship which she knew could not last. Several times between the Thursday and the Saturday she visited Gatehampton Farm set among the woods that line the banks of the river near the railway viaduct. Mrs Jane Gillam, who lived there with her family, said Alice asked for food and drink which she paid for. She appeared to be desperate for company since she asked, and was given permission, to go for walks with the Gillam children. She even asked if she could stay at the farm, and offered to pay six shillings a week, but Mrs Gillam would not agree to that, even though Alice lied to put a respectable face on things by saying that her husband, whom she named as Jewell, would be with her for part of the time.

Six shillings was probably the going rate for basic accommodation in those days as it is the sum quoted by J in his account of the Drowned Woman:

> Six shillings a week does not keep body and soul together very unitedly. They want to get away from each other when there is only such a very slight bond as that between them…

The remarkable thing about Alice's case is that she seems to have taken three days to summon up the nerve to end her life, days she spent wandering in those beautiful woods, alive with the cheerful chatter of people on holiday. Her family had the resources to come to her aid, but she was too ashamed to ask for help. She recorded her feelings in a notebook which was produced at the inquest. In one entry she wrote; 'Had I been able I should have done the deed last night, but meeting with a young Oxford man who so kindly talked to me (sic). How can I forget his sweet manners? I am glad I met with him, for he unknowingly prolonged my stay on earth. I only wish I had met him before, perhaps this would never have befallen me.'

Finally, she left a note for her family:

> Mother, my dearest Mother, forgive your child. I have been much trouble and sorrow to you. Dearest, forgive me now. I am thinking my dearest of you. Father, I also ask your forgiveness, and my brother's. I ask God's mercy and forgiveness, for I am a sinner. May he grant me a little mercy. If I cannot receive it, Oh Heavenly Father, let my soul rest in peace. Father, forgive me, I am so unworthy and am not fit to ask even this mercy.

J echoed these words when he wrote: 'Anyhow, she had sinned – some of us do now and then – and her family and friends, naturally shocked and indignant, had closed their doors against her'[6].

The body was not really discovered by the Three Men. The alarm was raised by two women rowing down the river who saw a hat and bag on the bank. They called at the Gatehampton Ferryman's cottage, which can still be seen just down-stream of the railway bridge. The ferryman's son went to investigate and found Alice's belongings. He saw her body under the water where it had been for three days. Sticking vertically out of the mud was her umbrella. The water was shallow and she must have waded out to her death.

The coroner was a compassionate man. He went out of his way to avoid a suicide verdict, saying that in spite of the notes Alice had left 'there was nothing to show the state of the deceased's mind at the time.' The simple verdict of 'found drowned' was returned.

So Alice could be buried in consecrated ground in the churchyard at Goring, but since nobody came forward to pay for a headstone we do not know where. There is only this certainty: when the river overflows its banks in the winter floods, her remains are taken once again by Old Father Thames into his gentle arms, as J poetically puts it.

On the 8th of October 1887 The *Berkshire and Oxfordshire Advertiser* commented that the villagers seemed to think Mr Jewell ought to have given a much fuller account of his dealings with Alice in view of the fact that she was well dressed and was wearing jewellery obviously provided by him.

Despite all the sermonising and sympathy from J, he dismisses the whole affair rather brusquely by saying that it was fortunate that some men on the bank took charge of the body, as they did not want to be kept hanging about a coroner's court. The finders of the body would have been able to claim a bounty of 10 shillings, a bit of luck for them. J and his two friends, their appetites unaffected, went on to lunch at The Bull in Streatley, much to Montmorency's satisfaction.

The body of Alice Douglass was actually found lying underwater by two women rowers who were alerted by her handbag and umbrella left on the bank.

14

Fishy Fishermen's Tales

Goring to Moulsford with a walk to Wallingford: Crafty ladies without corsets – How to date a girl Victorian style – A tale of two geniuses – Alfred the Great builds a New Town – Why a plaster fish could be genuine – A sport you can enjoy while asleep.

ENOUGH of sad tales: the river took on its 'sweet smiling face' again when the Three Men reached Streatley and Goring. As the trees thin out along the river's edge, the gentle chalk fells of the Chilterns reappear. This is the famous Goring Gap through which, half a million years ago, the Thames carved its way with the help of melting glaciers. It then took on a more southerly route, and the map of Southern England as we know it came into being. A corridor of communication was opened up from the coast of Kent into the Cotswolds. The tidal limit of the estuary became its natural port, and London came to be where it is. All this is entirely due to those primordial geological ancestors of Goring and Streatley who so generously stepped aside and left London to reap all the glory.

The two villages on either side of the river were overpopulated by artists, according to Leslie RA, who noted that the River, the two mills, the bridge, the hill, the eyots and backwaters all lent themselves to the painter's skill. However, he objected to the number of sketching tents and white umbrellas perched on every vantage point, while 'geniuses and their aesthetically dressed wives' swarmed about the place.[1] By this I imagine he meant women in 'arty crafty' gear who didn't wear gloves, hats or corsets. Corsets became something of an issue in J's time after the aesthetic movement had encouraged the reform of underwear. But J seems to have been largely unsympathetic. In 1894 he wrote:

Cannot, for instance, the faddist allow one year… to go past without an anti-corset demonstration in some newspaper? [2]

It was a 'must' for tourists to climb the hill at Streatley. Elizabeth and Joseph Pennell described the view in *The Stream of Pleasure* published in 1891:

> It was the hour of sunset when we mounted and looked down the valley, spread out like a map below, the river winding through it, a patch of light between the open fields, a cold dark shadow under the wooded banks.

The couple, born in America, settled in England and wrote many books together, but Joseph's fame rests on his work as an illustrator and etcher. He worked with Carl Hentschel (Harris) on his new printing processes.

Such were the delights of the village that the Three Men were persuaded to stay for two days rather than press on to Wallingford. And it was here that they abandoned their experiment of washing their clothes in the river and handed the job over to a washerwoman – who charged three times the normal price because of their filthy state.

In those days you dressed properly for the river. The hoi-polloi might wear a mixture of agricultural and nautical gear, but young gentlemen on holiday believed they should look the part. A black and white photograph of J, Harris and George shows them nattily clad in blazers, white flannel shirts and white trousers topped off with cravats and assorted headgear. White shoes completed the picture.

The river was the one place where Victorian men were allowed to be colourful, although we must allow for the fact that J probably had his tongue in his cheek when he described their holiday outfits, and was lampooning the aesthetes of his day of whom he disapproved as much as Leslie.

He said he always liked a little red in his things – red and black.

> You know my hair is a sort of golden brown, rather a pretty shade I've been told, and a dark red matches it beautifully; and then I always think a light-blue necktie goes so well with it, and a pair of those Russian leather shoes and a red silk handkerchief round the waist – a handkerchief looks so much better than a belt.

Harris, he said, always kept to shades or mixtures of orange or yellow, although his complexion was too dark for yellow. George had bought some new things for the trip and the blazer was rather loud. The man who had sold it to him said it was of an oriental design. This was very much in the style of what the *Lock to Lock Times* called the 'toilet' of the 'Arry:

Wear the brightest tinted blazer you can purchase – a combination of violet, black, yellow, purple, green and magenta – or in fact any stunning colour you fancy.

George's preferred headgear was a tam o'shanter which he found practical because, as he said in later life, there were no berets available in those days. This must have given him a rather bohemian air as he pulled it well down over the right-hand side of his face. Fashionable casual wear then was the 'cricket cap', as worn by the other two.

He really does seem to have had a taste for snazzy dressing. A reporter interviewing him in 1933 noted that he was wearing a 'picturesque coloured jacket' and wondered if it was the 'grandchild' of the blazer that caused so much merriment.

★

Blazers and flannels are not what we would now call practical clothing for roughing it in foul weather. But they were a fashion statement in their day, and anyone who sauntered forth thus attired on a Sunday when England was a Sabbath-keeping land could be seen as challenging the moral order, and might be hissed or booed by the more puritanical Nonconformist members of society. The world was changing, it was chapel-goers like J's mother who had once been derided and pelted with stones and mud by supporters of the established church.[3]

The Thames was considered such a sinful place that in the spring of 1889 the newly formed Salvation Army announced that it was to launch a 'bombardment' of the river by its 'naval brigade' and 'iron horse artillery'[4]. They had chartered a steam launch for the summer which would be filled with 'lasses' under the command of Lucy Booth. J tells us in his autobiography that a Salvation Army lass once fell on her knees before him and prayed for his soul.[5] Perhaps it was during this campaign.

Washing your clothes was one problem, personal hygiene arrangements were another. A humble garden trowel was the answer. You could bury all your rubbish, even of the most noxious and intimate kind. Not everybody obeyed the rules and Dickens Junior complained of piles of debris and rusty tins being left about. Lavatory paper was a more delicate matter and was to remain so for many years. The Rev Paul Gedge, writing in 1949, included old railway timetables among his essential provisions: 'A toilet roll is a very blatant thing in a boat and somehow can never be hid.'[6]

Disposal of rubbish has become more difficult over the years. Instead of providing litter bins, local councils put up notices asking people to take their rubbish home. This is not so easy if you are spending a week or more in a small boat. Not every lock has a rubbish disposal point. I remember cleaning out a barbecue one morning before setting out to explore the countryside. I ended up with a lot of greasy smelly newspaper which I put in a plastic bag. I carried it around with me most of the day, unable to find a disposal point. Then I visited a great stately home expecting to find a litter bin the park, but there was none. I stepped into the library through an open glass door and asked the charming lady attendant if there was a litter bin anywhere. She said I could put it 'there', indicating a wastepaper basket under a beautiful inlaid escritoire. So I did!

★

Leslie notes a not unpleasant smell of tar and pitch from the boatyard next to the Swan Inn on the riverbank, where he enjoyed a memorable lunch. At the time J was passing through, the yard had expanded to a handsome boathouse across the river at Goring, and a young man who was two years older than him was making a name for himself in boatbuilding. It would be pleasing to believe that these two men of genuine, but very different, genius could have met. Both would rise from humble origins to the very peak of their professions, one as the writer of a book featuring a boat, the other as an engineer whose name would be linked to a giant flying boat.

Sam Saunders was the son of the alcoholic licensee of The Swan. Like many an inn along the river, it had a boathouse which not only let out boats but also built them. Sam inherited this part of the business and was soon demonstrating an exceptional talent. He built an ornate barge for University College Rowing Club at Oxford, but his real interest was in the advancing technology of his time; he experimented with some of the first electric launches and imported early Daimler internal combustion engines. He realised that to get the best performance out of the latter, boats needed lighter and stronger hulls. He developed the process of building up a boat's hull with thin layers of wood like *papier-mâché*, a system now used in the moulding of glass fibre craft. Wood ply was already available for making boards but it could not be moulded into shapes for boats because there was no suitable waterproof glue available. Sam hit upon the idea of stitching the thin sheets together with copper wire and sandwiching waterproofed canvas between them. The chance to prove the value of this technique came in 1896 when he was commissioned to build a fast launch for the umpires at Henley Royal Regatta. The 51ft boat, called Consuta, (Latin for 'sewn together') was powered by a steam engine from George Des Vignes of Chertsey, whom we met earlier, and reached a speed of 27.5mph with very little wash. Her high profile success must have boosted Sam's order books and she had a distinguished career throughout the twentieth century. In 1949 she carried television cameras to cover the Boat Race – the first time they had had been taken on the water.

By the end of the last century Consuta had fallen into dereliction, but a dedicated band of enthusiasts was determined to bring her back to life and refit her with her original steam engine. The Consuta Trust not only succeeded in this great task but has kept her in use on the river, and in the public eye, ever since. If you are lucky you may see her in action, her distinctive cigarette-like funnel showing high above the elegant lines of her hull.[7] Despite her antiquated looks she still has an acceleration fierce enough to knock an unwary umpire off his feet – the feisty spirit of old George, her engine builder, lives on.

Sam's patent material proved a great success in the building of early speed boats and a boon to the infant aviation industry. It was just the thing for building the gondolas of airships and the hulls and floats of the first flying boats. Saunders outgrew their yard on the Thames and moved to the Isle of Wight, where Sam went into partnership with the pioneer aircraft builder A V Roe. They founded the company of Saunders Roe, which in the latter part of the last century was famous for building flying boats and hovercraft.

Long after Sam's death in 1933, a magnificent Saunders Roe flying boat took to the skies. Called the Princess, it was designed to fly from London to New York at 350mph carrying 100 passengers. It seemed to fulfil every schoolboy's dream of the future when the enormous 148-foot long aircraft lifted off the water for the first time in August 1952. However, the newly-developed gas turbine engines proved unreliable, and in any case seaplanes soon became obsolete. All three of the aircraft built were mothballed, then scrapped in the 1960s.[8] In 2013 Goring held a day of celebration and unveiled a blue plaque to its most famous son. It is fixed to his old boat house, currently used as a mail sorting office[9] – and his story is a useful reminder that in those days someone with real ability, like J himself, could reach the heights of a profession without formal further education.

★

It was at Goring that Harris spent some time sprucing himself up and cleaning his shoes with white pipe clay before disappearing. As the 'real' Harris was married in 1889, the year the famous book was published, we must assume that he was taking the train to London to meet his fiancée. J notes that the station is handily situated for those wishing to do a moonlight flit from their hotel without paying the bill. Courtship rituals in those days were very basic. J tells us that the thing to do was to go down to Oxford Street after the shops had closed, presumably targeting the shop girls on their way home, and on seeing a likely young woman in the crowd asking her if by chance they had met last summer at some genteel resort such as Eastbourne. All going well, you walked by her side to Marble Arch, and perhaps, on a seat in the park, you held her hand. He was not successful, however, as his shyness handicapped him and he would take the lady's rebuff that he had made a mistake and shrink back scarlet-faced into the shadows.[10]

After Harris disappeared, J and George took a walk from Streatley to Wallingford. J says they admired the ancient stone in the old walls, which they assumed to be Roman, replacing the rude mud bricks of the Britons who 'squatted' there. In fact they were misled by young Dickens who said you could see these relics on the right hand side as you walked up from the river to the railway station. Wallingford prides itself on being one of the best preserved Saxon boroughs in the kingdom and the defensive earthworks date back to that time, so admiration for 'those old world masons' is plain wrong: there is no Roman stonework here.[11] The only ancient walls to be seen were built by the Normans.

Wallingford was one of Alfred the Great's new towns designed to protect Wessex from those very Vikings that J believed to be his ancestors. It was from that time on, as he puts it, 'an active centre for the making of English history'. At the time of the Norman Conquest in 1066 the town was the lowest point at which the river could be forded, and a local Saxon Lord, Wigod, allowed William to cross unopposed. The Conqueror rewarded the town by allowing them an extra hour before curfew, and it is still rung every night at 9pm, an hour later than it used to be everywhere else. In later life J was to recall hearing it echo across the fields to his farmhouse home on the other side of the river. Little is left of the most tangible Norman legacy – the castle. Stones were taken to help build Windsor, and the final act of destruction was carried out by Cromwell after the Royalists used it as stronghold.

The stone bridge of 16 arches, some of them spanning dry land, dates back to the thirteenth century. The balustraded middle three were replacements when the originals were washed away by a flood in 1809. It is one of the glories of the town, and I remember a rather embarrassing moment here. It is a torment to travel in an open boat if you have an upset stomach. You can travel for ages among the knotted roots of trees or reed banks that stop you from making a landing. I was in a desperate state when I finally managed to get off the boat just below Wallingford Bridge, and raced ashore to ask the first person I saw the quickest way to a public lavatory. Three people stood in the middle of the bridge, and as they turned to impart the vital information I noticed that one of them was wearing the mayoral chain of office and was clearly showing two distinguished visitors over the town. At least he was able to prove that all tourists' needs were conveniently catered for.

Wallingford is an interesting little town, even leaving aside its colourful history, and it is well worth a visit if you can find moorings. They have been improved over the last few years, but are very popular, and a large section is reserved for Salter's steamers. Further upstream on the left you might find a niche under the trees against the steep bank.

The glory of modern Wallingford is the number of independent shops, from hatters to violin makers. How refreshing it is to see a high street without the over-familiar shop fronts of the usual chain stores. There is even a charming little department store called Pettits, founded in 1856 in a sedate Victorian building, that J and friends could well have patronised. The town also ranks highly in the annals of crime fiction, for this is 'Causton' of *Midsomer Murders* fame, and Agatha Christie lived in the village of Winterbrook nearby. Her grave is in the churchyard at neighbouring Cholsey.

It was on their return from Wallingford that J and George called at a little riverside inn at Moulsford. This was the Beetle and Wedge, now an up-market watering hole for the suburbanites of Reading, rather than a place frequented by local farm workers eager to regale any newcomer with their fishermen's tales. A large fish in a glass case attracted the visitors' attention and four customers each took credit for catching it before the landlord himself made a claim. The weight of the fish grew in the telling from 18lb 6oz to a preposterous 34lb. Finally George accidentally knocked the case off the shelf and the fish, which turned out to be made of plaster of Paris, shattered into a thousand pieces. The implication is that it was all a fraud.

However, fishermen will tell you there are two ways of immortalising a memorable catch. One way is to skin the fish and stuff it, the other is to make a cast. As the scales quickly lose their colour, both methods rely on some artistry with the paintbrush – so there is little genuine about a fish in a glass case. Nowadays resins would be used for the cast, but in Victorian times it was plaster. So the broken cast could, after all, have been the record of a genuine catch.

The story of the biggest trout ever caught on the Thames, which weighed in at 16lb 15oz, supports this view. On April 18 1880, a professional fisherman called Wicks had spotted a large trout swimming in the Kennet, a tributary that enters the Thames at Reading. He had arranged for a client to come and fish for it but when the man was late, poor old Wicks paced the bank, tossed on the horns of a dilemma. He could hardly resist catching the fish himself in case it disappeared, but if the client turned up late and found he had taken it, his custom would be lost for good.

Wicks eventually succumbed to temptation and caught the monster fish. He was close to a brewery and sold it to the owner who had a plaster cast made before sending the trout off to Queen Victoria at Windsor. The queen gave £3 to Wicks as a reward for his skill, which must have gone some way towards compensating him for the loss of his irate client.[12] The plaster cast has managed to survive fumble-fingers like George for more than 130 years and can now be seen in the Green Gallery on the first floor of Reading Museum.[13]

In J's day Thames fishermen usually charged 8s to 10s a day (40-50p in today's money), which included providing a punt, bait and tackle if required. They were given their dinner and beer into the bargain, and if the angler was fortunate enough to bag an exceptional catch a substantial tip was expected. Fishing was also a spectator sport with the angler poised on top of a weir elegantly casting his line. Excursion steamers would stop in the hope of seeing a catch. There is little to attract you to the modern fisherman, as he sits alone and misanthropic-looking, surrounded by a plethora of kit, often beneath a giant umbrella-cum-tent. With a warning device attached to the rod it is perfectly possible to make this unique among sports and pastimes – you can actually fish while fast asleep.

I am, perhaps, being unfair to the angling fraternity. As a novice boater my view of them was prejudiced because they would frequently wave their fists and shout as I went by. At the end of the season when I lifted my boat to clean the bottom, I discovered yards of fishing line wound around the propeller. After that I showed more respect for them and kept out of their way.

The Beetle and Wedge Inn at Moulsford where the plaster fish was smashed. The inn as J knew it would have consisted only of the building with the three gables on the right.

15

A Bit of a Mix-up

*Moulsford to Abingdon: The lock that wasn't there and meeting a true 'Arry –
Technicalities of building a floor with chicken bones – Pyromaniac temptation of a
famous author – Unsightly giants of the river – Practicalities of living in an old gaol.*

T HERE is a bit of a mix-up over the journey onward from Streatley.
J writes: 'We left Streatley early the next morning, and pulled up
to Culham, and slept under canvas, in the backwater there.' But later on
he says that they spent the night sleeping on board at Clifton Hampden
and got off to an early start passing through Clifton Lock, the one below
Culham, by 8.30 in the morning.

Despite recommending the Barley Mow as a place to stay and providing
us with a classic description: 'Its low-pitched gables and thatched roof and
latticed windows give it quite a story-book appearance, while inside it is
still more once-upon-a-timey-fied', they did not stop at the inn on this
occasion. As J notes, they wanted to be in Oxford by the afternoon and:

> it is surprising how early one *can* get up when camping out. One does not
> yearn for 'just another five minutes' nearly so much, lying wrapped up in a
> rug on the boards of a boat, with a Gladstone bag for a pillow.

The river between Streatley and Wallingford was not considered
'extraordinarily interesting' and proved remarkable for what wasn't
there rather than for what was – that is to say, the disappearing lock at
Wallingford, an incident described earlier in the original book.

J was out with a young lady who was a cousin on his mother's side, so
the conventions of the time permitted them to be out alone. They were
attempting to get down from Dorchester to Goring in time for supper.

It was 6.30pm when they reached Benson Lock, and they believed they could reach Wallingford Lock before 7.00pm, then row the five miles to Cleeve Lock, which is immediately before Goring, arriving just before 8.00.

But Wallingford Lock never appeared and night began to descend. It was only when they met a group of 'Arries and 'Arriets out boating that they were told they had almost reached Cleeve and that Wallingford Lock had been removed over a year ago.

It is interesting to read of this confrontation between J, derided by his critics as an 'Arry, and the genuine article. The party in the other boat were singing a music hall song and playing a concertina. The old 'squeeze box' was invariably the accompaniment to rowdiness and its reedy tones were the precursor of those destroyers of rural peace, the wind-up gramophone and transistor radio. Nonetheless, in view of their alarming situation, J welcomed the sound as 'far, far more beautiful that the voice of Orpheus and the lute of Apollo'. (Note he has jokily got these two the wrong way round.)

J was clearly perceived as being of superior social standing because he was addressed by the 'Arry as 'Sir'. For all their noise they were clearly amiable representatives of their class.

'Blow me tight if 'ere ain't a gentleman looking for Wallingford Lock, Bill.'

The song they sang was 'He's got 'em on'. Tastes change and writers of comic songs in a more permissive age would have considered 'He's got 'em off' as being funnier.

The chorus ran:

He's got 'em on, he's got 'em on,
Don't he try to do the heavy:
He's got 'em on, he's got 'em on,
He's the Don at ev'ry levee,
He's got 'em on, he's got 'em on,
Ain't he got a funny Chevy,*
I declare he's all there,
Ain't he got 'em on.

*Chevy chase, Cockney rhyming slang for face.

I am grateful to R R Bolland for discovering the words to this old song[1], although he was baffled by their meaning. He only needed to consult a dictionary of slang to find that the expression dates from 1880, and means to be very fashionably dressed, or overdressed.

Wallingford Lock was one of the shortest-lived on the Thames. It was built in 1838 to prevent barges from running aground just below Wallingford Bridge. The difference in water level was only about 18in and when water was high the lock gates were left open and no tolls charged. It was called a summer or low-water weir.

The Thames Conservancy obviously considered that it was more trouble than it was worth, and by the 1870s were planning to remove it. The town wanted to keep the lock and weir, however, fearing that a drop in the river level might be detrimental to health – that is to say there would be less water to dilute all the sewage and rubbish they threw in it.

But the Conservancy had its way and after dredging below the bridge – a simple solution to the original problem – they demolished this obstruction in 1883. making the 6½-mile reach between Benson and Cleeve the longest without a lock on the non-tidal river. The location of the old lock at Chalmore Hole is marked by a modern white-stuccoed house with dormer windows that stands on the site of an old ferry house.[2]

J notes that from Wallingford up to Dorchester the neighbourhood of the river grows more hilly, varied and picturesque. He was not to know that years later he would make his home a mere two miles away on the Oxford side in a little gem of a Chiltern village – Ewelme. Its ancient stone buildings are tiered on a gentle hillside and it seems a dreamy, idle spot, but it once produced more history and watercress than it could consume locally. The village rose from obscurity when Chaucer's son, Thomas, married a local girl, and their daughter Alice, after early widowhood, married into one of the country's most powerful families. The school and almshouses built at her behest still fulfil their original purpose. They stood there on Ewelme's grandest day when Henry VII came on a visit.

While the buildings remain, the watercress beds, which were in their heyday at the beginning of the twentieth century, have fallen into disuse. They are being restored so that the village can retain an essential part of its character and assist wildlife rather than as a commercial operation. Most British watercress is now grown in Dorset, Hampshire and Wiltshire and harvested between April and October. Outside this season you might find US imports on supermarket shelves.

J came to live here from 1901 to 1909 when he had become a great man of literature. Conan Doyle and H G Wells were among the visitors to the old farmhouse at Goulds Grove. It is an austere building in a rather bleak location some distance from the village. J had a liking for being there on his own in winter time when he could fend for himself and be left undisturbed to think. There were two 'front' doors at opposite ends of the house and he had to remember which way the wind was blowing or he could be knocked off his feet if he opened the wrong one. An outbuilding was used as a theatre for trying out his plays.

In the garden was a summer house which J built as a place in which to write. A remarkable feature of this hideaway was the floor which was composed entirely of chicken leg bones. He wrote that he enjoyed slotting them in.

I was intrigued by this method of construction and wrote to *The Structural Engineer* to seek enlightenment.

They kindly published my query and there followed a letter from Mike Smith.

> In the grounds of the National Trust property of Killerton in Devon there is a 'Bear Hut', which was once used as a home for a pet bear. The Bear's Hut has a floor constructed from deer knuckle-joints. The leg-bones of deer have been forced into the ground lengthways, like closely-spaced tent pegs, so that only the rounded end tips are exposed. Friction between the bones and the earth holds them firmly in place.
>
> The Jerome family could probably obtain chicken leg bones more easily than deer knuckle leg bones, so maybe the floor of the summerhouse was of a similar form, using chicken bones to reinforce an earth floor.

It must have been difficult to find such a large number of the appropriate bones in the days before fast food patrons so helpfully throw them over the front garden wall.

In the churchyard of St Mary the Virgin are to be found the graves of J and his wife, together with a memorial stone to his brother, Milton, who died in infancy.[3] At the interment of J's ashes in 1927 George stood on this spot, he was to become the last survivor of the Three Men.

The biggest change to the area since his day has been the building of RAF Benson airfield, which is used for helicopter training. The sound of night flights will be familiar to all who camp out on the river.

J says Dorchester-on-Thames, not to be confused with Dorchester in Dorset, can be reached by paddling up the Thames (A clear printer's error that has never been picked up – he meant the small River Thame which joins the Thames here under the footbridge that carries the tow-path.)

This tributary is little larger than a brook, but it has given rise to more wrong-headed pedantry than more majestic streams. In days long ago antiquarians put it about that the correct name for the Thames above this point was the Isis, and after its confluence with the Thame it should be called Thamesisis. You might occasionally come across a tedious person who still believes this, but J was sensible enough to ignore it.

He is absolutely right about the best approach to Dorchester being from Day's Lock, which is a further mile and three-quarters upstream. The town is then approached by walking through those mysterious earthworks known as the Devil's Dykes, and the river is overlooked by the picturesque twin hills known as Wittenham Clumps, or more rudely in olden times as the Berkshire Bubs, or Mother Dunch's Buttocks. (The Dunches were the local landowners, and no doubt this particular lady was not small.)

The most popular spot for modern boaters to moor is just above the lock, and you will need to get there before lunch to be sure of finding a space.

Across the river and a short distance from the lock is Little Wittenham Church, whose treasure is to be found against the west wall below the tower. Sir William Dunch and his wife Mary recline in stone effigy dressed in full Jacobean finery, and if you are lucky to catch the evening sun casting its mellow light over them, you will experience a scene of timeless serenity. It is disturbed only by the spiders who busily seek to weave their own gossamer shroud – a task in which they have been frustrated for nigh on four centuries.

When I visited the church a gentleman of the road, or down-market rambler, was stretched out in the church porch, a modern parody of the tomb within. His sleeping bag was drying out on the bench – a reminder that J himself in the hard times of his youth once slept in similar circumstances.

Close at hand is the footpath that leads up to the Clumps, from the top of which there are magnificent views of the surrounding countryside. In his autobiography J tells how he walked up here with the writer Eden Phillpotts. He clearly allows his imagination to run away with him as he describes this prehistoric settlement as a Roman encampment – he believed he could 'trace the ordered streets', although the hill is crested by trees.

It was here that Phillpotts suffered from an attack of pyromania. While lighting his pipe he had struggled against the temptation to set fire to a rotten tree which might in turn have set the whole grove on fire. He confided to J as be put the box of Lucifers back into his pocket that a beastly little imp was urging him on. 'If I hadn't come away, I believe he would have nagged me into it.'[4] Phillpotts was a lover of nature, sometimes described as the Scribe of Dartmoor, whose novels were esteemed at the time as second only to those of Thomas Hardy – the last person on earth you might imagine, to have vandalised this well-loved beauty spot.

Perhaps the rotten old tree was the famous Poem Tree, a beech on which 20 lines of verses were inscribed in the 1840s by Joseph Tubb. In this case the 'imp' might have appeared in the form of a literary critic. Tubb's verses took some days to carve, and he needed the help of a ladder and a tent. They are not inspiring. Unfortunately the tree succumbed to bad weather in July 2012, but you can still read the poem on a stone carrying a transcription and a rubbing.

Dorchester is on the other side of the river, and having crossed at Day's Lock you may walk through the Devil's Dykes and around fields of golden wheat, where the skylarks sing overhead before reaching the long, straggling high street. Lift your eyes roof-wards from the modern pavements and you can imagine coaches rumbling and jingling through on their way from London to Oxford. J says that the village was very old and, very strong and great once – that was in the seventh century when it was the capital of Wessex

Its great glory is the Dorchester Abbey Church of St Peter and St Paul, which seems out of scale with the rest of the place. It has been much cleaned up since J's time, and medieval wall paintings have been revealed. One of the old monastic buildings has been converted into a tea room and small museum. If you are lucky you might catch a guided tour to the top of the tower.

J describes the river banks between Clifton and Culham as flat, monotonous and uninteresting. This is the second lot of rather boring river we have encountered over two days. Perhaps enthusiasm for the trip was beginning to wane. At least their view wasn't dominated by the cooling towers of Didcot Power Station that blighted the landscape here for forty years. The river winds so much that at one moment they appeared to be straight ahead, the next on your right or left. You thought you had got rid of them but there they were again. The six 375ft towers were built in 1970 and in 2003 they were judged the third worst eyesore in Britain by *Country Life* readers. Three were demolished in 2014 and the remainder in 2016, so these looming giants no longer stalk boaters and walkers along the riverbank.

From the Thames the dreamy little hamlet of Clifton Hampden, with its cottages nestling under tea cosy thatch among prolific gardens, has a primitive air almost akin to an African village. But a bird's eye view would show it to be sited next to a large industrial complex. This is the Joint European Torus establishment, JET for short, where scientists experiment with extremely hot gases confined in a circular chamber by magnetism in an attempt to find a way to create cheap limitless power by nuclear fusion. They say it has a pretty hefty electricity bill at the moment. When it all began in the 1960s querulous souls feared it might unzip the whole of creation with an unstoppable chain reaction, a fear echoed in recent years about the large Hadron Collider built by CERN, near Geneva.

J, quoting from Sir Walter Armstrong, refers to Culham as the deepest and coldest lock on the river. Armstrong also called it tomb-like and, being much narrower than Sandford, which is in fact the deepest, it would indeed have *seemed* deeper.[5]

After leaving the long lock cut, J observes that the scenery improves. But one of the river's most attractive backwaters, Sutton Pools, is hidden from sight. This has been one of the best-kept secrets of the Thames, and perhaps J wanted to keep it that way by not mentioning it.

The old course of the river winds through the trees to the village of Sutton Courtenay with ancient buildings composing a very attractive river bank scene. This place once boasted a great novelty. The basin of the old lock was under the floor of a water mill, and this was a nuisance when the river ran high as barges did not have sufficient height to get through. The problem was overcome when the old river course was by-passed with a lock cut and new lock.[6] To get to Sutton Pools by boat you have to pass the very large sign saying *Danger*. But if the river is low it is safe to do so with caution, as boats moored up past this point testify.

We are only two miles away from Abingdon which J rather unfairly describes as 'quiet, eminently respectable, clean and desperately dull'. He seems to have taken his cue from Dickens Junior, who described the place as quiet even to the point of dullness. Did he come here looking for a good time? In fact, the town puts on its best face for the river, and the alms houses, St Helen's Church and old wharves compose a scene that outdoes anything Henley, Marlow or Whitchurch have to offer the passing artist or photographer. Just upstream are the old gaol and ancient stone bridge with a pub in the middle.

Known as the Queen of the Thames, this was once the county town of Berkshire, but it was too proud to admit the railway, so it went into decline and Reading took its place. The Old Gaol closed in 1868, and in J's time was a grain store. A new county jail was built at Reading ready for Oscar Wilde.

Abingdon's prison holds the unenviable record for hanging the youngest criminal – a boy of eight accused of firing barns. The ghosts of the hanged are said to haunt the place, but this does not seem to discourage people from living there for, strange to say, the Grade II listed building, built by Napoleonic War prisoners in 1811, has been converted into luxury flats. As a publicity leaflet puts it: 'Your perfect life doesn't have to be a compromise of luxury over practicality. The Old Gaol offers both.' One wonders if small windows showing but 'a little tent of blue', might prove a slight impracticality.

Facing the prison is a pub called The Broad Face, and few of the revellers who celebrate the end of the Royal Swan Upping there can be aware of the macabre origin of the name. It was a prime spot for watching public executions, and the story goes that after the 'drop' the face of the victim swelled up or 'got broad'.

Harris seems to have had the upper hand here and the Three take to visiting tombs again in local churches. J notes that in St Helen's Church it is recorded that W Lee, who died in 1637, 'had in his lifetime issue from his loins two hundred lacking but three.' One assumes he did not beget them all directly as this would have required the help of too many loose women. No doubt they were all lawful children, grandchildren and great grandchildren.

The more tasteless guides to the Thames in those days advised visiting the town on a Sunday when 80 loaves of bread were distributed to the poor at Christ's Hospital alms houses. Making a public spectacle of charity seems to us now to be in very bad taste, but visitors found it entertaining to see the humble and respectful way in which men and women accepted their dole and recited 'The blessed Trinity upon John Roysse's soul have mercy!'

John Roysse was a public benefactor who also founded the local grammar school in 1563 – this is now an independent institution known simply as Abingdon School. But perhaps his motives were not so altruistic as they might appear. Dickens Junior cynically notes that he had a very profligate son who was kept out of jail only because of the esteem in which his father was held.[7]

Gould's Grove at Ewelme, near Wallingford, where J lived from 1901 to 1909.

16

Where Neverland was Lost

Abingdon to Oxford: The peril of the green slime – A truly gothic death – The original deserted village? – An American tourist fought off with a broom – A very good place to drown yourself – Fantastical story on which a great university is founded.

THE beauty of Nuneham Courtenay made it one of the most popular attractions of the Victorian Thames and a magnet for trippers from Oxford. J recommended his readers to visit the park and house on the Tuesdays and Thursdays when it was open in summer. Undergraduates were allowed in free of charge after boating down, and the lower orders came by Salter's steamboat. The house and grounds cannot be visited these days as it has been leased to the Brahma Kumaris World Spiritual University, which uses it as a retreat centre.

It happened to be a Thursday when the Pennells, those egalitarian American Thames enthusiasts, came by and noted: 'Whether they come from Oxford or from the outer world of common men, they are just as picturesque to look at' – a reminder that in those days visitors to the river wore their Sunday best.[1] Lockkeepers then kept the walls free of the dark green slime that now grows on them and makes a mess on your hands and clothes. It was part of their duty to scrub the sides of the chamber with a broom, but there are fewer 'lockies' now and they are expected to spend their time on more essential duties.

In the grounds you can still see the Jacobean Carfax Conduit, an elaborate fountain that once stood in the centre of Oxford until it got in the way of the traffic in 1787 and the University gave it to Lord Harcourt. It was a useful gift, as it saved him having to build a fashionable little gothic ruin on the knoll overlooking the river where the monument now stands. He wanted every 'must have' that fashion dictated, including the regulation grotto. Appropriately, like Lady Fane, he suffered a truly gothic fate by falling down a well. He did not become a ghost though, in this case the supernatural story associated with his death took the form of a premonition. It is said that his daughter had a vivid dream in which she saw the body of her father laid out in the kitchen with the clock showing four o'clock. She told the family about it at breakfast, but Lord Harcourt, unperturbed, went out onto the estate to mark some trees for felling. Nothing was heard of him until a labourer was attracted to a well by the sound of a barking dog. Harcourt's body was found headfirst at the bottom, and it was supposed that he had overbalanced while trying to rescue his pet dog. The body was carried back into the house, the nearest room being the kitchen, and laid on a dresser at exactly four o'clock. Dickens Junior, who tells this yarn, seems prepared to believe it, which is surprising for a generally cynical man. He says it is undoubtedly well authenticated.[2]

When the first Viscount Harcourt, Lord Chancellor in Queen Anne's reign, built the house in 1710, he didn't want the village to spoil the vast classically landscaped park he planned, so he demolished it and built a new one a mile away. Some say the ruins inspired Oliver Goldsmith to write his poem *The Deserted Village*, others that the place is based on Lissoy, Westmeath, in Ireland. It must be said the villagers here were given a well-designed alternative, each brick-built house being provided with a garden and broad grass verge separating it from the road in anticipation of the Garden City style. Harcourt's real act of vandalism was to demolish the ancient parish church and replace it with a Romanesque structure with a pillared portico – obviously designed to fit in with the landscape rather than the needs of the parishioners, who must have found it strange to worship in a 'Romish' basilica.

Nuneham House might seem a little on the plain side, but Dickens diplomatically describes it as free from the inconveniences of over magnificence. He says it was crammed full of curiosities, relics and old masters, but these have since been dispersed.

Some elaborately thatched cottages were built beside the river purely to cater for tourists; we may therefore count the Harcourts and their successors among those generously disposed to the river excursionists of their time. But their benevolence does not seem to have been shared by their tenants, at least during the early days of the last century.

The American tourist Wellington Wack tried to land his canoe here with a friend, but was fought off by an old woman with a broom, who showered him with gravel and water and pushed the boat away from the bank when he tried to take a photograph. 'A Kodaker from the fastness of New York seemed to be her particular *bête noir,*' he remarked.[3]

Charles Harper wrote that in fine weather the cottagers supplied open-air teas, but when the weather was wet, they refused visitors the shelter of their homes. It left their customers with head colds and savage thoughts about Nuneham.[4]

The next point of interest on the journey is Sandford Lock. Nowadays you can count the number of power lines crossing the river to tell how close you are getting to it (three). In J's day the leaning chimney of Sandford Mill made a good landmark, and had all the interest and beauty of the tower of Pisa, according to D MacCall writing in 1885. Others just thought it plain ugly.[5]

The most remarkable thing about this lock for J is the pool beneath the weir stream known as Sandford Lasher, which he says is a very good place to drown yourself. The undertow is extremely strong and an obelisk marks the spot where two undergraduates died in 1843 while bathing. He says the steps were used as a diving board by young men who wished to see if the place was truly dangerous. J is taking his cue from Sir Walter Armstrong, who witnessed a near drowning at this spot in 1873.[6] A student took a header from the steps of the obelisk and did not come up for several seconds. 'the swirl had clutched him and was turning his body helplessly over and over under the ledge of the fall.' Fortunately a man with a boat was at hand, and managed to hold out an oar which was grasped by the struggling swimmer.

This spot was destined to play a tragic part in the life of J's great friend J M Barrie. The two played cricket together and it was J who introduced Barrie to the actress who would become his wife, although the marriage was not a success. The story of how Barrie cultivated the friendship of the five Llewelyn Davies boys and informally adopted them after the tragic deaths of their parents is well-known from the 2004 film *Finding Neverland* starring Johnny Depp as Barrie and Kate Winslet as Sylvia Llewelyn Davies.

The two elder boys went off to fight in the First World War. George was killed and Peter, who was the inspiration for Peter Pan, scarred by his experiences in the trenches, suffered from depression and committed suicide under a tube train in 1960. John, who was described as very bitter about life, died in 1959, and Nicholas, the youngest and the least traumatised by the early death of his parents, survived until 1986. Michael, however, seems to have been the apple of Barrie's eye and the one who seemed destined for the greatest success in life. Barrie had paid for him to go to Eton and Oxford.

On the evening of May 19 1921, Barrie had been writing a letter to Michael, and on the way out of his flat in Adelphi Terrace (near The Strand) to post it, he met a newspaper reporter who asked him if he could give any more details of the drowning. Barrie asked him what drowning he was referring to, and the reporter, realising he had not heard the news, explained that Michael had been drowned that day while swimming in Sandford Pool with a fellow undergraduate, Rupert Buxton, who also died.

Given that Michael had been unable to overcome his fear of water and never learned to swim, many believed that the two deaths might have been suicide. It was thought Michael might have been wrestling with the possibility that he was gay.

For two days and nights Barrie did not sleep and looked like a man in a nightmare. Friends were worried that he might take his own life. He never fully recovered from the blow. Seven months later he wrote to a friend, Elizabeth Lucas, that 'All is different now: Michael was pretty much my world.'[7]

Kensington Gardens was where Barrie found his Neverland, and Sandford is where he lost it. The weir pool is now a dismal sunless place. Woodland has closed in around it, crossed by little muddy tracks which always seem to be strewn with litter. Iron railings enclose the top of the semi-circular weir to keep potential suicides at bay, for who else would wish to dive into to that maelstrom of white water? In the centre is a tiny island on which stands that grim monument described by J.

For all that, there is some cheer to be found at Sandford Lock. Besides it stands The King's Arms pub, a popular spot with boaters and walkers, where you can sit at tables on a terrace overlooking the river. It looks old, but is not an ancient hostelry like the Barley Mow as it was converted from a brewery malthouse in the nineteenth century. Wellington Wack appreciated the atmosphere of the old Thames inns, but did not like the beer or the coffee. His companion deprecated the English barmaid. Having women behind the bar, he thought, was a national scandal and he wondered what 'degraded' period of the British nation had produced the *genus*. He remarked:

> It was horrible enough that in England women of the lower class should have descended to drunkenness so generally, but for a government to tolerate an institution wherein young women to the number of 80,000 purveyed the arsenicated[8] beer which wrecked their sisters, that was indeed an ineradicable stain upon the nation.'

He had obviously studied the subject, and was, perhaps, an early prohibitionist. Be that as it may, barmaids still thrive on the Thames although to advertise for one would break sex equality laws.

★

Barely half a mile further on is Iffley Lock, once again a popular subject for artists. Leslie notes that from 50 yards below the lock the church, mill and lock, with poplar trees casting their long shadows across the water, form a composition that has been painted again and again. A little too often for J, who had seen so many idealised representations that he found the real article disappointing.

Iffley is the last lock before Oxford if you are travelling up-river, and it is at the start of the reach used by Oxford colleges for their annual 'bumps' races. As the river is too narrow here to allow racing side-by-side, one boat is set to chase another, and the winner is the one who succeeds in bumping the stern of the boat in front over several heats. Modern rowing was invented at Oxford in the early nineteenth century. In 1839 the University Boat Club was started, and as D S MacColl put it: 'The Oxford school of rowing shot up to overshadow the older faculties'.[9] An exaggeration, no doubt, but giving rise to the old joke about a theology student being asked at his public examination: 'How many persons in the Trinity?' To which he replied: 'Four and a steerer.'[10]

It was July when the Three Men passed through and the undergraduates had gone down for the summer holidays, so the river would have been relatively quiet. Nevertheless J found it the most difficult bit he knew, with currents taking the boat first to one side and then the other. It would take someone born here to understand it. He wrote that a man who could row a straight course from Oxford to Iffley ought to be able to live comfortably under the same roof with his mother-in-law, his sister and the old servant who had been in the family when he was a baby. Every Oxford cox who has ever lived would therefore be such a man.

The difficulty with steering resulted in the skiff getting in the way of other boats and leading to bad tempered altercations. J says he found it difficult to understand why everyone was so exceptionally irritable on the river. Little mishaps that you hardly notice on land would drive you frantic with rage when in a boat. Happily, things have improved over the years and you are more likely to get a friendly wave from a passing boater than a fit of bad temper, and if you have spent time sprucing up your well varnished wooden boat and polished the brass you will almost always get a compliment. Such is the general amiability of people on the water now, that I am sure that if you were to pass in some old wreck people would say: 'interesting old boat'. Of course you can still find great entertainment by standing at a lock and watching quite respectable looking couples lose their rag with one another if he or she misses a rope, or the boat comes in too fast and scrapes the lock wall. Then there is the skipper of the hire boat whose crew of 'friends' are unwilling to recognise his authority and studiously ignore his orders. But real rage can be occasioned if someone tries to sneak through the gates out of turn ahead of the lockkeeper's call. Then you find yourself shut up with people still trying to argue the point, their imprecations among others echoing around the walls of the dark, dank chamber: 'butterfingers!', 'you came in too fast!', 'we were first!', 'why is it that after 20 years of marriage you have still not trained me into a perfect person?'

I have not encountered any difficulty navigating this reach in a motor cruiser. But you need to be careful of Salter's excursion boats making a three-point turn just as you come out of the gates of Iffley Lock. Listen for the four short blasts on the boat's hooter followed by another two (I am turning right round to port) and you will not be surprised. You also need to give a wide berth to inexperienced rowers or punters who have hired a craft for an hour or two. There is always a large raft of punts moored by Folly Bridge which seems to vastly exceed the number of those competent to use them. Fortunately many will be used on the Cherwell, Oxford's own river, which joins the Thames near here.

The scenery has not improved since Victorian times when the bank at Christ Church Meadow was lined by ornate college barges used as the headquarters for the college rowing clubs. At first they bought old barges that once belonged to the London Livery Companies, but when these became rare or worn out, they commissioned new craft, adding even more quirky features and ornaments than on the originals. You may still come across one of these exotic juggernauts moored down river, for they have all been 'sent down' and replaced by boring utilitarian boathouses, more practical, no doubt, as they can cosset the high technology boats and gear now required for the sport.

Oxford undergraduates on the water were taken good care of in the old days. The University Boat Club set up green barges called 'receiving houses' which were stationed along the river from Oxford to Iffley manned by experienced watermen. They had all the necessary skill for saving the half-drowned and were equipped with essentials such as hot bricks, hot water, warm blankets and a cosy bed. Sir Walter Armstrong[11] noted that it was not so easy to be drowned if you took to the river here during the appropriate times and season and stuck to the main river. He wrote that nearly all those undergraduates who in the last 20 years 'met their death in the embrace of Isis' had done so in side streams or very late in the evening.

It is here that the Three Men would have moored up to spend their two days in Oxford, perhaps leaving their boat in the charge of Salter's boatyard and staying at a hotel. What the Three did in the city of dreaming spires is a mystery, but there were plenty of dogs, and Montmorency had eleven fights on the first day. We know from his autobiography that J once showed the city to some American friends, so no doubt he was familiar with it from his boating days and the Three spent the time, like most tourists, looking at the colleges.

We can imagine that Harris with his interest in tombs might have wished to visit the memorial to Oxford's patron saint in Christ Church Cathedral.

The story of St Frideswide would have been a difficult one for Harris to explain; it is a fantastical myth embellished with many incredible details, having its origins in Anglo Saxon England of the seventh century. Frideswide was the rich, good and beautiful daughter of the local king. She was obviously considered a great catch, but had dedicated herself to the church, and refused to marry. A handsome young prince, having been rebuffed, decided to forcibly carry her off, but her father got wind of the plan and she escaped down the river to Abingdon in a boat rowed by an angel disguised as a young man in a white robe. This marks her out as one of the Thames's earliest excursionists, although rules on chaperoning, apparently, were rather more lax than in Victoria's day. Frideswide remained in the woods thereabouts for three years, converting a pigsty into a dwelling place, another talent that showed she was ahead of her time. Her accomplishments included water divining, for a well miraculously appeared whenever she prayed for water.

The prince did not give up. He came back to Oxford and threatened to sack the city if Frideswide was not surrendered to him. The citizens, fearing for their safety, betrayed her whereabouts. Two messengers were sent to find her and persuade her to come to him, but they were struck blind. The same thing happened to the prince when he went after her himself. But Frideswide was charitable, and miraculously restored his sight while at the same time killing his desire for her. So the story ended happily with Frideswide retiring to a little village on the other side of the Thames called Binsey. There she miraculously created another well which was believed to have extraordinary powers of healing. This she used to practice the speciality of her House, which was to restore sight to the blind. She also established a priory at Oxford where her body is supposed to have been buried. This institution became an important place of pilgrimage and did much to enhance the status of the city, otherwise only noted for its muddy ford for oxen.

At the dissolution of the monasteries in 1522 Cardinal Wolsey seized the priory to create a college, but after his disgrace it was grabbed – like all his other possessions – by Henry VIII. A college was eventually built, now known as Christ Church and its chapel became the college chapel and eventually the cathedral.

Myth and legend can take on a greater importance than mere fact, and here we see that on such an improbable foundation as this fantastic tale there rests one of the world's greatest seats of learning.

Could Harris, with his enthusiasm for tombs, have missed this story? There would be little to see in the way of a memorial to this curious saint in his day, except for a dark paving stone in the lady chapel with the name Frideswide carved on it. But if the Three had taken the trouble to walk the short distance over to Binsey they would have been able to see the miraculous well next to St Margaret's Church that had been restored in 1874.

The other great fantasy associated with Oxford is of course *Alice in Wonderland*. The young mathematics lecturer, Charles Dodgson (Lewis Carroll), took young Alice Liddell and her sisters up river by boat to visit Binsey and Godstow, which are still favourite picnicking spots. He must have been familiar with Frideswide's well, known locally as a 'treacle well', treacle being an Old English word for an antidote to venoms and poisons. Hence we have the rambling story told by the Dormouse at the Mad Hatter's tea party about three sisters who lived down a treacle well. Flowers may occasionally be seen placed at the well, so the old saint is still remembered here, and in the heart of the University on every October 19, her feast day is celebrated at her shrine reconstructed in 2001 in the Latin Chapel of the Cathedral.

★

J is contemptuous of those who opt for an easy holiday rowing downstream from Oxford with the current. There was more satisfaction in squaring one's back and fighting the adverse stream – that was when George and Harris were rowing. He is scathing about the kind of boats hired out 'up-river,' and says rowers planning to start a journey from Oxford should take their own boat because of the bad state of the skiffs available here. A boat called *The Pride of the Thames* was once offered to him, which he said looked like the fossil of a pre-Adamite whale or an early Roman coffin. Boats hired above Marlow, J reckoned, were of such a kind that people were ashamed to be seen out in them. They had no shining varnish or polished metal.

The famous firm of Salter's was building high quality boats here in his day, so how was it that J had such a scathing view?

I asked Dr Simon Wenham, who has written a history of Salter's boatyard[12], about J's opinion. He told me that Salter's had a near monopoly of the river-front at Oxford and had an amazing 900 assorted craft for hire in J's day. Some of these would have been racing boats let to the Oxford colleges, but in their more leisured time, the young gentlemen from the University would, no doubt, have knocked some of this immense fleet about a bit. Of course, City clerks would not have been given the pick of the bunch. People who hired boats down beyond Maidenhead would have been more fashion conscious and anxious about their appearance. There was more competition among boat hirers closer to the metropolis. An old boat builder told me that at Richmond competition was so fierce among the yards that there was a real danger to life and limb. His father moved his business further up the river at the beginning of the twentieth century to get away from it all.

The sinister Sandford Lasher near Oxford described by J as
'a good place to drown yourself'.

17

The Ignominious Return

Oxford back to Pangbourne: The river takes on an urban aspect – A derided boat proves its worth – An uncomfortable spot for a game of cards – Where Oscar Wilde had the last laugh – When Old Father Thames takes his revenge.

A T Folly Bridge the Thames assumes the work-a-day clothes of an artisan and skulks around the edge of Oxford in the guise of a canal girded with terraced houses and allotments. I doubt that the Three Men would have ventured on to this stretch. Its narrow bends are a hazard to rowing men since there is hardly room to extend an oar on both sides of the boat. Once Cherwell embraces the Thames with its two arms at Christchurch Meadow, the waters are divided into various branches that made Oxford an easy crossing point. Folly Bridge is believed to be on the site of the old ford used by oxen that gave the city its name. It is the biggest obstruction to be met so far on the journey upstream.

The bridge crosses an island, and one side has a very narrow arch almost hidden behind excursion boats moored on Salter's pontoon. This is reserved for craft coming down river. As you approach the other side of the island, the three broad balustraded arches seem blocked by a huge raft of punts. The first stone bridge, built in 1085, had a tower over the roadway at the Oxford end in which the thirteenth-century alchemist Roger Bacon lived, and this earned it the name Folly. As lights burned from his turret late into the night to the wonder of local peasants, strange stories grew up about him: that he invented gunpowder and made a brass head that could talk. Today his fame rests on his rediscovery of ancient Arabic scientific texts, although facts about this ancient friar are as bald as his tonsured pate. The tower was an early tourist attraction until it was removed in 1779 to widen the road. Samuel Pepys thought it was worth a shilling (5p) tip to the guardian when he visited it in 1669.

This part of the river can well be described as 'the most difficult bit' rather than the reach down to Iffley which J found trying. There are blind bends and places where it is so narrow that two skiffs with oars extended would not be able to pass one another. Just above Osney Lock is the lowest bridge on the river, and this is the sentinel that bars the larger motor cruisers from the unspoilt upper reaches. There is ample opportunity for getting tangled with other boats, and I once came across a narrow boat firmly wedged across the river, its bow on one bank and its stern against the other.

Osney Lock has a small, unwelcoming lay-by beneath the steep sloping bank, and above the lock the weir stream runs across the gates, which makes navigation difficult when the river is high. But the real obstruction to rowing any further in J's day would have been Medley Weir.

This was the last of the primitive types of lock that existed on the Thames until the advent of the pound lock familiar to us today. A row of squared off poles called 'rymers' was set in a beam sunk at the bottom of the river. Against these rested spade-shaped paddles which acted as a dam. They were supported at the top by another beam along which the lockkeeper could walk to withdraw the paddles and rymers when a vessel needed to pass through. Going upstream a boat would need to be hauled through against the current with a capstan. Small craft had to perform a complicated manoeuvre in which one man got out of the boat and pulled from the beam while a companion took a line from the bank. Going downstream the craft would simply shoot the rapids. If it was a large boat, the top beam could be swung aside, but for a small boat the occupants would have to duck. Henry Taunt, the famous Thames photographer, wrote about having the skin scraped off his face and nose while lying on his back to pass through such a weir at Eaton Hastings further up the river.[1] Negotiating one of these weirs would not be an option when out for a quiet Sunday afternoon's boating. Medley weir was removed in the 1920s and in J's day there were boatyards above the weir where a skiff could be hired by Oxford people, like Charles Dodgson, intending to row further upstream.

Although they have all been replaced by pound locks, the paddle and rymer weirs were considered such an important part of Thames heritage that they have been preserved by the Environment Agency in the weir streams of locks at Streatley and Rushey.

Whatever the Three Men got up to in Oxford, the rain set in on the third day, and they started their journey home on Monday morning in a steady drizzle. This was a dispiriting experience as J notes: the Thames in sunlight is a 'golden fairy stream' whereas in the rain it becomes a 'spirit haunted water through the land of vain regrets'.

Not only is it miserable and uncomfortable, but persistent rain of this kind can bring the river up and make navigation a problem. A particularly tricky stretch in a fast stream is that between Abingdon Lock and the bridge, as the Pennells described in 1891.[2]

They knew nothing about boats, could not swim, and set off on their journey down the Thames when the rain was pouring down. Old Salter had given them a brand new boat, nothing like J's *Pride of the Thames,* and perhaps as he looked out of the office window and saw them swing helplessly about in the current he might have wished he had given them his shabbiest old up-river tub. They made just three miles on their first day, passing through Sandford Lock with much trepidation about going over the Lasher. They were attracted by the King's Arms and decided to stay the night there, but it was as deserted as the river: no one had stayed there for a month because of the weather, and the couple feared that they might have to pay for all of those who had stayed away. Fortunately the bill turned out to be reasonable and they learnt an important lesson: 'riverside inns were as comfortable as boats were uncomfortable', so they resolved to spend the nights of their holiday ashore. The following day the sun came out, and the river resumed its customary gaiety, but the stream remained treacherous.

After coming through the lock at Abingdon their attention was distracted by a distant view of the town and they were startled to hear shouts from the bank. A small crowd had gathered to watch their inevitable collision with the wall of an island that separates the river in two just before it passes under the bridge. It is testimony to the quality of the build of this 'up-river' boat that it withstood the impact, and all that the would-be rescuers standing ready with boathooks and lifebelts had to do was seize it and hold it hard before it could rebound against the wall. Unfortunately it was on the wrong side of the island for the pontoon of the Nag's Head Inn, and with great difficulty the Pennells managed to manoeuvre it around and moor up with another loud bang. They were so grateful to the Nag's Head staff that they felt obliged to stay there for the night.

Joseph Pennell complained that there was nothing in the guidebooks about the strong current here, and he was unprepared for what he believed to be one of the few really dangerous places on the river. He and his wife were inexperienced boaters, of course, and the Three Men had passed here in similarly bad conditions without incident.

But I can vouch for the power of the current at this spot. I was bringing a cabin cruiser down-river from Oxford and turned around beneath Abingdon Bridge to moor her with the bow facing the current in the approved text book fashion. My wife was standing in the bow, and as I brought the boat to the bank I stopped the engine, jumped out with the stern rope and prepared to take the bow rope from my wife. Somehow or other I missed it, and before I could try to take it again, the current snatched the front of the boat out into the stream and carried the whole boat further from the bank. I tried to pull her back with my rope but my shoes could get no purchase on the wet grass, and five tonnes of boat pulled me relentlessly towards the river. Fortunately, as the boat was swept down-stream it came close to a moored narrow boat, and I was able to loop what remained of my rope around a mooring iron and bring our craft to rest alongside. The owner helped pull us back to our intended mooring and said a similar thing had happened to him on the opposite side of the river. I told a passer-by of our adventure, and said I nearly lost my wife. He replied that I was unlucky, he had been trying to do that for years. But we learnt an important lesson – always secure the line at the front first when mooring in an upstream direction.

Rain is the scourge of the pleasure boater and the Three Men passed a melancholy time on the first day of their return. They hoisted the cover over the boat leaving just a little gap so they could see where they were going. George stuck to the umbrella.

In those days before antibiotics, 'catching a chill' was a real danger, and the Three began unnerving each other with health scares. They stopped for the night just below Day's Lock, a remote spot with a long walk over the Devil's Dykes to reach any chance of warmth and comfort. They tried to keep their spirits up by playing penny nap for an hour and a half in what must have been uncomfortably cramped conditions. J says sarcastically that the excitement was too much for them and George emerged the victor with the princely sum of fourpence (less than 2p).

Years later Harris told of a similar dismal night in a wet boat. Late in the afternoon, as the sky darkened, they agreed to pull up and have a frugal meal of a leg of Welsh mutton – 'bought from a famous supplier in The Strand' – and salad. As they were preparing the food on the bank the threatened storm burst and they hastily put the canvas up over the boat and bundled everything inside. It was dark, but for some reason the lamp would not light so they used two candles. They took a mouthful of the salad and both George and Harris thought it tasted queer. J thought nothing was wrong, but Harris says he always did have a peculiar taste. The next morning they discovered that, owing to their carelessness in using two medicine bottles for the vinegar and the lamp oil, they had mixed them up.[3]

The rain continued on the second day, and despite their brave assertion that they had planned a fortnight's enjoyment on the river and a fortnight they would have even if it killed them, their resolution soon weakened and the temptation of catching the express train to London from Pangbourne proved too much.

J describes a dishevelled and dispirited procession from the Swan boathouse to Pangbourne Station after they had left the skiff and its equipment in charge of the waterman there. It was not unusual to leave a boat at a different place to the one you set off from. Wellington Wack wrote that a boat could be taken from a boatyard and left at the end of a journey with any waterman, a postcard to the boat's home yard was all that was required, and a van would collect it and take it back.

Ignominious as their departure was, the Three were careful to conform to the dress code of the time. Gone were the white canvas shoes of the sort that had been so assiduously pipe-clayed at Goring by Harris. They were replaced by black leather ones, although rather muddy. Men could not go hatless into Town in those days, and sporting caps were inappropriate, so they wore brown felt hats that had been badly battered at the bottom of the boat. They reached Paddington at seven and drove to the West End. Their goal was the Alhambra music hall that dominated the eastern side of Leicester Square where now the Odeon cinema stands. It was built in an impressive Moorish style with minarets, hence its name. They must have been hungry after those wet days on the river for they had a light meal which was followed by a solid supper after the performance.

It was 'a capital little out-of-the-way restaurant in the neighbourhood of —', as J described it in a footnote in his autobiography, but he declined to give the name because he wanted to keep its delights to himself. With the help of his description it is not difficult to discover the place, however – The Florence at 57 and 58 Rupert Street, which is just off Coventry Street and an easy stroll to Leicester Square.[4]

It provided what seems to us an extraordinary service to its customers by looking after their dogs while they went to the theatre – that is if J is to be believed. Of course he had to explain how Montmorency was disposed of, but as the dog was a complete fiction, this would not ordinarily have been a problem.

The restaurant was owned by Luigi Azario, but you would be wrong to think that because of its name and the nationality of its proprietor this was a place to enjoy Italian dishes. There was only one kind of cooking in those days: the *haute cuisine Franglaise*.[5] Signor Azario would have kept the Italian dishes for his family and friends and the occasional English Italophile. So it is not surprising that J wrote in the same footnote that you could get 'one of the best-cooked and cheapest little French dinners or suppers that I know of here'.

This was the restaurant where J snubbed Oscar Wilde and his companions, though if the place was as small and cosy as he described it, this must have been quite a difficult social manoeuvre. Despite J's reluctance to name it, this establishment grew in popularity and size, extending from No 53 to 58 by the beginning of the twentieth century and becoming the haunt of even more celebrities. A sushi bar now stands in the middle of the site, renumbered as 19.

In J's day it was a well-known haunt of bohemians and he used to meet a 'dear friend' of his here. She was Amy Hogg, nine years his senior, who lived on her own in lodgings opposite the British Museum, frequented restaurants and Aerated Bread shops alone[6], and had many men friends, all of which was considered very shocking then. The two would sit at a window table, obviously not afraid of gossip. Amy married Arthur Machen, a pioneer writer of tales of the supernatural, in 1887. So J was a frequenter of this restaurant in his bachelor days prior to Amy's marriage and at the time he was making his boating trips with George and Harris. J says Amy owned a vineyard near Beaune in Burgundy, and supplied wine to The Florence. I think he meant her family owned it, as she spent the early part of her married life in near poverty. J mentions in the footnote that the food was served with an excellent bottle of Beaune, all for 'three and six' (17½p) – a plug for the wine associated with his former girlfriend.

The Three Men's bronzed faces and picturesque clothes – overcoats worn over boating rig – marked them out at the Alhambra, and the box office man mistook them for a troupe of Himalayan contortionists who had come to the wrong entrance. The theatre provided a programme of lively and exotic music hall acts in those days, but it was the ballet in which it excelled. It began by following the French style and lost its dancing licence for a while in 1870 after a performance of the *can-can*. The French repaid the compliment by imitating the Moorish architectural decorations of the Alhambra for the *Folies Bergere* theatre in Paris.[7]

It was a wise move to leave the theatre at 10.30pm for their supper at The Florence. This was the interval after the first ballet and it lasted for nearly an hour. It gave young men about town a chance to meet up with the ballet girls who had caught their eyes, entertain them in the basement café and arrange for assignations later. The less well-heeled or physically attractive had to trawl the bars looking for the successors of Harriet Buswell. Perish the thought that our three gentlemen should be among them. They were enjoying the end of their culinary deprivations, savouring the smell of French sauces, the aroma of Burgundy, and welcoming the sight of clean napkins and long loaves.

And they drank a toast to Three Men well out of a boat.

So we take our farewell of the river to whom I have, perhaps, not paid sufficient tribute. For he is there for us still in all his moods, smiling and bejewelled under the sun, dark and threatening in his dreadful floods. Our attitude to him has changed since J's day, and he takes on the role of an open-air gymnasium rather than a relaxing holiday haunt. Joggers and cyclists crowd the banks while canoeists, kayakers and rowers pit their strength against his power. J's book was born when three young men gave voice to their hypochondria. Their successors today would have been obsessed by fitness and their prowess in the gym.

There is nothing that seems as timeless as a great river, yet its banks are ephemeral, mere walls of earth that crumble away at the least provocation of burrowing animals, tree roots and the wash of passing boats. But our brief human life span allows us to see but a freeze-frame image. To view it as the truly living thing it is, you would have to observe it over the course of thousands of years. Then it would look like a snake wriggling on its bed, sloughing off the occasional ox-bow lake. We have been looking at the river with all its changing faces for but the twinkling of an eye. Old Father Thames we call him, or the stream of pleasure, as if he exists purely for our convenience and amusement. We try to imprison him within steel and concrete embankments, build houses on his playgrounds, and hope that a little play pen called the Jubilee River will propitiate him. But he is his own master and will roam where he will, as he did when he roared through the Goring Gap all those thousands of years ago. J believed the science of his day that we were heading for another Glacial period.[8] Now we believe that temperatures are going the other way and that London's river, as he is sometimes patronizingly called, will one-day rise and sweep a way through the centre of the great city, But this will not be any day soon. In a thousand years' time perhaps, when all London's great monuments will take on a new beauty, reflected in the water like the ruins of Abu Simbel.

The Swan Inn boathouse at Pangbourne where The Three ended their holiday.

18

Postscript

In which J tells what happened after The Three returned from their holiday, and how they were set an unfair challenge.

OUR early return to London was not the end of the story. I wrote what proved to be a very successful book about our exploits, but Harris and George took exception to the way that I had portrayed them. You might have thought they would have been grateful to me for making them the heroes of a work that would eventually find its way on to every station newsstand from Penzance to Inverness. But not a bit of it. George said that as serious rowing men, who had known their way about the river for years, it was very unfair of me to suggest we did not know one end of an oar from another and couldn't rig a camping skiff cover without falling over each other. We were men of more than average athletic powers, yet our rate of progress had been pathetic. Our decision to cut the holiday short had been an honourable one taken out of consideration for my health he insisted. I had looked pretty much done-in because of the dangerously damp weather and they had probably saved my life by deciding to cut off home.

He said our friends and acquaintances had been putting two and two together and it hadn't taken them long to work out who those described in the book really were. He had suffered a great deal of ribbing as a result. 'Dash it all J', he said, 'you make me out to be such a sluggardly fellow. Fat too – you say I weigh about 12 stone, while I'm not a pennyweight more than ten. At least, I suppose, that might be to some advantage, as those who really know me will think: 'George Wingrave lazy and fat? Can't be the same fellow at all.'

Harris said his situation was worse. Chaps were coming up to him and saying: 'thought you only drank lemonade, old boy. Different story on the river, hey? Can't keep you off the whisky or out of the pub. When are you off for another soak?'

Of course a mild dispute among friends is one of the pleasures of life. One can, *without risk of seriously injuring a relationship let rip with a few home truths. It gets them off your chest; you feel the better for it and any frostiness between you and your friends melts away like the snows of winter before the rays of the waking spring sun in that precious moment when the first smile of reconciliation appears as they accept your point of view.*

★

George was the first to come round to my way of thinking that any kind of celebrity is better than spending your life in the shadows. We shared rooms in Tavistock Place, and had managed to 'chum' along together cheerily enough during the few months after our trip, provided that that contentious issue between us was never mentioned.

Then a month after the book was published George came home from the bank and told me the most remarkable story. For one of such a phlegmatic disposition he showed a surprising amount of dramatic flair in telling it.

He had been summoned upstairs to see old Mr Humbrage, one of the senior partners, and as this was the usual preliminary to getting the sack, he went weak at the knees. 'One knows who one's friends are at such a time', said George, and judging by the amount of sniggering by his fellow clerks, he realised he had precious few. The old man was standing in the middle of his magnificent office holding my book in one hand and a copy of The Lock to Lock Times[1] *in the other. He said that he had read in the latter that the George described in a certain vulgar and racy book – which he was waving about – was in fact Mr George Wingrave of the London South Western Bank (Head Office).*

Of course old Humbrage would not admit to having read it himself. He and Mrs Humbrage only perused literature of an improving kind on a Sunday, which was a day of rest, a day of rest, he emphasised, being most suited to that kind of relaxing pursuit. He had therefore asked a minion with less refined taste to read it for him and note the offending paragraphs.

In the book was a scrap of paper which marked a page from which he read.

'George goes to sleep in a bank from ten to four each day, except Saturdays, when they wake him up and put him outside at two.'

Humbrage shook his head and cleared his throat. 'We also have here comments by a fellow called Harris:

' "Bank be blowed! What good was he at the bank.... whenever I go in he sits behind a bit of glass all day trying to look as if he was doing something.... and what's the good of their banks? They take your money, and then, when you draw a cheque, they send it back smeared all over with 'no effects', 'refer to drawer."

'Clearly this friend of yours is a habitual bouncer of cheques', Humbrage remarked. 'A dastardly abuser of all the principles on which credit, the foundation of our institution, is based.'

George began to stammer with embarrassment at this point. I can only guess the extent to which he felt obliged to blackguard me to stave off the wrath of his superior. He admitted that he secretly cursed me at that point and rued the day I had come to lodge with him and that he had allowed me to cajole him out on to the Thames. He thought that I had betrayed his simple trust and become the author of his ruin to promote my own success. He bit his tongue, but more bad things were to follow.

Humbrage said he had been told the book described George as a habitué of bohemian restaurants and frequenter of music halls, and that on that boating trip he had played cards for money. All these things were expressly forbidden in the indenture George had solemnly signed when he joined the Bank.

'Well, young Wingrave, What have you to say for yourself?'

A lesser man than George might have tried to dig himself out of that hole by simply calling me an untruther and a cheat. But he did the gentlemanly thing and said that as a writer, exaggeration was my stock in trade. Harris was in fact a respectable business man and a teetotaller. The card game referred to was just penny brag. ('And so it begins!' snorted Humbrage) The restaurant was a modest little place and the Alhambra a respectable house of entertainment.

The old man sighed a deep sigh and said that all these disgraceful goings on by an employee reflected badly on the reputation of the Bank. The matter was serious enough to have been considered by the Board, who at first were minded to run him out of the building without his feet touching the ground.

However, there was one among them, a new, young appointee, who spoke up on George's behalf. He said there was a new class of client: writers, actors, singers. People, who just a few years ago, would have been considered as on the fringes of respectable society. They were now making very good money and looking to banks to manage it for them. This was a growing class, he believed, and it would be of benefit to the Bank to have someone familiar with their milieu. He was a persuasive man, and managed to swing the board around in George's favour.

The upshot was that they decided to transfer him to the bank's branch in the Strand. 'Work there with due diligence Wingrave – be careful of your friends – and you could well end up in a very senior position', George had been told.

Old Humbrage then turned his anger on the writer of the offending paragraph. He said he had good authority to believe that it was written for money. Selling information sensitive to the Bank was a very serious matter indeed. Almost the worst offence an employee could commit.

George returned to his desk hardly able to conceal his delight. To the disappointment of his curious colleagues he calmly resumed his work. Among the most histrionic of the sniggerers when George had been called up was Styvings, a man senior to him and of overweening ambition. The fellow had been boasting that it was he who was the author of the paragraph. He did not snigger when it was his turn to be summoned before old Mr Humbrage, and when he returned his face was as white as a sheet. He put on his coat and walked out of the office, never to be seen again.

'So you see', said George, 'all that discomfort, and the insults resulting from a literary conceit, have produced a happy ending for me, making it all worthwhile'.

★

It was shortly after this that Harris came to call on us. He remarked that Montmorency's bark of welcome seemed less enthusiastic than in former times. It is a sad spectacle when a fox terrier, the scourge of fellow dogs, street urchins and cats reaches doggy late middle age. The first sign of his decline had been when he slunk away from a belligerent tom cat that day in Marlow. Now he seemed to prefer to spend his time sleeping on a soft chair and rolling over on his back to be tickled. George said we should make him the subject of experiments to see if we could disprove the adage that old dogs can't learn new tricks.

George told us a story about an old dog he had heard of that had learnt to swallow sixpenny pieces. How it came about he did not know, but the chap who owned him would put him out of his digs every morning when he went to work, and the dog had found a welcome in the shop of a local pawn broker. It seems that from his connection with that establishment the animal had come to esteem money above all other things. You could leave a steak out and he would never touch it. But if he came across a penny or threepenny bit it would be gone in a trice. That dog could tell the value of coins as well. If you offered a penny and a sixpence, it would always take the sixpence.

George had spent an evening with friends in the rooms of the dog's owner. They had all given it a sixpence and a penny to test its extraordinary ability. As they were breaking up to go home one of the chaps, who was rummaging in his pocket to find the bus fare, suddenly went pale.

'I had a half-sovereign in it when I came out', he said in a shaky voice, 'and it's gone. I need it to pay my landlady tomorrow, or she will throw me out.'

Of course we all concluded, said George, that he had accidently fed the money to the dog. He was all for choking the beast in the hope that it would be sick, or failing that, to open him up with a carving knife. But the dog could not be found. Its owner had let it out into the street a quarter of an hour before to do its nightly business. That young man left his friends there and then looking very crestfallen. He was going to carry out a search of the streets. No one offered him any help, although it was suggested he might have more success if he came back the following night, allowing for the normal course of a dog's digestion.[2]

After George's story we all began telling dog stories of our own. We began chaffing one another about the age of these hoary old tales. They were the sort of stories our grandsires might have told each other when they were still in petticoats.

But how we laughed! A cloud seemed to lift from us and we slipped into the old, easy affable companionship, quite like old times before that last trip on the river. We spoke about what we had been doing during those few embarrassing days when we were supposed to be still on holiday.

I said I had spent the time hidden from my friends in the British Museum Reading Room. Harris said he hoped I hadn't been reading medical dictionaries again as it was apt to turn me into a hypochondriac. I said that at least it had given me a good yarn for my book, but there was one curious detail I had kept to myself. My medical man is an old chum and I did not wish to embarrass him in any way. He had listened to my health worries and prescribed plain honest food, fresh air and exercise. Then he had gone beyond the bounds of reason and told me to give up smoking. I thought for the sake of his reputation I had better not mention it.

'Quite right', said Harris, 'no one in their right mind would believe in a physician who told them to give up their baccy, specially someone who had actually dedicated a book to his pipe.'

I said it was an undisputable fact that smoke was good for the lungs and a natural preservative, as in the case of kippers.

George said real advances in civilisation had only begun after the introduction of tobacco; one of the few good things to come from America. It had enabled people to regard life in a more reflective light, come up with all sorts of revolutionary new ideas, and generally made mankind less savage. Besides, what could chaps talk about if they couldn't discuss the merits of their favourite tobacco mixture?

George never admitted what he did to fill in those missing few days. When I went off in the morning he said he thought he would have a bit of a lie-in. And when I returned in the evening he said he'd though he should have an early night to compensate for all the exercise on the river – this from a man who had considered himself 'more than averagely athletic'.

But only a man of stone can bear the reproaches of his friends who feel he has in some way done them a wrong. I was rather hurt. They thought my 'scribblings' had belittled them, and I felt called upon to make amends. It was agreed that I should write another book showing us all in a more heroic light, and a week or two later Harris turned up with a letter he had cut out from The Field. [3]

It was a very old letter as it turned out. Harris had found a 14-year-old copy of the popular sporting journal lining a drawer. Although a little yellow, the advice it contained, he said, was still good. The writer noted that a large number of men were seen annually doing the trip from London to Oxford, but after this had been accomplished once or twice, they naturally sought for some further field of operations.

'There is no honour in doing things the easy way' said Harris, and he was all for following the extraordinarily convoluted route from Oxford to London proposed in the letter, a journey of some 455 miles compared to the 180 we had set out to achieve.

'You start at Oxford', said Harris, 'Not on the Thames, but on the Oxford Canal, which you follow all the way up to the Midlands, where you take a turn to the left by some other canal which takes you to – um – um – Warwick, and then by means of the River Avon to that Shakespeare place. After that there is a difficult bit where you have to carry the boat and launch it over the bank into the River Severn. Then you went all the way to Gloucester.'

He said the Severn was an interesting river to navigate because it had no locks. There were ferocious rapids instead, which you had to shoot, being careful not to wreck your boat on the rocks.

'I have heard about something like that trip,' said George. 'I suppose you then go down into the Severn Estuary and take the Avon to its junction with the Kennet and Avon Canal joining the Thames at Reading.'

'You would do no such thing', said Harris. 'By taking such a short cut you would deprive yourself of some of the most beautiful scenery to be seen in England. No, from Gloucester you must take the canal up to Hereford, then join the Wye to enjoy its magnificent views before you get back to the Severn Estuary. You also pass a little church somewhere which has an elm tree growing through one of the pews.

'The Estuary is in any case too dangerous for a skiff. When you get to Chepstow at the mouth of the Wye, it is only a short way across to Avonmouth and Bristol, so you get a fishing boat to tow your empty boat across. Then as George said, it is a simple matter to return by canal to the Thames.'

Harris had warmed to his subject, I had rarely heard him speak for so long and be so single minded about anything before. He had sought out the writer of the letter, one Howard Williams, who was just 21 when he made the trip.

Williams had read my book and had been very encouraging about us engaging in such an adventure. On the Thames, said Harris, a passing skiff is just taken as a *matter of course, but on those provincial rivers a group of rowing men passing through a town is the cynosure of every eye, and people come out and line the bridges to cheer you on your way. As for the girls – apparently they are very friendly.*

He said Williams, who had shown him his journal, and his friends were all good god-fearing men who went to church and refused to have their photographs taken of a Sunday. But when they came across a Sunday school treat at Chepstow they invited the young lady teachers to start a game of Kiss in the Ring. To their delight they agreed, but it was spoilt by the little brats wanting to join in. One of the party had disappeared for the evening and worried by his late return the others were about to alert the police to start dragging the river. When he turned up, all he would say was that he had been to visit his grandmother's grave – Harris gave a knowing look. A bit like you at Streatley, said George, trying to bring him back down to earth.

George and I were getting irritated by Harris. He was throwing down a challenge which we felt we should have some difficulty in avoiding without loss of face.

But the banker in George was already at work. They must have been pretty well off, those chaps', he remarked. 'If in gainful employment – as opposed to gentlemen – they would have had to be absent from work for how long?'

'Just over three weeks', said Harris.

George continued: 'And they stayed in country inns paying for their meals for 22 nights. Then they would have to pay the various licence fees for the waterways, plus the tolls for the locks. How many did you say?'

Harris looked at the cutting. 'It says here 221', he replied.

I said you would never find a boathouse on the Thames prepared to hire out a skiff for such a journey as there would be a very good chance that it would be wrecked and never come back. 'I suppose those fellows had their own boat?'

'That is true', said Harris,' they brought it up to Oxford from lower down the Thames on a railway truck. It cost them thirty-seven shillings.'

'And did they manage to avoid all those rocks while shooting rapids on the Severn?' I asked

'No', said Harris, 'the boat was pretty well bashed about and had to have extensive repairs before they could cross the Severn Estuary.'

'If we intended to do this trip we would have to buy our own boat,' I said, 'and buy it at Oxford where it would be an inferior sort of up-river boat. And they had a crew of five', I added, 'Would we need that number?'

Harris said he thought so if we did what they did, and carried the boat off the water every night and put it in a barn to keep everything dry. Some locks on the canals were closed on Sundays so you had to carry the boat around them.

He thought we might invite Jim if he was not off on a cricketing tour. And a good all-round sportsman like Doyle would come in handy. 'All you writing chaps seem to have bags of time on your hands', he added.

But George was totting up some figures on the back of an envelope. 'It would be going it a bit on the financial side and I can't see us getting much change out of £100 at today's prices.

'I don't know about you chaps, but there's not much left from my salary at the end of the month, after living expenses, baccy and doing those little things that make life bearable; visits to the theatre, restaurants, and so on.'

We left it at that. Nobody wanted to reject the idea out of hand. But as it turned out, the three of us would never take to the Thames together again. The next time I rowed out on those familiar and well-loved waters, it was quite a new experience. I had my wife with me.[4]

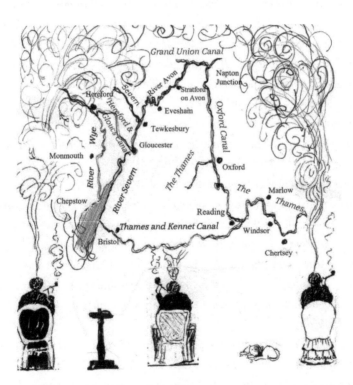

A pipe dream.

APPENDIX I

Author in Search of a Hard Consonant

The story of a strangely reversible name.

J'S REAL family name was Clapp, a name prevalent in the West Country, particularly around Bristol, and as you might expect from such a region of seafarers and Dissenters, Clapps were well represented among the first emigrants to America. Their descendants over there, anxious to proclaim their kinship with the founding fathers, have links to many genealogical websites. But sadly they remain unaware that the author of *Three Men in a Boat* is, perhaps, the most famous of the tribe.[1]

Grandfather, Benjamin Clapp, was living in Bath at the time the writer's father was born c. 1805.[2] One imagines Benjamin, a watch-maker and Nonconformist, to have been a meticulous and pedantic man as suggested by the name he chose for his son. He preferred the classical 'Jerome' rather than the traditional English Jeremy, although there is evidence that it was pronounced by the family as Jeromee.[3] His reverence for scripture would perhaps have made the name of a saint acceptable to him as St Jerome translated the Bible into Latin (the Vulgate) and is the patron saint of scholars.

In addition to the family name, Benjamin, as a West Countryman, must have passed on to his son and grandson the belief that they were descended from a Dane called Clapa who came to Appledore circa AD 1000.

A search on the internet will reveal that many present-day Clapps believe that their ancestor was Osgood Clapa, mentioned in The Anglo Saxon Chronicle, who died in 1054. Tradition has it that at a riotous party to celebrate the marriage of Clapa's daughter, King Hardicanute drank himself to death in 1038. Lovely people![4]

Jerome Clapp was a lay preacher in a Nonconformist sect called the Independents. They were subsumed into the Congregational Church which in turn merged with other churches to become the United Reformed Church. It is from records kept locally within this organisation that details of Clapp's early career have been preserved. These were explored by a local historian Peter Christie.[5]

During his ministry in North Devon there is strong evidence that he became the father of an illegitimate child and that the scandal pursued him after he moved to Walsall in 1855, probably accounting for him changing his name from Jerome Clapp to Jerome Clapp Jerome. He was never thereafter referred to as 'the Rev' or climbed into a pulpit. It used to be said that candidates for the Nonconformist ministry should wear their underpants the wrong way round as well as their collars, and in not heeding that advice the Rev Jerome Clapp, it seems, was driven to reverse his own name.

That such a fate should befall a talented and charismatic man was a tragedy. Although he never preached again, J described him as a Nonconformist Minister on his marriage certificate. Clapp had striven to educate the local farm workers with lectures against drink and in favour of pacifism, and to drive his message home he published tracts.

He must have been an exceptionally good communicator, a talent he passed on to his son. We find an unexpected touch of pulpit prose in the middle of the hilarious tale of planning and packing supplies for the Thames excursion. Coveting too many material things leads to the wagging of a finger.

> ... oh, heaviest, maddest lumber of all! The dread of what will my neighbour think? with luxuries that cloy, with pleasures that bore, with the empty show that, like the criminal's iron crown of yore, makes to bleed and swoon the aching head that wears it!

Then there is the commentary on the woman found drowned near Goring: '... she had sinned – some of us do now and then...'

After the sins of Jerome Clapp had caught up with him he left Walsall and bought a ships' chandlery business at Limehouse in East London. The family, with the three-year-old J, moved down to Poplar to join him. It was not a pleasant place to grow up, with streets of anonymous terraced houses in this newly built suburb, where bullies lurked on street corners.

There was little money and Mrs Jerome struggled to keep up standards. Young Jerome had to travel across London to get to a decent school – Marylebone Grammar.

His father died from a heart attack when he was 12 and his mother when he was 15. It was an uphill struggle for J to support himself and he turned to a variety of occupations – railway clerk, school teacher, actor, penny-a-line journalist and solicitor's clerk. But always before him was the ambition to be a writer.

★

With regard to the family roots, myth is often more compelling than fact, and when the Rev Jerome Clapp had moved to Appledore at the invitation of the local Independent congregation in 1840 he believed he was returning to his ancestral lands. In 1842 he married Marguerite Jones, the daughter of a draper in Swansea, South Wales. When her mother died he either inherited or used the money to buy a dairy farm.

J wrote that the farm in Devonshire:

> … is marked by a ruined tower, near to which, years ago, relics were discovered proving beyond all doubt that the Founder of our House was one 'Clapa', a Dane, who had obtained property in the neighbourhood about the year Anno Domini one thousand. It was Clapa, I take it, who suggested our family crest, an upraised arm grasping a battleaxe, with round about it 'Deo omnia data' … my mother never seems to have got over the idea that by some inalienable right the farm still belonged to us.[6]

In fact, there is nothing to suggest Clapa had any connections with North Devon. Peter Christie notes that the Viking in North Devon is usually referred to as Hubba, and his presumed tomb was excavated in September 1841 when nothing much of interest was found. Vikings did not use Latin, and it is not surprising that the crest is different from those offered on US web sites ($15, framed for your wall, or on a coffee mug for $13.90!). By the time heraldry came into fashion the Clapp family tree had grown many branches.

It has been suggested that J's reference to his ancestry was tongue-in-cheek, but given his views on 'breeding' in common with most Victorians, I think he took his family history very seriously.

He would have seen the supposed family crest engraved on a gold watch given to his father by his mother on their wedding day. He used it as a letterhead while struggling to establish himself as a writer, so the man dubbed by some as an 'Arry might seem a bit of a snob, although this self-promotion is understandable given the class consciousness prevailing at the time, and the fact that he was desperately trying to claw his way back up the social ladder so brutally kicked away from under him in childhood.[7]

For a romanticised view of the virtues he believed his family had inherited from their Danish ancestors, we can turn to *John Ingerfield*, his short story published in 1897. This is also interesting for the way it reverses the fortunes of his father. John Ingerfield is descended from a long-haired, sea bronzed personage called Inge who came from out of the wild North Sea. With nothing more than a two-handed battle axe he acquired wide lands and many head of cattle.

> They are a money-making race. In all times, out of all things, by all means they make money.
> ...the Ingerfields, hard men and grasping men though they be – men caring more for the getting of money than for the getting of love – loving more the cold grip of gold than the grip of kith and kin, yet bear buried in their hearts the seeds of nobler manhood, for which, however, the barren soil of their ambition bears scant nourishment.

So John Ingerfield was a man of Norse descent and 'very typical of his race'.[8] His family, originally from Yorkshire, moved to London where he attended Merchant Taylors' School. (J claimed his father also attended this school although this is disproved by school records). It is the time of George III, and John successfully makes his fortune in the unpleasant trade of tallow and oil refining near the Thames at Limehouse. J's father set up in business at Limehouse, but it was a failure. In contrast, John's success enables him to buy a house in Bloomsbury and contract a loveless marriage with a woman of superior social position. The story describes how the couple eventually fall in love and die of the plague while looking after its victims. This loving devotion seems to underline Jerome senior's infidelity.

It is tempting to believe that J saw this ancestral obsession for making money as an explanation for his father's apparent addiction to business speculation, which seems to sit awkwardly with his career of preacher and idealistic promoter of good causes.

In the first of these financial debacles the Rev Clapp fell prey to two fraudsters who convinced him that silver lay under his land. Much of his money was lost in a futile mining operation. J euphemistically called it stone quarrying, but he must have known the truth. In his play *The Passing of the Third Floor Back*, Samuels, the swindler, having fallen under the benign influence of the Stranger, confides to his associate that land for a silver mine he has been promoting in Ireland would be a far better investment as a dairy farm.

After his move to Walsall, Clapp embarked on another speculation. He bought rights to sink a coalmine which was then a sure-fire investment in that part of the world. But he lost all his money digging the pit and when it flooded he was bankrupted. To rub salt into his wounds, the man who bought it from him struck coal and made a fortune.

Clapp's desire to create wealth was perhaps a little more altruistic than it seems at first sight. The money that came to him after his marriage in 1842 allowed him to promote his causes on a wider stage. In 1841 he attended a meeting of Nonconformist ministers at Manchester campaigning against the corn laws, and it is recorded that he attended the Peace Society Congresses in Brussels (1848) and Paris (1849). No doubt this would have involved much personal expenditure. To an ambitious man it would have been obvious that wealth would enable him to campaign for pacifism, temperance and social justice from a much more elevated platform than the pulpit of a small-town chapel. It might even enable him to become a great philanthropist like J Passmore Edwards, with whom he toured towns in Cornwall in 1849 in support of the Peace Congress Movement for Arbitration Instead of War.[9]

★

To return to J's belief in his Danish roots. After his death in 1927 *The Times* published an obituary on June 15 which included the following sentence:

'His father, an Independent preacher, the Rev. Jerome Clapp Jerome – the middle name was derived from that of 'Clapa' a Danish ancestor of the family – was at that time the proprietor of coalmines on Cannock Chase'.

This provoked the following letter published on June 22:

MR. JEROME K. JEROME.

It might interest your readers to know the real origin of Mr. Jerome Klapka Jerome's middle name. To my knowledge there was no question of Danish ancestry. When the Fort of Komárom surrendered on October 3, 1849, during the Hungarian War of Independence the Press of the whole world glorified George Klapka, the courageous young General of Artillery, 29 years old at that time, who was able to hold the fort against the united Austrian and Russian armies and only surrendered when he secured an amnesty for his fellow combatants. After the surrender Klapka went abroad. When he arrived in London, Francis Pulszky, Kossuth's secretary, considering the young hero's precarious position, advised him to write his memoirs for Messrs. Chapman and Hall, the publishers, who immediately granted him an advance of £100. It was a question now of finding a quiet retreat, as the book had to be finished within two months. Klapka gladly accepted the invitation of the Rev. Jerome Jerome. In Walsall he found a home, and even in later, years, whenever tired of restless wandering, he always returned to his kind host. When, in 1859, a son was born to the Rev. J. Jerome, in honour of his famous guest he named him Jerome Klapka.

Professor Michael M. Bálint, 3, Nemetvölgyi ut 42, Budapest

★

This is a very remarkable letter. Apart from 'air-brushing' out the Rev Jerome Clapp Jerome's middle name, it contains a whole catalogue of errors concerning the famous author, yet it was quoted uncritically by Alfred Moss in his biography of J published in 1928, Joseph Connolly's biography of 1982 and in *In the Wake of Three Men in a Boat,* by R R Bolland in 1995.

★

I examined the letter in detail: *To my knowledge there was no question of Danish ancestry.* How could a Hungarian living in Budapest claim personal knowledge that a man born in England with the name Clapp was not of ancient Danish ancestry?

The facts about George Klapka are correct, except when we come to: *Kossuth's secretary, considering the young hero's precarious position, advised him to write his memoirs for Messrs. Chapman and Hall, the publishers, who immediately granted him an advance of £100.* The publisher was in fact Charles Gilpin, a Quaker, and this is of significance as we shall see. *Klapka gladly accepted the invitation of the Rev. Jerome Jerome. In Walsall he found a home …* According to the advertisement for the memoirs published in *The Times* in June 1850 they were written in two parts over the winter of 1849-50. At that time Jerome Clapp was living in Appledore.

…in later, years, whenever tired of restless wandering, he always returned to his kind host. This is most improbable given the Jerome Clapp's difficulties during their years in Walsall, and the fact that Klapka was then playing an active part in the wars of Italian independence.

When, in 1859, a son was born to the Rev. J. Jerome, in honour of his famous guest he named him Jerome Klapka. A simple check through census returns on the internet will show that JKJ was named after his father – Jerome Clapp Jerome – and only assumed the middle name of Klapka around the time of the publication of his first book *On the Stage and Off.*

Although most of the facts in this letter fall down under scrutiny like ninepins, it is not so easy to dismiss the possibility that Klapka did stay with Clapp while writing his memoirs, though it would have been during what was then a relatively tranquil period of the preacher's life in North Devon rather than in Walsall. It seems improbable that such a military celebrity should come into contact with an obscure pacifist parson, but their paths came surprisingly close, although it cannot be proved that they actually met.

At this point we need to look into the life and career of General George Klapka.

He was of German descent and his name, Klapka, was the Germanic equivalent of Clapp, the suffix 'ka' meaning small – 'little Klap'.[10]

In 1848 the Hungarians rose in revolt against the Austrians. Klapka was one of the officers in the improvised rebel Hungarian army – freedom fighters we would call them now – and he was made a general at a surprisingly early age. He commanded a small rebel enclave at Komárom, which fought on after the general collapse of the uprising and the surrender of its leaders. That put him in the fortunate position of being able to negotiate the terms of his own surrender. While most of the Hungarian patriots faced summary execution in Vienna or, if they were lucky, escaped to Turkey, Klapka was able to arrange his own exile in England.

As almost the sole survivor of those who had courageously risen against the unpopular and reactionary Austrian Empire he was lionised by the Victorian public in the same way that they were to take Garibaldi to their hearts during the Italian wars of independence. Being a Protestant and revolutionary, Klapka found himself at home in England among Nonconformists, radicals and pacifists, the *milieu* in which the Rev Clapp was active.

This is well illustrated by a report of a meeting of the Peace Society in London that appeared in *The Times* of October 31, 1849. It was no meeting of obscure utopian eccentrics, the paper devoted 3½ columns to it. In attendance were Richard Cobden the anti-Corn Law campaigner, Charles Gilpin the publisher and politician, mentioned above, and Samuel Gurney of the famous banking family. Victor Hugo sent his apologies for absence through the French delegation.

The chairman, Mr W Ewart, MP, noted:

> Among the illustrious foreigners who had honoured that (sic) meeting with their presence, there was one of a class not very usually found at peace meetings, but one whose presence he was sure would be hailed by the audience; he meant General Klapka (great applause), who came, he supposed, with the view of twining the peaceful olive with the laurels of war.

The Rev Clapp had attended the Peace Congresses held in Brussels and Paris. Unfortunately we have no evidence that he attended this London meeting.[11]

It was at this time that Klapka was seeking 'a quiet retreat' and Clapp would have been in a good position to provide it. He was prosperous and lived in a large house in a quiet part of the country and was therefore better placed than most Nonconformist clergymen to host such a distinguished guest.[12] Wanting peace and quiet Klapka might have arrived in Appledore incognito, hence no reference in local newspapers to the presence of such a famous man.

Against this possibility we have to consider that there is no acknowledgement in Klapka's book that he had received 'kind' hospitality allowing him to write it. All letters quoted in it have a London address. No correspondence exists between Clapp and Klapka and this is strange if we are to believe in the close relationship described in the Bálint letter.

And J made no reference to it in his own autobiography, something he would no doubt have been proud to include – if it had been true.

Taking into account all the other discrepancies in the Bálint letter I am not inclined to believe that the General ever stayed with Clapp.

If Clapp had intended to honour the General by naming his son after him then surely this would have been in 1855 when his first son, Milton Melancthon, was born, although at that time the family name was Clapp, and Klapka Clapp would have sounded ridiculous.

One wonders who the letter writer was, and his motive.

The most distinguished bearer of this name was Michael Maurice Bálint, then working at the Budapest Institute of Psychoanalysis. He had changed his name from Mihaly Maurice Bergmann on converting from Judaism to Unitarianism. With the advent of fascism in Hungary in the 'thirties he took refuge in Britain, becoming President of the British Psycho-Analytical Society before his death in 1970.

If he was indeed the writer, what was his motive? It must be remembered that anti-semitism was prevalent in Hungary in the 1920s and 30s and it was particularly directed against intellectuals. The tone of the letter suggests the writer was anxious to establish himself as a patriot as much as attempting to explain the Klapka connection. Perhaps the clearly Anglophile writer of the letter to *The Times* took J M Barrie's maxim to heart that writing a letter to *The Times* was the 'legitimate ambition of every Englishman' – or would-be Englishman.[13]

★

Whether or not Clapp and Klapka ever met, there were three good reasons why the name of the General should resonate in the Jerome household: As a contemporary hero, as a supporter of the peace movement and, possibly above all, as a representative of the Germanic branch of the tribe of Clapp.

Jerome senior had more than an average interest in names – Milton Melancthon for a son, Blandina for a daughter – so Klapka (little Clapp)[14] must have seemed an almost irresistible nickname for his elder son, and few boys would have been in greater need of one.

When J embarked on his career as an author it is not difficult to understand his desire for a hard consonant as a middle initial. Jerome C. Jerome, 'Jeromesyjerome' sounds weak and may well have carried unpleasant memories of the schoolroom. It might also have revived memories of a scandal down in the West Country. He did not have far to look for a substitute. Klapka must have faded from the public consciousness by then, but it is reasonable to assume that it had been cherished in the Jerome family. Adopting it was a way of remaining in touch with his Clapp roots while abandoning his true surname.

And so in 1885 a memorable and strangely reversible name came before the public:

> My first book! He stands before me, bound in a paper wrapper of a faint pink colour, as though blushing all over for his sins. 'On the Stage – and Off. By Jerome K Jerome'. (the K very large, followed by a small j; so that by many the name of the author was taken to be Jerome Kjerome).

Writing this in *My Life and Times,* J seems to be teasing us. He doesn't say what the K stands for.

APPENDIX II

An Interview with George aged 71

From the Oxford Mail, Tuesday April 25 1933

Revelations of the One who Survives

"GEORGE"

Why The Historic Thames Trip Was Taken

"George", who made the world laugh – by accident – more than almost any other man in the world, lives quietly now in a flat in St John's Wood [London].

He is the last of the famous "Three Men in a Boat", whose adventures have been so beloved of our fathers, our grandfathers and ourselves.

Those three jolly sailors on that merriest of voyages were Jerome K Jerome, who wrote the book, Carl Hentschel, who appears as "Harris", and George Wingrave, the original of "George"

Now Jerome and Hentschel are dead, and A C Goodinge[1] – a friend of the three, although not as sometimes thought, one of the men in the boat – has just died too.

STILL INTERESTED IN LIFE

George of the irrepressible antics is over 70 now, with the snow-white hair, rosy cheeks, shrewd eyes, and as intense an interest as ever in London life and the things that are going on in the world.

In fact, there are two distinct personalities, "George" of the jests and "Mr Wingrave", the serious-minded man of affairs.

And Mr Wingrave chuckles as much as anyone when he recalls those deft jokes about George.

George and Harris and Montmorency, the dog, are not poetic ideals, but things of flesh and blood – especially George, who weighs about 12 stone.

"George goes to sleep at a bank from ten to four each day, except Saturdays, when they wake him up and put him outside at two."

THE "LOUD" BLAZER

"George has a 'loud' blazer, Harris said that as an object to hang over a flower bed in early spring to frighten the birds away he should respect it, but that considered as an article of dress for any human being except a Margate [minstrel]. It made him ill.

"George fancies he is ill, but there is never anything really the matter with him, you know."

Well, Mr Wingrave told an "Oxford Mail" reporter to-day, that "George" has retired now from his bank. But as he sat and talked, he wore a picturesquely coloured jacket which is perhaps a grandchild of the blazer that caused so much merriment.

"I'm over 70 now, you see," he said, "and although I am still active I suppose I am really getting old."

AN OLD PHOTOGRAPH

"It is 44 years ago or more since we three young fellows went together on that holiday cruise which Jerome turned to such good account in the book.

"Here is an old photograph of the three of us in flannels sitting on the river bank. Jerome is wearing the cricket cap and I am the one in the tam o' shanter – there were no berets in those days.

"**Yes, we all three lived together, but not as you suggest, in a triple-bachelor flat. The truth is we starved in one room. That room had to do for the three of us then. We were all making our way in the world, you see.**

"**As for the river trip which led to the book – well, it was a case of doing that or having no holiday. The important thing was it cost practically nothing.**[2]

"There was the beautiful river very near us and the boat, with room for us all to sleep on it, could be hired for a guinea a week."

THE POWER OF TRUTH

"I think the secret of the wonderful popularity of the book lies in the fact that that it is a description of things that actually happened. The incidents in it are true. You see we three lived together for years, and so no end of funny things happened to us, naturally enough.

"Yes, we remained fast friends all through, but even the jolliest voyage must come to an end.

"I still get many letters from people who have read of us and want to know more of the author and Harris and George."

And on that adventurous river holiday 44 years or so ago not one of the three young men dreamed that their little mishaps and amusements would send peals of laughter echoing far into the future.

The photograph referred to by George from the cover of Jerome K Jerome, His life and Work, *by Alfred Moss, 1928, the first biography of the author. Jerome is on the right.*

NOTES

CHAPTER 1

1. The whole of the north side of Tavistock Place was demolished for redevelopment at the end of the nineteenth century. This suggests leases on the properties had not been renewed and they had declined into a shabby state.

2. A list of 32,00 congregational ministers from the mid-seventeenth century to 1972 compiled by Charles Surman is available on line. It lists Jerome's ministries in Cirencester (1829-1835), Dursley, Gloucestershire (1835-1839), Southam, Warkwickshire (1839), Appledpre, Devon (1840 – 1850). His name does not appear in the Congregational Year Book from 1856 onwards either as Jerome or Clapp. A note on a card index states: Alex. Gordon says Mr Clapp Jerome, deacon of Bridge Street, Walsall left in 1857 to build Ephratah Chapel, Bradford Street, Walsall.

   For details of the sexual scandal involving the Rev Clapp Jerome and research by local historian Peter Christie see Appendix 1. It seems that he never entered a pulpit after leaving Walsall and that J is unlikely to have heard him preach, although he gave his father's occupation on his marriage certificate in 1888 as 'Non-conformist minister.'

3. Charles Booth's Poverty Map of London of 1899 shows Sussex Street, Poplar, where J lived as being a mixed neighbourhood, some comfortable and others poor. Middle class and well-to-do households were only a few streets away.

4. *My Life and Times,* J's autobiography, published by Hodder and Stoughton in1926 (Birth and Parentage).

5. *On the Stage and Off,* memories from J's career as a travelling actor, Field and Tuer, London 1885.

6. Carl's ingenious way of overcoming anti-German sentiment affecting his business is described in an article published in the *Straits Times* of Singapore on December 30, 1914. Under the headline "Case of

Carl Hentschel Ltd: Development Arising Out of War Feeling", it says the arrangement was "probably without precedent" though perfectly legal. Cutting made available by Singapore Government Archive.

7. Carl Hentschel quoted in *Twenty Years of My Life*, by Douglas Sladen, page 86. Published by Dutton 1913 and reprinted in facsimile form by ULAN press, available from Amazon. Sladen was a friend of J's and editor of one of his magazines. Carl referred to his workplace as a studio because the rather crude chemical and mechanical means he used to produce printing blocks required delicate re-touching by artists.

8. The incident of Carl Hentschel accidentally sipping alcohol is told in Alfred Moss's biography of J, *Jerome K Jerome: His Life and Works*, Selwyn and Blount, 1928.

9. The *Lock to Lock Times* was published for just over a year from 1888. It opens an invaluable window on the river at that time before being subsumed into a more general leisure interest journal. It may be found bound in frail volumes at the British Library's newspaper section.

10. Obituaries on Carl Hentschel and George Wingrave appeared in *The Times* on January 10, 1930 and March 25, 1941 respectively.

11. *Jerome K Jerome, His Life and Work* by Alfred Moss.

12. The interview with George Wingrave was published in the *Oxford Mail* on Tuesday, April 25, 1933, page 5. I am grateful to Dr Simon Wenham for drawing my attention to it in his book *Pleasure Boating on the Thames, a History of Salter Bros 1858 – Present Day*.

13. George Dunlop Leslie, Royal Academician, wrote his book *Our River* in 1881. It was published by Bradbury, Agnew and Co, London, British Library Shelfmark DRT Digital Store 10349.pp.1.

14. *Novel Notes* appeared in 1893. In it J tells the story of a group of writers who meet regularly to plan the 'perfect' novel. The proposed book is never published.

15. The anecdote set on Maidenhead Bridge is recorded in the *LTLT* of June 27, 1888.

16. The favourable review of Jerome's book appeared in *LTLT* September 14, 1889.

17. *Three Women in One Boat – A River Sketch*, by Constance MacEwan was published in 1891 by F V White & Co of London. An article on the Friends of Rowing website by Göran R Buckhorn gives excerpts includijng part of one of their "hymns".

The kingdom of women has yet to come,
The race for wealth is not half begun,
In the heart of a man there is room for all,
Three women afloat in a boat, Yo-ho!

www.rowinghistory.net

CHAPTER 2

1. *MLAT,* Preface: 'I was living close by in Tavistock Place. The site of the house is now occupied by the Passmore Edwards Institute (Settlement).'
2. Professor Richard Ekins of the University of Ulster published his findings in *Jerome K Jerome's Residences in Fitzrovia and Bloomsbury,* Camden History Review 37, Camden History Society.
3. *Twenty Years of my Life,* page 86.
4. R. R Bolland, the Thames historian, visited 12 Coram Street shortly before it was demolished and stood in the murder room. In his book *In the Wake of Three Men in a Boat* (Oast Books, Tunbridge Wells, 1995) he gives an extensive account of the murder hearings but fails to connect Biggs with Fleck. This is because he believed Jerome had Newman Street, much further west, in mind as the starting place for his story. There was once a pub there called The Blue Posts, but he was following the wrong boy.
5. Coincidentally Joseph Connolly has the same name as the author of a biography of J published in 1982. *Jerome K Jerome, a Critical Biography,* Orbis Publishing, 1982.
6. Accounts of the murder, inquest hearings and committal proceedings were carried in *The Times* from December 27, 1872 to the acquittal of Dr Hessel on January 31, 1873. Leaders criticizing the conduct of the inquest appeared on January 8 and 17, and criticism of the police and conditions in which remand prisoners were held on February 4.
7. The biography of Harriet Buswell is based on evidence given by Supt Thomson, of E Division, Metropolitan Police, at the inquest and reported in *The Times* of January 16, 1873.

CHAPTER 3

1. *London Signs* by Bryant Lillywhite, Allen and Unwin, 1972 has the following entry. 'Blue Posts, or Two Blue Posts in place of a hanging sign, reflect an ancient custom of having coloured posts as a means to identify a house prior to the numbering of streets which took place in London in the 1760s. The practice probably dates from Roman times. It was usual to paint door posts or posts erected to mark an entrance and in London blue appears to be the predominant colour.'

2. *Dickens's Dictionary of the Thames, 1887,* republished in facsimile form by Old Books in 1993, used by permission of Bloomsbury Publishing Plc.

3. '...so I read up Dugdale and a vast number of local guides...' J quoted in *Twenty Years of My Life*, by Douglas Sladen, page 89. *The Topographical Dictionary of England and Wales* (By Thomas Dugdale. Edited by L L Blanchard.) London 1848. British Library Shelfmark DRT Digital Store 10348.e.8

4. For those interested in the fate of the villagers of Birches, contemporary accounts, which date the occurrence to May 1773, report no fatalities.

5. *The Thames from its Source to the Sea,* Sir Walter Armstrong, British Library, Shelfmark DRT Digital Store 10348.k.14

6. *The Book of the Thames from its Rise to its Fall,* Mr and Mrs S C Hall, first published London 1859. Republished in facsimile form by Charlotte James Publishers, Teddington, 1975.

7. The touts are described in *The Stream of Pleasure,* by Elizabeth and Joseph Pennell, who were American visitors at the time, Their book was published by Macmillan and Co, New York, 1891, republished Bibliolife, PO Box 21206, Charleston, SC 29413. Pennell was born in Philadelphia, but made his home in London. He wrote many travel books with the help of his wife, and was noted for his etchings, lithographs and illustrations. He also assisted Carl Hentschel with his platemaking.

CHAPTER 4

1. My thanks to Lynne Jackson of the Architectural Review for providing me with a copy of the journal dealing with Oatlands Grotto.

2. *In the Wake of Three Men in a Boat*, R. R Boland.

3. When the journey was first discussed, Chertsey, two miles further up river was the planned meeting point: 'Harris and I would go down in the morning and take the boat up to Chertsey…'
4. *LTLT* January 19, 1889.

CHAPTER 5

1. I am indebted to the Steam Boat Association archive for details of the Des Vignes boatyard.
2. The following letter appeared in *The Times* of September 19, 2013. 'Sir, The Thames does not "saunter aimlessly through the industrial estates of Staines". There are no industrial estates near the river in Staines-upon-Thames, to give the town its correct name. It is the picturesque focal point of this green and leafy town to the west of London. Ali-G put the town upon the map, but it is the river that ensures the world knows more precisely the whereabouts of Staines-upon-Thames, thus making it a small part of an urban wonder of the world.' Alex Tribick, Staines-upon-Thames, Surrey.
3. The Woodland Trust gives a history of the Ankerwycke Yew tree on its website www.woodlandtrust.org.uk A booklet by Janis Fry, 'Living Link to Magna Carta', explores the connection between this historic event and the tree.
4. J might have raised an eyebrow at American lawyers paying tribute to Old English rights. They did nothing to stop US publishers from pirating his books, and while on a lecture tour in the Deep South, he spoke up for the rights of Afro Americans and got a very ugly response. Segregation was still widespread when the monument was unveiled in 1957.

CHAPTER 6

1. The account of the Dockett Point tragedy is based on reports in *The Times* on the three days of magistrates' court proceedings and the official record of the Old Bailey trial.
2. J records his trip on the last completed moonlit cruise of the Princess Alice in his biography *My Life and Times,* (The Wheels of Change).

CHAPTER 7

1. *The Book of the Thames,* Mr and Mrs S C Hall, first published 1859, republished in facsimile by Charlotte James Publishers, Teddington, 1975.
2. I am grateful to Robin Newlands, a retired river inspector, for the story about the brothel house at Boveney.
3. The Gregory painting of Boulter's Lock can be seen in the Lady Lever Art Gallery, Liverpool.
4. The Second Duke of Cambridge's fiery temper was noted by Charles Harper (Charles G Harper, *Thames Valley Villages,* 1910) commenting on the encounter in 1910 after the duke was safely dead. His full title was Prince George, Duke of Cambridge. He married an actress, Sarah Fairbairn in 1847 contrary to the Royal Marriages Act and she was never recognised as Duchess, he preferred to be buried with his mistress, Louisa Beauclerk. He became head of the Army under Victoria and his statue, mounted on a horse, can be seen outside the Ministry of Defence in Whitehall.
5. *The London Journal* peddled fiction of mainly women's interest for one penny.
6 *The Thames Highway Vol II: Locks and Weirs* by Fred S Thacker, was published in 1920, and with his first volume, a general history, became the standard work on the history of Thames navigation. It was republished in facsimile by David & Charles in 1968.
7. The paragraphs on Hedsor Water are based on an article I wrote for *The Boater,* journal of the Thames Vintage Boat Club, Winter 2002/3, in which I acknowledge the help of Robin Newlands.

CHAPTER 8

1. Ben Hoyle, in a report in *The Times* September 24, 2005, wrote: 'Losing to anybody but Marlow might have been bearable, but the similarities between the towns are so strong that the easiest way to tell them apart is probably by remembering which one has the Britain in Bloom regional crown. Henley and Marlow, separated by seven miles, are exquisitely preserved, conspicuously affluent market towns. 'Competition in every sphere is intense.'

2 *My Life and Times* (Trials of a Dramatist).

3. *The New York Times* archive.

4. The plinth carries the following inscription: 'For it is not right that in a house the muses haunt mourning should dwell – such things befit us not'. It comes from a fragment of verse by Sappho.

5. A description of Monk's Corner and photograph of the interior as it is now were published in *Idle Thoughts* No 30, Summer 2008 when the house was for sale. It included five acres of grounds. A description of the external tiles can be found in *Glazed Expressions*, the journal of the Tiles and Architectural Ceramics Society No 6.

6. *Times* obituary of Alfred Baldry, May 20, 1939.

7. The story of Station Victor at Hurley is told by local historian Phillip Williams in *OSS Station Victor: Hurley's Secret War*, published by Amberley 2016.

CHAPTER 9

1 *Thames Portrait,* E Arnot Robertson. Ivor Nicholson, London, 1937.

2. The story of King George's bread rolls is told by George Dunlop Leslie in *Our River,* page 84.

3. The unfortunate end of Charles Phillis is recorded by Fred Thacker in *The Thames Highway, Vol II.*

4. The painting of Charles Jewell's luncheon party is reproduced and described in Phillips Henley sale catalogue 1997.

5 *Henley Royal Regatta: A Celebration of 150 years*, by Richard Bernell, William Heinemann, 1889.

6. J interviewed by Douglas Sladen *TYOML* page 91.

7. J's views on the Royal Henley Regatta are taken from *My Life and Times* (The Author at Play). 'We spent our honeymoon, my wife and I, in a little boat... We stayed a day at Henley for the Regatta.'

CHAPTER 10

1. The Thames Traditional Boat Rally (renamed Thames Traditional Boat Festival in 2015) is held at Fawley Meadows, Henley-on-Thames

in July every year. It is Europe's largest gathering of traditionally-built craft with up to 200 boats attending.

2. The *Reading Mercury* dated March 16th 1895 carried the following obituary: 'WARGRAVE. Death of an Army Veteran. The frequenters of the river during the summer months will miss the familiar figure of Charles Avery, the one-armed boatman of the George and Dragon Hotel, who died last week from bronchitis after only a few days' illness. He was 63 years of age and served in the Indian Mutiny where he lost his arm.' I am grateful to Peter Delaney, secretary of the Wargrave Local History Society for passing this on and providing me with the memorial verse to Thomas Day reproduced below.

3. Victor, the grandson of the famous waxworks owner Marie Tussaud, married Elizabeth Elliott in 1864. Elizabeth's parents, William and Amelia, lived in Wargrave, and when Elizabeth died she was buried in her father's grave, her name being carved on the back of his headstone. 'Tussaud in Wargrave' by Peter Delaney, *The Second Book of Wargrave,* Wargrave Local History Society.

4. J in conversation with Douglas Sladen, recorded in *TYOML,* page 89.

5. Preface to *The Idle Thoughts of an Idle Fellow,* Jerome K Jerome, 1886: 'This book wouldn't elevate a cow.'

6. Day's experiment with two teenage girl orphans is the subject of Wendy Moore's book *How to Create the Perfect Wife,* published in 2013 by Weidenfeld and Nicholson. The memorial to Day on the wall of the south aisle read as follows:
Beyond the rage of time or fortune's Power,
Remain cold stone! remain and mark the hour,
When all the noblest gifts which heaven e'er gave,
Were centr'd in a dark untimely grave.
Oh! taught on reason's boldest wings to rise
And catch each glimmering of the opening skies;
Oh! gentle bosom! oh, unsullied mind!
Oh! friend to truth, to virtue and mankind!
Thy dear remains we trust to this sad shrine,
Secure to feel no second loss like thine!

7. The death of Day's wife is described in a foreword to the 1840 edition of *The History of Sandford and Merton.*

8. J's view on suffragettes is based on his reaction to the Parish Council's Bill of 1894 which gave women the right to vote in local council

elections. He is quoted by Carolyn W de la L Oulton in *Below the Fairy City, A Life of Jerome K Jerome,* Victorian Secrets, 2012.

9. The story of the man who revered Tennysons's *Wedding Day* poem is told by Alan Wykes in *An Eye on the Thames*, Jarrolds, 1966. Wykes also recounts how an old inhabitant told him about the local swains taking their girlfriends to see the Tussaud tomb.

CHAPTER 11

1. The Ehrlich Brothers are two German stage illusionists.
2. E Arnot Robertson *A Thames Portrait*. The story of John Ruskin witnessing a spitting incident was told to Elizabeth and Joseph Pennell, *The Stream of Pleasure.*
3. R R Bolland suggested Hallmead Eyot as the site of Harris's mythical battle.
4. Fred Thacker says the Thames Conservancy ordered the eel bucks to be removed in 1892.
5. The first story about the disappearing goose appeared in the *Daily Mail* in December 2011 and was said to have occurred in the waters of the Olympic Park. On February 20, 2013 the *Reading Post* reported a similar story complete with artist's impression of a crocodile's head emerging from the Thames near Caversham Bridge.
6. Jerome's view of Wilde appears in *MLAT* (The Wheels of Change). Wilde's view of Jerome comes from *The Unmasking of Oscar Wilde*, by Joseph Pearce, Harper Collins, London, 2000.
7. The most recent account of Amelia Dyers activities can be found in *Amelia Dyer Angel Maker, the Woman who Murdered Babies for Money,* by Alison Rattle and Alison Vale, published by Andre Deutsch, 2007.

CHAPTER 12

1. *The Thames from Source to the Sea,* by Paul Atterbury and Anthony Haines, Weidenfeld and Nicholas, 1998.
2. *Thames Journey,* Paul Gedge, George G Harrap & Co, 1949
3. Charles G Harper, *Thames Valley Villages,* 1910. Available as an e-book from the website of the University of California.

4. In the first of the Forsyte novels *The Man of Property,* 1906, Chapter III, June, at that point engaged to the architect Bossiney, is trying to get her uncle James to buy a plot of land for a villa so that her fiancé will be given some work. 'I stayed with the river on my way home Uncle James and saw a beautiful site for a house.' It was near Pangbourne. Could Galsworthy have had Evans's speculation in mind?

5. Stephen Salter (1861-1954) a member of the Salter family famous for its boating business at Oxford. He built houses of a similar style on the Isle of Wight (*Pleasure Boating on the Thames, a History of Salter Bros 1858-present day. Simon Wenham* The History Press, 2014)

CHAPTER 13

1. History of Beale Park, confirmed by Richard Howard, trustee.
2. Website of the Waldorf Astoria Hotel, New York.
3. The details of this tragedy are taken from the *Berkshire Chronicle* report of the inquest, July 3, 1886.
4. The description of The Grotto comes from *The Grotto House, Toil and Leisure in a Modest Country House in Berkshire,* Pam Pheasant, published by the Institute of Leisure and Amenity Management, 2003.
5. Details are based on an inquest report carried in the *Berkshire Chronicle,* August 16, 1879.
6. The discovery Alice Douglass's body and the inquest was reported in the *Berkshire Chronicle* in July 1887. There was no evidence given that the drowned women had a daughter as J suggests. The inquest is also covered at great length in R R Bolland's *In the Wake of Three Men in a Boat.* Bolland makes the interesting point that one of the witnesses in the Coram Street Murder case was named Alice Douglass. Could she be the same girl who drowned herself in 1887, 15 years after the murder? She would have been 15 at the time, old enough to have been a waitress, so it remains an intriguing possibility.

CHAPTER 14

1. *Our River,* George Dunlop Leslie.

2. Carolyn W de la L Oulton *BTFC* page 149.
3. *MLAT* (Birth and Parentage). 'It was not until the middle of the (nineteenth) century that the persecution of the Nonconformists throughout the country districts may be said to have entirely ceased.'
4. *The Lock to Lock Times* report, February 23 1889, was scathing, but it had to admit later in the year: 'few, indeed hardly any, frequenters of the Thames, have so much as caught sight of the emissaries of "the General", and what is more to the point, the vast majority hope they never will'.
5. *MLAT* (More Literary Reminiscences).
6. *Thames Journey,* Paul Gedge.
7. Consuta Trust www.consuta.org.uk
8. *From River to Sea, the Marine Heritage of Sam Saunders,* Raymond L Wheeler, Cross Publishing, Newport, Isle of Wight.
9. Organised by Goring and Streatley Local History Society and Oxfordshire Blue Plaques Board.
10. *MLAT* (Record of a Discontented Youth)
11. I am grateful to Judy Dewey, of Wallingford Museum, for confirming that Wallingford's defences are of Saxon origin and the best preserved in the country with the possible exception of Wareham in Dorset. They contain no stone work, and Norman stonework was wrongly interpreted as Roman by Kirby Hedges, who wrote a two-volume history of Wallingford in 1881.
12. A E Hobbs tells the story in *Trout of the River Thames* published by Herbert Jenkins Limited in 1947. It is included in an anthology compiled by Peter Rogers published by the Little Egret Press, St Germans, Cornwall, 2008.
13. Angela Houghton confirmed to me that the plaster cast of the record trout that was given to Queen Victoria is still on display at Reading Museum.

CHAPTER 15

1. *In the Wake of Three Men in a Boat.*
2. *The Thames Highway.*
3. The gravestone of Milton Melancthon, Jerome's brother, was discovered in Stourport and brought here by the Jerome K Jerome Society in 2009.
4. *My Life and Times* (I Become an Editor).

5. *The Thames from Its Source to the Sea Vol 1,* Sir Walter Armstrong.
6. *The Thames Highway.*
7. *Dictionary of the Thames,* entry under Abingdon.

CHAPTER 16

1. *The Stream of Pleasure,* Elizabeth Robins Pennell, Joseph Pennell, Macmillan and Co. 1891. Republished BiblioLife in facsimile.
2. *Dictionary of the Thames,* Nuneham Courtenay.
3. *In Thamesland,* Henry Wellington Wack, The Knickerbocker Press, 1906
4. *TVV,* Charles G Harper.
5. *The Royal River,* First Published 1885 republished Bloomsbury Books, London 1985, Chapter II, Oxford to Abingdon, D MacColl.
6. *The Thames from Its Source to the Sea,* Sir W Armstrong.
7. *Hide and Seek with Angels, a Life of J M Barrie,* Lisa Chaney, Hutchinson, London, 2005.
8. This refers to an outbreak of arsenic poisoning among beer drinkers in the Manchester area in 1900. Arsenic had contaminated sugar supplied by a chemical company to the brewers. Six thousand people were made ill and at least 70 died.
9. *TRR,* MacColl, Chapter I.
10. Printed in the *London Literary Gazette,* 1824, but it must have been doing the rounds.
11. *The Thames from Its Source to the Sea* (two volumes), Sir Walter Armstrong, JS Virtue and Co., London, 1886, republished in facsimile by British Library.
12. *Pleasure Boating on the Thames, a History of Salter Bros 1858-present day,* Simon Whenham, The History Press, 2014.

CHAPTER 17

1. Henry Taunt's *New Map of the River Thames,* was published in 1872. It was republished, as *The Thames of Henry Taunt,* by Alan Sutton, Gloucester, in 1989. Taunt's account of his narrow squeak at Hart's Weir appears on page 20.
2. *The Stream of Pleasure,* Elizabeth Robins Pennell, Joseph Pennell,

Macmillan and Co. 1891. Republished BiblioLife in facsimile.

3. Charles Hentschel in conversation with Douglas Sladen, *TYOML*, page 87.

4. *MLAT (*More Literary Reminiscences).

5. *Gourmet's Guide to London, 1914,* by Lieut Col Newnham-Davies. He was a noted author of restaurant reports in the last decade of the nineteenth century and wrote: 'The Florence is not too wholeheartedly Italian to please diners of other nationalities.' He says the prevailing taste in those days was for the *haute cuisine Franglaise.*

6. The Aerated Bread Company was founded in 1862 by a Scottish doctor John Dauglish, who aimed to exploit a way of making additive-free bread. This involved passing carbon dioxide through the dough instead of using the normal yeast fermentation process. Kneading the dough was thus eliminated and this was believed to be healthier than working it with hands, or even feet. The company then opened tea shops, the earliest in London, in which unaccompanied women could be served. Known as the 'ABC' its shops survived until the 1980s.

7. Theatre Trust Theatre Data base website.

8. *MLAT* (The Wheels of Change).

CHAPTER 18

1. The paragraph in the *Lock to Lock Times* was referred to in Chapter I.

2. The dog story is adapted from one told by J in *Novel Notes.*

3. The letter from Howard Williams to *The Field* appeared in October 1876. He kept a full diary of the exploits of the five men which was prepared for publishing by a descendant, Felicity Catmur in 1981. *The Diary of a Rowing Tour from Oxford to London via Warwick, Gloucester, Hereford & Bristol, August 1895,* was published by Alan Sutton. From it I have taken the story of gate-crashing the Sunday school treat, the mysterious disappearance of one of the characters, and the church with an elm tree growing through a pew. Alas, this latter novelty no longer exists, the suckers from the tree having died in the 1880s. But a creeper growing over an iron frame in the church of St Mary, Ross on Wye, commemorates it.

4. Purists might point out the J was married before writing *Three Men in a Boat.* But the supposed conversations reported here involves the imaginary characters rather that the real ones.

APPENDIX I

1. Websites devoted to the Clapp family may be found on www. houseofnames.com, and www.ancestry.com.

2. The date of Jerome Clapp's birth is from the 1871 census of the Jerome household. There are no certainties about the year, Caroline W de la L Oulton, (*Below the Fairly City*, p 19) gives 1808 and 1810 as alternatives.

3. 'He used to call himself something like "Jerrymy", said an old miner whom I met one day in Norton.' M Wright quoted on page 34 of *Idle Thoughts on Jerome K Jerome*, published by the Jerome K Jerome Society 2009.

4. Osgood Clapa is mentioned in the Anglo Saxon Chronicles, but is a difficult figure to pin down. The story of the drinking bout appears in Daniel Lyson's *Environs of London*, published in 1792. He placed the event in Clapham a fact that has taken 200 years to disprove. Modern historians believe he was born in Hereford of Danish ancestry and died in exile in 1054. His estates were in East Anglia. Genealogists appear fascinated with him, and claims are made that he has direct family connections with George I and Winston Churchill (see Osgood Clapa on fabpedigree.com).

5. Peter Christie's fascinating article on *The Reverend Jerome Clapp in Appledore 1840-1855* was published in the journal of the Jerome K Jerome Society, *Idle Thoughts* No 30, Summer 2008. It stated 'There is, in fact, still an oral tradition in Appledore that Clapp was the father of at least one illegitimate child.'

6. The account of the family crest appears in *My Life and Times* (Birth and Parentage). The most recent dismissal of J's belief about his ancestry appeared in 2012. '.... there are places where he tells, what in a biography, would be termed outright lies, such as his claim to be descended from Clapa the Dane.' *BTFC*, p216.

7. The raised battleaxe and motto appear at the top of a letter sent by J to the manager of the Drury Lane Theatre from 19 Tavistock Place dated February 16, 1886. The letter is in Columbia University Rare Books and Manuscripts Library, and was reproduced in *Idle Thoughts No 34*, Spring 2013.

8. Referring to J's beliefs on breeding and birth I quote here: 'Inclining to a eugenicist view of humanity based on racial, gender and intellectual hierarchies, Jerome initially mistrusted socialism on just these grounds.' *BTFC* page 56.

9. The pacifist campaign in the West Country is mentioned in *BTFC* page 20.

10. I am grateful to Dr Gabriel Ronay, specialist writer on Hungarian affairs for confirming that Klapka was of German descent.

11. Although *The Times* referred to this meeting in its headline as a 'Peace Congress' it was in fact intended to review the past year's activities and announce a full congress the following year at Frankfurt. Clapp seems to have continued with his involvement in the Peace movement until at least 1866. An entry in J's mother's diary for May 22, 1866 reads: 'Peace Meeting in Cannon Street Hotel. Papa made a beautiful speech ...' *My Life and Times* (Birth and Parentage). The outbreak of the Crimean War in 1853 caused many to see the movement as unpatriotic, and it went into decline.

12. Peter Christie, in his article quoted above, says Clapp was recorded as living in Odun House 1847 when his daughter Blandina was born. 'One of the grander houses in the village. (Appledore).'

13. I am grateful to Dr Ceri Dornan of the Bálint Society for passing on my query about the identity of the *Times* letter writer for consideration by his members. The result was inconclusive. Heather Suckling noted that while Bálint was not formally a professor at the time, in Eastern Europe a professor is a senior teacher of medicine, not someone with a chair. I enjoyed the comment made by John Salinksy: 'Why would he be interested in J K Jerome? It's obvious to me now. Didn't one of the characters in *Three Men in a Boat* (actually JKJ himself) suffer from overwhelming somatisation, exacerbated by reading a medical tome, after which he concluded he was suffering from every ailment under the sun except Housemaid's Knee. What a patient for the father of psychosomatic medicine!'

14. The suffix 'ka' (kin in English) is also a term of affection e.g. Poeska, little cat, in Flemish.

APPENDIX II

1. I have not been able to discover anything about this mysterious 'fourth man'.

2. The paragraphs in bold are as printed.

BIBLIOGRAPHY

Suggestions for further reading

Biographies

Twenty Years of My Life, Douglas Brooke Wheelton Sladen, Constable & Co, London 1914. Republished as facsimile edition, ULAN Press, available through Amazon UK.

Far Off Things, Athur Machen, Martin Secker Ltd, London, 1922. Reprinted in facsimile, Forgotten Books, 2012.

My Life & Times, Jerome K Jerome, first published by Hodder and Stoughton Ltd in 1926.

Jerome K Jerome, A Critical Biography, Jospeh Connolly, Orbis Publishing, London, 1982, ISBN 0-85613-349-3

Jerome K Jerome, His Life and Work, by Alfred Moss, Selwyn & Blount, 1928.

Below the Fairy City, A Life of Jerome K Jerome, by Carolyn W De la Oulton, Victorian Secrets, 2012, ISBN 978-1-906469-37-5.

Hide-and-Seek with Angels, A Life of J M Barrie, Lisa Chaney, Hutchinson, London, 2005, ISBN 0-09-179539-7.

Charles Frohman: Manager and Man, by Isaac Frederick Marcosson and Daniel Frohman, et al, 1916, Harper Brothers, New York and London. Available Gutenburg Project.

The River

Our River, George Dunlop Leslie, Bradbury, Agnew & Co, London 1881, republished Kessinger Legacy Reprints.

The Thames from its Source to the Sea, (Two Volumes) Sir Walter Armstrong, J S Virtue & Co, London, 1886 republished in facsimile British Library,

Historical Print Editions, available through BiblioLife Network.

The Thames from its Source to the Sea, Paul Atterbury and Anthony Haines, Weidenfeld and Nicolson, 1998, ISBN 0-297-82414-7.

The Three Men in a Boat Companion, Stephen Lambe, 2012, Amberley Publishing, The Hill, Stroud, ISBN 1445607786.

Three Men in a Boat annotated edition, Christopher Matthew and Benny Green.

The Stream of Pleasure, Elizabeth Robins Pennell, Joseph Pennell, Macmillan & Co, 1891. Republished BiblioLife in facsimilie.

In Thamesland, Henty Wellington Wack, G P Putman's Sons, The Knickerbocker Press, 1906. Republished in facsimile by Nabu Public Domain Reprints.

Dickens Dictionary of the Thames 1887 Facsimile edition published 1994 by Old House Books, Newton Abbot, Devon. ISBN 1-873590-12-1.

The Thames Highway, Vols I & II, Fred S Thacker, 1914. New impression 1968, published by David & Charles (Publishers) Ltd Newton Abbot, Devon.

Small Boat on the Thames, by Roger Pilkington, Macmillan, London, 1966.

The Book of the Thames from its Rise to its Fall, by Mr and Mrs S C Hall, 1859. Facsimilie edition published by Charlotte James Publishers, Teddington, Middlesex, 1975, ISBN 0-9503990-9-4.

The Victorian Thames, by D G Wilson, Sutton Publishing Ltd, Stroud, Gloucestershire, 1993, ISBN 0-7509-0183-7.

The Upper Thames, J R L Anderson, Eyre and Spottiswoode, London, 1970, SBN 413-27400-4.

An Eye on the Thames, Alan Wykes, Jarrolds, 1966.

Portrait of the Thames, from Teddington to the Source, J H B Peel, Robert Hale, London, 1967.

Thames Sacred River, Peter Ackroyd, Vintage Books, ISBN 978-0-099-42255-6.

The Thames, A P Herbert, Weidenfeld and Nicolson, London, 1966.

The Thames of Henry Taunt, edited by Susan Read, published Alan Sutton, 1989, ISBN 0 86299 616 3.

Time on the Thames, Eric de Maré, The Architectural Press, London, 1952.

The Historic Thames, Hilaire Belloc, 1907, J M Dent & Sons edition.

The Thames, England's River, Jonathan Schneer, published 2005, by Little, Brown, ISBN 0-349-11929-5.

The Thames, a cultural history, Mick Sinclair, Signal Books, Oxford, ISBN 1-904955-27-4.

Thames Portrait, E Arnot Robertson, Ivor Nicholson and Watson, London, 1937.

The Diary of a Rowing Tour from Oxford to London in 1875, Alan Sutton Publishing, Gloucester, ISBN 0-904387-70-4.

The River, The Thames in our Time, Patrick Wright, BBC Worldwide Ltd, 1999, IBSN 0-563-38478-6.

The Grotto House, Toil and leisure in a modest country house in Berkshire, Pam Pheasant, published by Institute of Leisure and Amenity Management, 2003.

The Golden Age of the Thames, Patricia Burstall, David and Charles1981, ISBN 0-71538171-7.

Thames Bridges from Dartford to the Source, Neil Davenport, Silver Link Publishing Ltd, 2006, ISBN 1-85794-229-9.

Pleasure Boating on the Thames, a history of Salter Bros 1858-present day. Simon Wenham, The History Press, 2014, ISBN 976-7509-5633-2.

The Princess Alice Disaster, Joan Lock, Robert Hale, London, 2013, ISBN 978-0-7090-9541-5.

Amelia Dyer, Angel Maker, Alison Rattle and Allison Vale, Andre Deutsch, 2007, ISBN 978-0-233-00224-8.

Crochet Castle, Thomas Love Peacock, Penguin Classics.

From River to Sea, the Marine Heritage of Sam Saunders, Raymond L Wheeler, Cross Publishing, Newport, Isle of Wight, 1993.

Idle Thoughts on Jerome K Jerome, a 150th Anniversary Celebration, Edited by Jeremy Nicholas, The Jerome K Jerome Society, 2009.

The Hellfire Clubs, Sex, Satanism and Secret Societies, Evelyn Lord, Yale University Press, 2008, ISBN 978-0-300-11667-0.